100 THINGS
BYU FANS
SHOULD KNOW & DO
BEFORE THEY DIE

100 THINGS BYU FANS SHOULD KNOW & DO BEFORE THEY DIE

Jeff Call

TRIUMPH
BOOKS

Library of Congress Cataloging-in-Publication Data is available upon request.

This book is available in quantity at special discounts for your group or organization. For further information, contact:
   Triumph Books LLC
   814 North Franklin Street
   Chicago, Illinois 60610
   (312) 337-0747
   www.triumphbooks.com

Printed in U.S.A.
ISBN: 978-1-62937-425-3
Design by Patricia Frey
All photos courtesy of AP Images

To my wife, CherRon, and our sons, Ryan,
Brayden, Landon, Austin, Carson, and Janson.
You're my home team—and my favorite team.

Contents

Foreword

I decided to return to Brigham Young University as the offensive coordinator in December 2015, almost 25 years after finishing my career as a BYU quarterback. The time seemed right to make this move, and I knew what I was getting into. The fans and everybody at the university have been really welcoming.

When we played our first home game at LaVell Edwards Stadium against UCLA in September 2016, I was flooded with memories as we came down that tunnel from the locker room to the field. In that environment, with the crowd cheering, I had nerves, just like when I played here. The only difference was I wasn't wearing a helmet and pads.

There are two things BYU fans enjoy talking about most with me: our historic 28–21 win over No. 1 Miami on September 8, 1990, and the Heisman Trophy.

Everyone says they were there for the Miami game. We must have had 200,000 fans there that night. That win was a big moment for us, and for the program. We played UTEP in the 1990 season opener, and we had to manage that one and get through it knowing our next game would be against No. 1 Miami, the defending national champion. We had played at Miami a couple years before during the regular season, in the Orange Bowl, and I always remembered that game. They beat us by a few touchdowns. I learned so much from that experience, just playing against those guys; they had incredible speed.

When game week of the Miami contest arrived, it seemed like everyone was really dialed in and focused like never before. That single-mindedness gave us the win. After our victory, there was a lot of national attention on us. That one put us on the map and got everybody around the country watching us every week.

That win over Miami early in the season opened the door for me to win the 1990 Heisman Trophy at the end of that season. When you win the Heisman, it almost becomes part of your name for the rest of your life. Even when I was playing in the NFL, it wasn't "Ty Detmer, 14-year NFL veteran," it was "Ty Detmer, Heisman Trophy winner." It's been a lot of fun to be able to go back to the Downtown Athletic Club in New York City to participate in some of the events and announcements over the years. The Heisman Trophy is something I'll always cherish and appreciate.

But there were so many players who helped the program become a national power that year; the Miami win simply gave us newfound credibility. As a quarterback, I relied so much on the guys around me to be successful. The Heisman is an individual award but how do you really pick the best player? To me, it's the team, the guys around you, that really make it special. And, of course, our phenomenal coach, LaVell Edwards.

LaVell had such a big influence on me as a player, as a coach, and as a man. He just had that calming effect. He was never too high during the high times or too low during the low times. He kept that steady, even keel. That's something I appreciated as a quarterback, because my emotions could swing so much in a game. For us as players, even when we got behind, there was no panic. LaVell allowed us to go play and not get too caught up in the emotional part of the game. Which isn't to say that emotional aspect isn't important. It is essential, and we all saw it at times in LaVell. He was a competitor. He just allowed us to enjoy the process at BYU and to learn all the stuff off the field on our own, though he was there to guide that too, if needed. The whole atmosphere around the program centered around LaVell's calm approach. He allowed guys to be themselves and play football and learn life lessons along the way.

Our current head coach, Kalani Sitake, has a similar type of mentality as LaVell, and I love coaching with him. When we opened our first season with a 1–3 record, there was no panic. It wasn't, "We have to meet longer and work harder." There was none of that. It was about staying the course; it was about doing the right things and knowing everything was going to click. Sure enough, we ended up winning eight of our last nine games. You can see LaVell's influence on Kalani's coaching style. For me, that was a big reason for coming back to BYU and being a part of the program again.

The future of BYU football is bright, and I don't see any reason why we can't continue to play at a high level as we've always done. I see that continuing and, at some point, BYU getting into the College Football Playoff. That's the goal.

When I go out recruiting, my pitch is based on my experience at BYU and all that it did for me. It's a home away from home, and current players can still have the same experiences preceding generations of players did. BYU is different. It's like no other place. The word *unique* gets thrown around quite a bit. Other schools claim they're unique too, but where besides BYU can you talk about religion, have an opening prayer to start every team meeting, and be around such positive influences? Many of the young men in the program have been away on their own for two years serving a mission for the school's sponsoring institution, the Church of Jesus Christ of Latter-day Saints. They come back and are changed; it is apparent in their demeanors and attitudes. It's like no other program. There may be a few guys at different schools who served missions, but not to the extent we have here. It's the foundation of what the program is built on. No other place has that.

We've established a great tradition here at BYU, and players want to be a part of it. They know they're going to come to a place where they're going to win a lot of football games and have some exciting times. That's the way it's been year in and year out, no matter the schedule or the conference. That expectation has been built by past teams, and we coaches know that and feel those expectations. We've got a national championship. We've got guys with

individual honors. We've got All-Americans. We have everything
that every other school has. That tradition and history just carries
on.

This book, *100 Things BYU Fans Should Know & Do Before
They Die*, is a terrific resource for every generation of fan, because
the younger ones probably don't know a lot about the traditions
and the people who helped build the program. The older fans will
recall at least some of the information presented here, and there are
probably a few things they have forgotten.

This book will help all fans appreciate what BYU athletics is all
about. It's great to relive some of these memories, and we all look
forward to making many more.

—Ty Detmer
BYU quarterback, 1988–91
BYU offensive coordinator, 2016–present

Introduction

I've found it fitting that I spent a significant chunk of time during the fall of 2016 researching and reviewing many of the stories about the history of Brigham Young University football and its legendary coach, LaVell Edwards. When Triumph Books approached me about writing this book, I jumped at the chance. I've been covering the Cougars since my undergraduate days at BYU, starting in the early 1990s. Before that, as a kid, I closely followed Edwards and the BYU football program. One of my first introductions to Edwards came before I became a journalist. For an assignment in a college writing class, I decided to write about BYU football. Who better to talk to than the man who all but invented BYU football?

Being idealistic and naive (though a part of me figured it was a long shot), I walked into the BYU football offices, introduced myself to LaVell's secretary, Shirley Johnson, told her my purpose for coming, and asked if it would be possible to set up an appointment to talk to the coach for just a few minutes. To my utter shock, just minutes later I was sitting across from Edwards in his office. How many coaches, especially of Edwards' stature, would allow that? That day, he granted me what would turn out to be the first of many interviews with him.

Though I probably stammered through my questions during that first interview opportunity, Edwards didn't treat me like a random student writing something that, as far as he knew, only my professor would read. He treated me with a respect that made me feel as if I were a reporter from a prominent newspaper or magazine. My experience with him that day was one of the reasons why I decided to become a sportswriter.

I eventually became the sports editor of the school's *Daily Universe* in 1993 and I've been writing about BYU sports for the

Deseret News in Salt Lake City since 1997. I was fortunate enough to cover the last several seasons of Edwards' 29-year head-coaching tenure in Provo. His final two weeks at the helm—when the name of Cougar Stadium was changed to LaVell Edwards Stadium, followed by, six days later, the Cougars' last-minute, come-from-behind victory against archrival Utah in his final game—were unforgettable.

After he retired, Edwards continued to be gracious with interview requests, whether it was reminiscing about the 1984 championship season or providing valued perspective on issues at BYU and college football in general. Edwards answered questions and offered insights with candor, warmth, and humor. When he returned home with his wife, Patti, from a mission to New York City for the Church of Jesus Christ of Latter-day Saints, in 2004, I called him for an interview and he invited me to his modest Provo home, the same one in which he had lived in for decades. Looking around the living room, there was scant physical evidence that the home belonged to one of college football's all-time-winningest coaches. Surely there had to be a shrine that displayed memorabilia, championship rings, and awards somewhere. I asked him where he kept all of it. Edwards shrugged. "Everything is packed away in boxes," he said.

In 2011, LaVell's grandson, Cougars senior tight end Matthew Edwards, caught the first pass of his career, a nine-yard touchdown late in the third quarter in his final home game. A couple of days later, I called LaVell and asked about his family's reaction to the unexpected touchdown. "There was jumping up and down, just like [Jim] McMahon had thrown the touchdown pass to Clay Brown [in the 'Miracle Bowl']," LaVell said with a chuckle. "It was that spontaneous and that exciting. I even jumped out of my seat. That was very special."

LaVell Edwards passed away on December 29, 2016, at the age of 86. As I watched the tributes pour in from all over the country, and attended the memorial service in his honor, I was reminded that much of this book, which I had spent the previous months working on, wouldn't have been possible without him. Many of the chapters involve him and his athletes. His influence on this book, just like his influence on BYU's campus, is ubiquitous.

This book isn't all about football, however. BYU also has a rich basketball tradition, to which I've dedicated considerable space. The most difficult challenge about a book like this isn't what to put in, but what to keep out. Plenty of worthy chapters were left on the proverbial cutting-room floor. In truth, I could have written *200 Things BYU Fans Should Know & Do Before They Die* had space and time permitted. Ranking these events and athletes was simultaneously thrilling and painstaking. I realize not everyone will agree with the order, but I welcome differences of opinion. That's part of what makes sports enjoyable. My hope is that the spirit of BYU sports is captured within these pages.

A few of the individuals that have made a lasting impact at BYU are known by Cougars fans all over the world by their first name—Jimmer, Kalani, Ziggy, Bronco, and Taysom. But one name, LaVell, stands above the rest.

1 LaVell Edwards

To BYU, Reuben LaVell Edwards was much more than just a football coach. What he meant to the football program, the university, his players, and the fans transcended what he accomplished as a coach, which was staggering in and of itself.

It's amazing to consider what might have happened had BYU passed on hiring the defensive coordinator with no collegiate head coaching experience in 1972. It took a group of BYU players showing up at the home of school president Dallin H. Oaks to help convince him the school should hire longtime assistant LaVell Edwards, who had never been a head coach at the college level and had been a part of only a few winning seasons in his coaching career to that point. Edwards had grown up on a dairy farm in nearby Orem as the eighth of 14 children. He played football at Utah State. Even in Provo, he wasn't exactly a household name.

Hiring Edwards was risky, but of course it proved to be a stroke of pure genius; it altered the trajectory of the BYU football program's future forever. Prior to Edwards, BYU had only had two coaches with winning records, and the program was, if not perennially downtrodden, mired in mediocrity. Edwards guided the Cougars to heights never dreamed of previously. During 29 seasons at the helm, he logged 257 wins—which ranks sixth in Division I history—22 bowl appearances, 19 conference championships, one unlikely national championship, two National Coach of the Year honors, and a 2004 induction into the College Football Hall of Fame. That is just a fraction of his legacy.

Edwards helped revolutionize the sport in the late 1970s and 1980s. While most schools were running the football, he installed

1

When LaVell Almost Became a Lion

In 1999 LaVell Edwards coached in a domed stadium for the first time in his storied career when the Cougars faced Marshall in the Motor City Bowl in Detroit, Michigan. But if it had been up to the Detroit Lions, Edwards' first game on the sideline at the Pontiac Silverdome would have happened a lot sooner, and a lot more often.

After BYU defeated the Michigan Wolverines in the December 21, 1984, Holiday Bowl and claimed the 1984 national championship, Edwards was contacted by Lions officials about filling their head coaching vacancy. The opportunity was intriguing to him at first. "I had decided I wouldn't go anywhere else unless it was an NFL job," Edwards said.

But he was so busy when the Lions came calling that he had a difficult time meeting up with team officials. His hectic schedule included coaching in the East-West Shrine Game in San Francisco, the National Coaches Association banquet to pick up his National Coach of the Year Award, and a visit to the White House at the request of President Ronald Reagan, who wanted to congratulate Edwards on his team's championship season.

It was at a Washington, DC, hotel that Edwards finally discussed the job opening with Lions general manager Russ Thomas. When Edwards returned to Provo, Lions owner William Clay Ford called and officially offered him the position over the phone. Ford asked Edwards to fly to Detroit, but Edwards said he couldn't leave that weekend because he had some recruits coming into town. "It became evident in my mind I couldn't pick up and leave," Edwards said. "I realized I wasn't willing to drop everything for this. It wasn't right for me." So he turned down the job offer.

It wasn't the first time Edwards had been courted. The University of Minnesota, the University of Colorado, and the University of Miami are among the schools that each had expressed interest in him prior to the Lions' offer. But the Detroit Lions' offer was the closest Edwards ever came to leaving BYU, and he said he never regretted the decision. "The guy they ended up hiring, Darryl Rogers, they fired three years later," Edwards said. "That would have been me."

and unleashed an unconventional, relentless passing attack that produced a string of All-America quarterbacks. Edwards became universally respected not only for winning and changing college football by emphasizing the forward pass but also because of the way he coached. Like an effective CEO, he surrounded himself with talented, driven people on his coaching staff. He delegated responsibilities and he let his assistants coach. Unlike most other coaches, he didn't wear a headset and he didn't micromanage. *USA Today* once called him "a national coaching treasure."

Without Edwards, there probably would be no 63,000-seat stadium, and BYU would probably just be known as some religious school in Provo surrounded by large mountains. Edwards, in many ways, was a visionary man. "Brigham Young arrived in the desert 149 years ago, on the banks of a sea made of salt, and saw what hadn't been seen: a place to build a home," wrote Berry Tramel of the *Daily Oklahoman* in 1996. "We don't think much about Brigham Young when it comes to American pioneers, but we should; he was more at home on the frontier than Davy Crockett and Daniel Boone. LaVell Edwards arrived as a college head coach in 1972, on the campus named for the Father of Utah, and saw what hadn't been seen: a place to throw the football. We don't think much about LaVell Edwards when it comes to American football coaches, but we should; Bobby Bowden and Joe Paterno have nothing on him when it comes to building programs. Brigham Young put Utah on the map. Then along came Edwards to do the same for Young's university."

In 2000 Edwards retired, leaving players and fans with a lifetime of memories. Among many other things, he'll be remembered for his stoic sideline demeanor. He'll also be remembered for his courtesy, humor, and love for his players and for his family. He and his wife, Patti, who celebrated their 65th wedding anniversary in 2016, had three children: Ann Cannon (a writer), John (a doctor), and Jim (a lawyer). Edwards was not only synonymous with BYU football, he was a man for all seasons. To his family he was a devoted father and loving husband. To the players he coached, he was a father figure.

It was his style and personality that set him apart. Edwards was never consumed by football, nor was his perspective clouded by an obsession with winning. He didn't have the big contract with the big ego to match. He found time to listen to Willie Nelson's music, read voraciously, travel, golf, work in his flower garden, and serve his church and community. Integrity, humor, and humility were hallmarks of his career. While known for his stern outward appearance and for frequently folding his arms during games, he never took himself too seriously. "Someone once said I'm actually a happy guy," he said, "I just forgot to tell my face."

Edwards' serene approach and dry sense of humor belied his competitive nature. But his calm demeanor was at least partly responsible for BYU's ability to pull out so many close games and trademark comebacks. Perhaps the only person who doesn't

BYU's All-Time Head Football Coaches

Coach	Years	Overall Record (Pct.)
Alvin Twitchell	1922–24	5–13–1 (.289)
C. J. Hart	1925–27	6–12–2 (.350)
G. Ott Romney	1928–36	42–31–5 (.571)
Eddie Kimball	1937–41; 1946–48	34–32–8 (.514)
Floyd Millet	1942	2–5 (.286)
Chick Atkinson	1949–55	18–49–3 (.279)
Hal Kopp	1956–58	13–14–3 (.483)
Tally Stevens	1959–60	6–15 (.286)
Hal Mitchell	1961–63	8–22 (.267)
Tom Hudspeth	1964–71	39–42–1 (.482)
LaVell Edwards	1972–2000	257–101–3 (.717)
Gary Crowton	2001–04	26–23 (.531)
Bronco Mendenhall	2005–15	99–43 (.697)
Kalani Sitake	2016–present	9–4 (.692)

see Edwards as a legend is Edwards himself. Fittingly, on the day he coached his last home game, the school and the LDS Church, which sponsors the school, changed the name of Cougar Stadium to LaVell Edwards Stadium. It was, after all, the House that LaVell Built.

After retiring, his autumns were free from football for the first time in 56 years. He spent his time with his beloved Patti, children, and grandchildren. He fulfilled a dream of serving an LDS mission in New York City with his wife.

Super Bowl–winning quarterback Steve Young, who arrived at BYU as a walk-on in 1980, credits Edwards for helping instill confidence and launching Young's NFL Hall of Fame career: "I remember going on my recruiting trip to BYU, and there was a big line of guys wanting to talk to LaVell outside his office. I was the last guy. LaVell knew my name but not much else. I didn't know if he was going to offer me a scholarship or not. In his office he was sitting in his chair, and I saw a bunch of spiritual books—I was pretty impressed. I didn't think the two could mix. As he sat there I thought for a second he had fallen asleep. He started chewing on his tongue, like he was looking for inspiration. Then he said, 'I think we'll give you a scholarship.' I'm grateful he gave me, an option quarterback, a chance. He [saw] more in you than you [could] see in yourself. That's the greatest compliment you can give a coach."

Edwards died on December 29, 2016, at the age of 86. That evening, the lights at LaVell Edwards Stadium lit up the night sky in tribute to the legendary coach . . . and legendary man.

2 1984 National Championship

More than three decades later, it still reads kind of like a made-for-Disney movie script. The story of BYU's improbable 1984 national football championship season had unlikely heroes (Adam Haysbert, for example), villains (Bryant Gumbel and Barry Switzer come to mind), dramatic moments (who can forget the image of Robbie Bosco hobbling around on one leg in the Holiday Bowl?), serendipitous events (one by one, teams ahead of the Cougars in the polls fell), an unmistakable underdog quality (devoid of star players at the time, BYU started the season unranked), a certain moxie (four fourth-quarter comebacks), and a penchant for accomplishing something unprecedented (how in the heck did a team from the Western Athletic Conference, from the Mountain time zone, win a national title?).

"The way it all came together, it almost had to work just the way it did for it to happen," recalled legendary coach LaVell Edwards. "It was a magical year." Maybe it was magic. Maybe it was fate. Maybe it was destiny. Maybe the Cougars were somewhat lucky, too. "In spite of everything we did, it still took a little bit of luck," admitted Glen Kozlowski, a wide receiver on the 1984 team. "It still came down to a lot of factors that we had no control over."

"It was the confluence of the right group of guys with the right scheme against the rest of the college football world of that moment," explained 1984 offensive lineman Trevor Matich, who is now an ESPN college football analyst. "BYU was the mouse that roared. Nobody knew who we were. We were the first school nobody had ever heard of that rose up and grabbed the college football world by the neck and said, 'You will know who I am. You have no choice.'"

1984: 13–0, National Champions, WAC Champions

Date	Opponent	Location	W/L	Score
September 1	Pittsburgh	Pittsburgh	W	20–14
September 8	Baylor	Provo	W	47–13
September 15	Tulsa	Provo	W	38–15
September 22	Hawaii	Honolulu	W	18–13
October 6	Colorado State	Fort Collins, Colo.	W	52–9
October 13	Wyoming	Provo	W	41–38
October 20	Air Force	Colorado Springs, Colo.	W	30–25
October 25	New Mexico	Albuquerque	W	48–0
November 3	UTEP	Provo	W	42–9
November 10	San Diego State	Provo	W	34–3
November 17	Utah	Salt Lake City	W	24–14
November 24	Utah State	Provo	W	38–13
December 21	Michigan	San Diego	W	24–17

The 1984 season catapulted the BYU football program—as well as the LDS Church and the state of Utah—into the national consciousness. "It was really crazy with all of the media [attention]," said Bosco. "I can remember after the Pitt game going up to Salt Lake with LaVell to be on *Good Morning America*. It was like, 'Why do they want to talk to us?'"

The season began with a stunning upset over No. 3 Pitt on the road and culminated in a victory over a Michigan team with an average record in the Holiday Bowl, which led to controversy as people around the country debated BYU's worthiness as the nation's top-ranked team. The undefeated 13–0 Cougars had to wait two weeks after defeating the Wolverines before they were officially voted No. 1 by both the Associated Press and United Press International polls on January 3, 1985, touching off a celebration around the state. Not long after securing the national championship, Edwards visited the White House and met with President Ronald Reagan.

BYU still stands as the last team to enter a season unranked and win a national championship. The Cougars are also the last team from a non–Power 5 conference to win a national title in football. For those who played on that national championship team, that accomplishment is sweeter than ever. "One of the great things about winning a national championship is the whole team is involved," Bosco said. "It's a team award. You can celebrate that with everybody, and you can talk about it forever."

Of all the great seasons BYU enjoyed in the early 1980s, 1984 seemed the least likely to end in a national championship. The Cougars had lost quarterback Steve Young, tight end Gordon Hudson, and linebacker Todd Shell from a 1983 team that went 11–1, winning its last 11 straight games and finishing with a No. 7 national ranking.

Final Associated Press Poll 1984

Rank	School	Record	Points
1.	BYU (38)*	13–0	1,160
2.	Washington (16)*	11–1	1,140
3.	Florida (6)*	9–1–1	1,092
4.	Nebraska	10–2	1,017
5.	Boston College	10–2	932
6.	Oklahoma	9–2–1	883
7.	Oklahoma State	10–2	761
8.	SMU	10–2	864
9.	UCLA	9–3	613
10.	USC	9–3	596
11.	South Carolina	10–2	557
12.	Maryland	9–3	552
13.	Ohio State	9–3	497
14.	Auburn	9–4	432
15.	LSU	8–3–1	314
16.	Iowa	8–4–1	228
17.	Florida State	7–3–2	207
18.	Miami (FL)	8–5	166
19.	Kentucky	9–3	152
20.	Virginia	8–2–2	119

* first-place votes

Not only were the '84 Cougars unranked, but in its preseason college football preview, *Sports Illustrated* picked them to finish No. 3—in the WAC. It looked like a rebuilding year in Provo for a team breaking in a new starting quarterback and several others at skill positions. "Going into spring football, there were low expectations around the conference and around the country," said Kozlowski. "We had been so dominant in our conference, everybody thought '84 was the year they could beat us. By the end of spring ball, we made a commitment to each other that we were going to try and prove everybody wrong."

When the season-opening opponent, Pittsburgh, debuted at No. 3 in the national rankings, the Cougars sensed an opportunity. On the eve of the season opener, in a Pittsburgh hotel, the team convened for a meeting. "We talked about the fact if we could win that game, and go undefeated, we could win the national championship," said Kozlowski.

The relatively low expectations going into the season may actually have helped the '84 team. "With the enormous pressure [a national ranking] places on a team, I don't know if we would have been able to do what we did," said return specialist Vai Sikahema. "We started the season with such low expectations, and as the expectations grew, our team grew. We peaked at the right time."

During the 1984 season, Oklahoma coach Barry Switzer and *Today* show host Bryant Gumbel complained loudly that the Cougars didn't deserve a No. 1 ranking or a national championship. They contended BYU played a weak "Bo Diddley Tech" schedule. The Cougars' most notable wins came against a Pitt team that finished with only three victories and a 6–5 Michigan team in the Holiday Bowl.

That '84 title is still one of the most disputed college football championships. But to safety Kyle Morrell, the record speaks for itself: "We went out and played our schedule and beat 13 teams in a row. Other teams would come to play us like they never came to

JEFF CALL

play in any other football game. We were undefeated. Our schedule wasn't the toughest in the nation, but we were 13–0, and I believe we deserved the national championship." And indeed this is the most compelling argument in favor of the '84 squad when BYU fans debate which Cougars team is the best all-time; no other team in school history has recorded an undefeated season.

Matich said what he misses most about his days at BYU is the camaraderie with his teammates. Their brotherhood was galvanized through a grueling yet rewarding national championship season. "That bond is something we'll have the rest of our lives, whether we have lunch every day or whether we see each other every ten years. When we get together, it's like we've never been apart. It's like it's 1984," he said.

3 Ty Detmer Wins the Heisman Trophy

Toward the end of a long, grueling, and record-breaking junior season, BYU quarterback Ty Detmer found himself surrounded by his teammates at the Princess Kaiulani Hotel in Honolulu on December 1, 1990, and waiting on history.

They were sitting poolside, and in front of them were cameras and a satellite hookup with national television network CBS. Detmer had an earpiece and listened as Downtown Athletic Club president C. Peter Lambos, presiding from the New York landmark, uttered those immortal words: "The winner of the 1990 Heisman Trophy award, whose name is Ty Detmer. Ty Detmer of BYU. Ty Detmer!"

Detmer, wearing a Hawaiian lei around his neck and flanked by BYU athletic director Glen Tuckett and coach LaVell Edwards,

Heisman Voting 1990

Name, School	Class	Position	Votes
1. Ty Detmer, BYU	Jr.	QB	1,482
2. Raghib Ismail, Notre Dame	Jr.	WR	1,177
3. Eric Bieniemy, Colorado	Sr.	RB	798
4. Shawn Moore, Virginia	Sr.	QB	465
5. David Klingler, Houston	Jr.	QB	125
6. Herman Moore, Virginia	Jr.	WR	68
7. Greg Lewis, Washington	Sr.	RB	41
8. Darren Lewis, Texas A&M	Sr.	RB	31
8. Craig Erickson, Miami	Sr.	QB	31
10. Mike Mayweather, Army	Sr.	RB	20

pumped his fist upon receiving the news and said, "We got it!" Edwards raised both arms before giving Detmer a bear hug, and the Heisman winner's teammates celebrated and cheered. Defensive tackle Rich Kaufusi tossed Detmer into the pool.

As Detmer said when he informed his team about capturing the award—using the word "we"—this wasn't just an individual recognition; it was about the team and the program. The Texas native understood this completely. After earning the Heisman, he continually acknowledged those who came before him—from Gary Sheide to Gifford Nielsen to Marc Wilson to Jim McMahon to Steve Young to Robbie Bosco. During the 1980s, no other program had more top-five Heisman finishers—five—than BYU. The school finally had its first Heisman Trophy winner after coming so close for so many years. "They all had great seasons, and a couple of them should have won it," Detmer said. "They set the tone here. Now we finally have it.... There have been a lot of great players, like my teammates and previous BYU quarterbacks, that contributed to it. They opened the door." The week after winning, Detmer graced the cover of *Sports Illustrated* with the headline TY'S PRIZE.

Bosco's first season as an assistant coach at BYU was in 1990, and he relished Detmer's Heisman victory. "This was a great moment in BYU history. Ty deserved it. No doubt in my mind," said Bosco, who had finished third in the Heisman balloting twice. "Ty has a little bit of every BYU quarterback in him. Of all the great points of all our games, he has those points in his game. Plus he is just a great kid. I'm happy for him."

Detmer's Heisman campaign had begun in earnest at the end of his sophomore season, when he threw for 576 yards in a loss to Penn State in the Holiday Bowl. Then his performance early in his junior season, when BYU upset the defending national champions, No. 1–ranked Miami Hurricanes, 28–21 in Provo, sprung him to the top of the Heisman race. "Is it possible to win the Heisman Trophy in September?" wrote Ed Sherman of the *Chicago Tribune* after the game. "It is if your name is Ty Detmer and you rip apart Miami on national television."

That year, BYU launched a Heisman campaign to promote Detmer for the Heisman by mailing cardboard ties to the media while fans wore makeshift ties in support of Detmer. He ended up throwing for 5,188 yards and 41 touchdowns in 1990.

Detmer received 1,482 points in the Heisman voting, ahead of Notre Dame's Raghib "Rocket" Ismail at 1,177. He finished first in all six voting regions to become the first college player from the Rockies to earn the 25-pound Heisman Trophy, awarded annually to the outstanding college football player of the year since 1935. In 1991, as a senior, Detmer finished third in the Heisman balloting.

For years, a portrait of Detmer hung alongside the many other recipients on the third floor of the Downtown Athletic Club in New York City. A duplicate hangs in the Cougar Room of LaVell Edwards Stadium.

Hours after Detmer received the Heisman Trophy, BYU got thumped by Hawaii 59–28. Weeks later, in the Holiday Bowl, Texas A&M crushed the Cougars 65–14. But nobody could take away Detmer's—and BYU's—Heisman Trophy.

4 Kalani Sitake

After spending 10 seasons as an assistant at archrival Utah, and another year at Oregon State, Kalani Sitake took the reins of BYU's program in December 2015, becoming the Cougars' 14th head coach, replacing Bronco Mendenhall.

At the introductory press conference, legendary coach LaVell Edwards—Sitake's coach at BYU—was in attendance, along with dozens of former Cougars players who had come out to show support. Sitake, a former Cougars fullback, had come home. It seemed fitting that *Kalani* means "a gift sent from heaven" in Tongan. He became the first Tongan head coach in college football history. "I'm proud to be part of this family. I've never left," said Sitake. "I've always been part of BYU. I've always bled blue."

Not long after returning from his LDS Church mission to Oakland, California, nearly two decades earlier, Sitake had a tattoo inked on his left arm. It depicts the letter *S* (for *Sitake*) inside a compass. "My ancestors were navigators," he explained back in the late 1990s. "It's a compass leading me home, even if I'm far from home. It helps me remember who I am."

Sitake's hiring reconnected the football program to the Edwards era, which spanned 29 seasons. Sitake played for Edwards, and his final game as a Cougar was Edwards' final game as coach—a dramatic victory over archrival Utah in 2000. "This is a new era in BYU football. It's the dawning of a new day," said athletic director Tom Holmoe. "There are things in this program that will remain the same. Some things will be a common thread from LaVell all the way to Kalani. We're not going to throw out everything else and start over. There's some richness in this program. We're going to keep that and add to it."

Even after spending a decade as an assistant coach with the Utes, Sitake's heart never strayed far from BYU. He emphasized how happy he was to return home and how passionate he is about his alma mater. Kalani Sitake is a BYU guy, an Edwards guy. "Coach Edwards has been a huge influence in my life," he said. "I'm very thankful to LaVell and all he's done for me." During his inaugural season, Sitake paid homage to Edwards once again: "I want to be here as long as I can," he said. "I want to be the Polynesian LaVell Edwards."

Sitake returned to Provo with a strong reputation as a recruiter and a players' coach. Not only did he win over the fans right away

Flash the Y Sign

One of Coach Kalani Sitake's signature influences on the football program, and the entire athletic department, came in the form of a hand gesture. Sitake repurposed the famous shaka sign, a well-known surfers' gesture, to fit BYU. He flashed the shaka when he was introduced to BYU fans at the Marriott Center in January 2016, shortly after being hired, in part as a tribute to his heritage.

The shaka sign, or Y sign, is made by extending the thumb and pinky finger while holding the three middle fingers curled into the palm. Surfers used it all the time, and it came to mean "hang loose." For Sitake's purposes, it signifies support for BYU. "To me, it makes a lot of sense," Sitake explained. "It's the [letter] Y in sign language. It fits perfectly."

In truth, this new use of the shaka at BYU, and its origins, has come full circle. Hamana Kalili, a member of the LDS Church and fisherman from Laie, [Hawaii,] lost the three middle fingers on his right hand in an accident at the Kahuku Sugar Mill while pressing sugarcane through rollers. Later, while working at the sugarcane railroad, Kalili lifted his right hand, revealing his two fingers to conductors, signifying the track was clear. Soon kids started using that sign.

Today a 7'4" bronze statue of Kalili, credited as being the father of the shaka, stands in the Hukilau Marketplace at the Polynesian Cultural Center in Laie. And for Cougars fans, the shaka also represents BYU.

Head coach Kalani Sitake holds the reins of the Cougars football team.

but he won over his players too. It didn't take BYU running back Jamaal Williams long to embrace Sitake's leadership style. "The first thing he said was, 'I'm not here to be your elder or your bishop or none of that. I'm here to be your football coach,'" Williams recalled of that first team meeting. "After he said that, I was sold. He's a great person. He's a real players' coach."

"I love Coach Sitake. He's a great man, a great coach," said quarterback Tanner Mangum. "A lot of it is, internally, as a team, he talks to us about loving each other and really making this a brotherhood. Making this our team. He's the leader, he's going to help us, but he wants us to take responsibility for it and to be accountable to ourselves and make sure we're looking out for each other and loving each other. He's a good example of that. He loves people. He loves his family, he loves his assistant coaches, he loves us. He's making sure we're tight-knit and together and a team. That's going to carry us throughout this season and years to come."

In his first season at the helm, Sitake led the Cougars to a better-than-expected 9–4 record despite a challenging schedule, all while installing a new offense and a new defense. BYU set an NCAA record with four losses by a total of eight points, marking the fewest points separating a four-loss team from an unbeaten season. On the other hand, the Cougars won three games by a total of 11 points. BYU tied another NCAA record—most games (seven) decided by three points or less. The Cougars started the season 1–3 but finished 8-1.

Sitake's skills as a coach are surpassed only by his passion for BYU. "BYU is a special place. When I look at a young man in his eyes and I look at his family and parents, I can tell them that I'm living proof that this is a special place," Sitake said. "It's a special place and it's unique. I played here, I lived this life, I met my beautiful wife here. I made great friends here who became my brothers.... There are a lot of young men who come here and it changes their lives. I'm going to build on that."

5 The Miracle Bowl

Going into the 1980 Holiday Bowl, BYU had never won a bowl game and coach LaVell Edwards was feeling the pressure. Against Southern Methodist University, it appeared the Cougars were about to lose a bowl for the fifth consecutive time.

BYU trailed SMU early in the fourth quarter by the seemingly insurmountable score of 38–19. After another fruitless drive for the Cougars offense, and with many of the fans at Jack Murphy Stadium already streaming to the exits, Edwards decided to punt.

Quarterback Jim McMahon was livid. He called a timeout and headed to the sideline to confront his coach. McMahon wasn't a quitter. And he hated losing. He knew what the prolific offense was capable of doing, even when down by 19 points. With fire in his eyes and in his voice, McMahon insisted that the Cougars go for it on fourth down and two from their own 46-yard line. "If we punt," he yelled, "we lose!"

So following some confusion, Edwards sent McMahon back out onto the field. McMahon got a first down. Then he got a touchdown as BYU cut the deficit to 38–25. That was a positive sign, until the Mustangs promptly answered with a 42-yard touchdown run by Craig James.

With 3:58 remaining on the clock, BYU found itself down 45–25. Game over, right? Not so fast. Not when you have McMahon at quarterback. In order to pull off this improbable upset, the Cougars needed an improbable string of events over the final four minutes to go their way.

First, McMahon marched BYU on a 72-yard drive that culminated with a 15-yard touchdown pass to Matt Braga. BYU's two-point attempt failed, to make the score 45–31. Then came a successful onside kick recovered by Todd Shell on the 50-yard line. McMahon drove BYU for another touchdown, this time in four plays over 34 seconds, capped by a one-yard run by Scott Phillips. That was followed by a two-point conversion. Suddenly it was 45–39 with 1:57 on the clock.

The Cougars' next onside kick was recovered by SMU, but the Mustangs were unable to run out the clock and were forced to punt from their own 43-yard line. SMU took a delay-of-game penalty after letting the clock run down to 18 seconds. Bill Schoepflin charged the punter and blocked the punt with 13 seconds left.

With the ball resting on the SMU 41-yard line, McMahon returned to the field with a shot at winning the game. His first two passes were incomplete, leaving three seconds remaining. Offensive coordinator Doug Scovil dialed up the play—his last, as he had already accepted the head coaching job at San Diego State—simply called Save the Game.

McMahon dropped back and hurled a high-arching rainbow pass that landed in the sure hands of tight end Clay Brown in the end zone, with two SMU defenders draped all over him and no time remaining. Touchdown Cougars! BYU 46, SMU 45.

Radio announcer Tony Roberts called the play this way: "And now it's third down and 10 from the 41.... This is it.... Back to throw...no time on the clock. It is...it is...what? Caught! He caught it. Touchdown on the last play. Brigham Young has won. A miracle catch. Everybody went up in the air for the football. I don't believe it.... I don't believe it, and yet I saw it!"

All BYU's receivers had raced into the end zone to await a last-gasp Hail Mary by McMahon, and Brown somehow came up with the ball. As Edwards pointed out afterward, it was an LDS returned missionary, Kurt Gunther, who provided the winning margin, 46–45, with an extra point to cap what was at that time the greatest comeback in college bowl history and one of the most dramatic finishes of all time. BYU had completed an implausible bowl comeback as the Cougars scored 27 points in the fourth quarter, 21 in the final four minutes.

McMahon's stubborn resolve and competitiveness sparked an unbelievable finish in the Holiday Bowl, which is simply known by BYU fans as the Miracle Bowl.

6 Steve Young

In the fall of 1980, a left-handed option quarterback from Greenwich, Connecticut, arrived at Brigham Young University with exactly zero fanfare. At the time, his greatest claim to fame was being the great-great-great-grandson of the school's namesake, Brigham Young.

As for his prospects as a QB at pass-happy BYU, the future didn't look bright for Jon Steven Young. His freshman year, he was buried behind seven other quarterbacks on the depth chart, including starter Jim McMahon. And upon taking his first snap at a BYU practice, Young tripped while backpedaling and fell to the ground. At one point, the Cougars coaching staff almost moved Young from quarterback to safety. To say the least, he recovered quite nicely from that inauspicious start.

A veer quarterback in high school, Young decided to attend one of the nation's top passing schools. "Back then, it was all beyond me; so was just passing the football. Because I'd never really done that before," Young said. "In high school, if they called a pass, I'd drop back and run."

As a Cougar, Young set 13 NCAA records and led the NCAA in total offense, passing, and pass efficiency in 1983, his senior season. That year, he guided BYU to an 11–1 record, capped by a game-winning touchdown catch in a 21–17 victory over Missouri in the Holiday Bowl. It was his final play in a BYU uniform. That image of Young high-stepping and celebrating in the end zone is stamped forever on the minds of Cougars fans.

Young established himself as one of the most popular athletes in school history, and not only did he play football at BYU, he also graduated with a law degree. After a year in the USFL, he signed with the Tampa Bay Buccaneers in 1985 and was traded to the San Francisco 49ers in 1987, where he would stay until his retirement in 2000. It was with the 49ers that he really began to come on in the professional ranks, and he turned almost the entire state of Utah into die-hard 49ers fans during his tenure there.

During a pro and college career that featured eye-popping plays and amazing comebacks, he was named the NFL's MVP in 1992 and 1994 and led the 49ers to a convincing Super Bowl title in 1995. In 1999, at the beginning his 16th season in the pros, Young suffered his third concussion in four years. The previous March, at 38 years old, Young got married, and he and his wife, Barbara, had their first child in December. With health concerns and his new family playing major factors, he announced his retirement from the game in June 2000.

In 2003 BYU retired Young's No. 8 jersey. It serves as a reminder that Young started his Cougars career No. 8 on the depth chart. He became so discouraged that he seriously considered quitting, leaving school, and returning home to Connecticut. But when he called his father, Grit, and told him his plans, Grit replied, "You can quit, but you can't come home." Quitters weren't allowed in Grit Young's house. So Steve remained at BYU and had a meteoric rise up the depth chart, filling in for an injured Jim McMahon in 1981 and becoming the full-time starter in 1982. Young learned how to throw a football by watching McMahon.

Among Young's many accomplishments:

- As a senior at BYU in 1983, Young led the nation in total yards passing (3,902), total offense (4,346 yards), and touchdowns (33).
- His career totals: 592-of-908 passing for 7,733 yards and 56 touchdowns. He gained 8,817 yards of total offense in 31 games.
- In 1983, Young was selected as a consensus All-American, won the Davey O'Brien and Sammy Baugh quarterback awards, and finished second in the Heisman Trophy balloting.

- During his 15-year professional career, Young won the NFL MVP award twice (1992 and 1994) and was the only quarterback in league history to win four straight passing titles.
- In 1995 he guided the San Francisco 49ers to victory in Super Bowl XXIX with a record six touchdowns, for which he received Super Bowl MVP honors.

After football, Young got involved in business, started the Forever Young Foundation, and made a name for himself as an NFL analyst for ESPN. In 2016 he published a memoir titled *QB: My Life Behind the Spiral.*

7 The Feel of Cotton

Perhaps never did BYU play with more of a chip on its shoulder during the LaVell Edwards Era than in the 1997 Cotton Bowl in front of 71,000 fans and a national television audience.

It was the program's first and only New Year's Day bowl game, but the Cougars had been snubbed by Bowl Alliance and the more prestigious and lucrative Fiesta Bowl ($8 million payout) despite their No. 5 ranking and 13–1 record. The Cotton Bowl's payout was $2 million.

The Bowl Alliance had an at-large bid open for the Sugar and Fiesta bowls, and instead of choosing BYU, No. 2 Nebraska, which fell to Texas in the Big 12 Championship Game, went to the Sugar Bowl and No. 12 Penn State earned a Fiesta Bowl invitation to face Texas.

"If [everyone wasn't] talking about BYU, they were talking about the alliance, whose agenda has invited more conspiracy theories than the Kennedy assassination," wrote *Sports Illustrated*'s Richard Hoffer. "For some reason, at least as people at Brigham Young saw it, the alliance was conspiring to keep the Cougars out of any of its bowls." By the time the season ended, Western Athletic Conference commissioner Karl Benson and league presidents threatened a lawsuit, which led to congressional hearings.

BYU's Cotton Bowl opponent, No. 14 Kansas State, showed similar disrespect for the Cougars all week long during bowl festivities in Dallas. The Wildcats refused to talk or shake hands with Cougars players. They saved their talking for the field, where they belittled BYU and its conference.

The Cougars didn't cotton to all of this insolent treatment. "They were disrespecting us at all the events—not shaking our hands and stuff—and we took it personally," said cornerback Tim McTyer. "They wouldn't shut up," said quarterback Steve Sarkisian. "They were saying things like, 'Hey, Sark, this isn't the WAC. This is the big time.'"

The Cougars let their play do most of the talking with a couple of the biggest plays in school history in a dramatic 19–15 triumph.

Coach LaVell Edwards recalled that his team was prepared and eager to back up its lofty ranking going into the game. "We've never done a better job of focusing on the task at hand," he said.

It was a contest that featured a safety by BYU and a 41-yard Hail Mary touchdown pass by Kansas State on the final play of the first half, sending the two teams into the locker room at halftime with the Wildcats ahead by the baseball-like score of 8–5.

Things didn't go much better for the Cougars in the third quarter as Kansas State grabbed a 15–5 lead. But BYU mounted a comeback, punctuated by Sarkisian's 28-yard touchdown pass to K. O. Kealaluhi with about four minutes left in the game to put BYU ahead 19–15.

Sarkisian completed 21 of 36 passes for 291 yards and a pair of scores to earn co–outstanding offensive player honors. He was also

Final Associated Press Poll 1996

School	Record	Points
1. Florida (65.5)*	12–1	1,673.5
2. Ohio State (1.5)*	11–1	1,585.5
3. Florida State	11–1	1,529
4. Arizona State	11–1	1,486
5. BYU	14–1	1,360
6. Nebraska	11–2	1,316
7. Penn State	11–2	1,293
8. Colorado	10–2	1,228
9. Tennessee	10–2	1,172
10. North Carolina	10–2	1,070
11. Alabama	10–3	977
12. LSU	10–2	849
13. Virginia Tech	10–2	786
14. Miami (FL)	9–3	690
15. Northwestern	9–3	663
16. Washington	9–3	643
17. Kansas State	9–3	625
18. Iowa	9–3	535
19. Notre Dame	8–3	511
20. Michigan	8–4	466
21. Syracuse	9–3	451
22. Wyoming	10–2	314
23. Texas	8–5	169
24. Auburn	8–4	130
25. Army	10–2	130

* first-place votes

sacked seven times for minus-45 yards. "Steve was playing in a lot of pain in the fourth quarter," Edwards said, referring to Sarkisian's ailing throwing shoulder. "It was a gutsy performance."

But the win was preserved by the Cougars' stingy defense. The Wildcats were driving deep into BYU territory and had a first-and-10 at the 12. The Cougars figured out Kansas State was going to try a slant pass, as they had done earlier in the game. Waiting

1996 Schedule, Results

Date	Opponent	Location	W/L	Score
August 24	Texas A&M	Provo	W	41–37
August 31	Arkansas State	Provo	W	58–9
September 14	Washington	Seattle	L	29–17
September 21	New Mexico	Provo	W	17–14
September 28	SMU	Provo	W	31–3
October 4	Utah State	Logan, Utah	W	45–17
October 12	UNLV	Provo	W	63–28
October 19	Tulsa	Tulsa	W	55–30
October 26	TCU	Fort Worth	W	45–21
November 2	UTEP	Provo	W	40–18
November 9	Rice	Provo	W	49–0
November 16	Hawaii	Honolulu	W	45–14
November 23	Utah	Salt Lake City	W	37–17
December 7	Wyoming	Las Vegas	W	28–25 (OT)
January 1, 1997	Kansas State	Dallas	W	19–15

on that play, cornerback Omarr Morgan, nicknamed the Blanket, intercepted a Brian Kavanagh pass intended for Jimmy Dean on the Cougars 3-yard line with 55 seconds left. "After I caught it, I cradled it like a baby," Morgan said. "I wasn't going to drop it. It was the greatest feeling in my life."

The oft-overshadowed defense also delivered in other ways: Linebacker Shay Muirbrook tallied 11 solo tackles and a school-record six quarterback sacks, including the first-quarter safety. For his performance that day, Muirbrook was inducted into the Cotton Bowl Hall of Fame in 2012. "This is probably the best defense we've ever had at BYU," said Edwards after the game.

Some argue it was the best *team* the Cougars have ever fielded. Not only did the Cotton Bowl triumph secure BYU's top-five finish in the final rankings, it also gave the Cougars a then-NCAA-record 14th win that season. "Winning 14 games is a great accomplishment," said running back Brian McKenzie. "It could be duplicated in the future, but we'll always be the team that accomplished it first. It's something that you can look back on and tell your kids."

Kansas State coach Bill Snyder credited the Cougars. "They're ranked No. 5 in the country and deserve to be," he said. With the win, BYU sent a message to Kansas State, the Bowl Alliance, and the rest of the college football world. That message? "We proved," Muirbrook said, "we're for real."

8 Danny Ainge

Danny Ainge is the author of the most iconic play in BYU basketball history, and one of the most famous in NCAA tournament history. That play sent the Cougars to their first and only Elite Eight appearance in the team's history. In 1981 Ainge helped BYU explode onto the national stage with a spectacular performance in that tournament.

It began with Ainge writhing in pain with a back injury on the eve of the Cougars' opening-round win over Providence. At the last moment, when nobody expected him to play, he ended up leading BYU to a victory. Then came his 37-point effort to defeat UCLA.

In the East Regional semifinals against Notre Dame at the Omni in Atlanta, BYU trailed by one after the Fighting Irish hit a 16-foot jumper with eight seconds left. The game ended with Ainge's coast-to-coast dash through the entire Notre Dame five with a layup over the outstretched fingertips of Orlando Woolridge just before the final buzzer.

"The ball came into Ainge, who looked neither right nor left but to the basket. He broke into a dribble, went behind his back to the center-line, cut through heavy traffic like a fire chief late for lunch, his siren blaring, roared into the circle, found the door open and drove on to the hoop, sank a little, simple playground layup, and everywhere Irish were left in grief," wrote Furman Bisher of the *Atlanta Journal-Constitution.*

"We tried to stop him. But he's just too good an athlete," lamented Notre Dame coach Digger Phelps. "He reads so well that he just went to the opposite direction, got the ball, and took it down the floor, right through five people."

With that, the Cougars reached the Elite Eight before falling to Ralph Sampson and Virginia. But BYU relished reaching those heights. When Ainge arrived on campus, the proud BYU basketball program was coming off four consecutive losing seasons. As a freshman, Ainge made a big impact, but the Cougars were a sub-.500 team again. In each of the next three seasons, the Cougars won at least 20 games and advanced to the NCAA tournament.

When Ainge was a sophomore, he poured in 40 points in a victory over visiting Oral Roberts, whose coach, Lake Kelly, made the politically incorrect observation, "He's the best white basketball player I've ever seen."

During his four-year career, Ainge was a consensus All-American, Western Athletic Conference Player of the Year, and set an NCAA record with 112 consecutive games scoring in double figures. He also broke the school scoring record with 2,467 points—a mark that stood for 30 years. What makes that career scoring number even more impressive is that he did it without the benefit of the three-point line, which wasn't implemented until 1986.

Ainge was a consensus All-American by winning the Eastman and John Wooden Awards. He also held the school's assists and steals records until they were broken in 2002 and 2011, respectively.

If that weren't enough, in the summers, the Eugene, Oregon, native played professional baseball in the Toronto Blue Jays organization. The Boston Celtics ended up selecting Ainge in the second round of the 1981 draft, which led to a protracted legal battle with the Blue Jays over Ainge's services. The Blue Jays won the trial, but the Celtics ended up buying out Ainge's contract.

Ainge made the right choice to pursue professional basketball. In his three seasons as a Toronto infielder, he had a major league batting average of .220. "I'm reminded of adversity every time I look at the back of my baseball cards that the kids make me sign," he said. "And I usually try to sign the back of them so I can cover up all my statistics."

Ainge was a key part of the Celtics' NBA championships in 1984 and 1986, playing alongside superstars Larry Bird, Kevin McHale, Robert Parish, and Dennis Johnson. He also played on the 1988 NBA All-Star team.

"Danny Ainge was always a delight. He was smart, accessible, and witty," said *Boston Globe* columnist Bob Ryan. "He loved to talk baseball. After a good game that he had early in his career, I asked him if this was his best day, and he said, 'No, I went 3-for-4 at Yankee Stadium.' I used to kid him that he hit two home runs but never one outdoors. He hit one in Seattle and one in Toronto."

Later, Ainge went on to play for the Sacramento Kings, Portland Trailblazers, and Phoenix Suns in a 14-year NBA career. He finished with 1,002 three-point field goals and having played in 193 NBA playoff games. After he retired, he coached with the Suns.

On March 8, 2003, in front of a sellout crowd of 22,702 at the Marriott Center, Ainge became the first Cougars basketball player to have his jersey—No. 22—retired. It hangs in the rafters of the building.

Ainge is currently the president of basketball operations for the Celtics. He was named the 2008 NBA Executive of the Year after Boston's NBA championship.

9 Jim McMahon

Sporting a suit coat bedecked with a bright flowered pattern, an earring in his ear, and his signature sunglasses, former BYU quarterback Jim McMahon was inducted into the BYU Athletic Hall of Fame in September 2014, at the Marriott Center. "I better not screw this up," McMahon joked when he stood to deliver his acceptance speech. "I just passed public-speaking [class]."

McMahon has worn sunglasses, inside and outside, throughout his life. At age six he accidentally severed the retina in his right eye with a fork while trying to loosen a string. Because of that injury, he has been sensitive to light. But it certainly didn't interfere with his field vision. McMahon saw things unfold during a play more than most quarterbacks.

During his BYU career, McMahon broke 75 NCAA records and guided the Cougars to their first two bowl victories. But it wasn't until he recently completed his last four classes to graduate—including a public-speaking course—that he was eligible for induction into BYU's Hall of Fame. "I studied more the last eight months than I did in five years of college when I was here," McMahon said. "I never would have guessed 32 years ago when I left here that I would be standing here today."

When McMahon was inducted into the College Football Hall of Fame in 1998, he returned to campus and was honored during halftime ceremonies. "Ninety percent of my memories here were made down there on that field. I came here to play, not to go to school," he said at the time. "I'd make sure I was eligible, but I didn't come here to be a doctor. I never did like school. Of course, I would have been that way at any college. Now I'm trying to tell my kids to go to college."

Before "The Super Bowl Shuffle," Jim McMahon was a fresh-faced QB in Provo.

Legendary coach LaVell Edwards, who presented McMahon for the BYU Hall of Fame via a video tribute, said McMahon nearly left BYU after his sophomore season. "I wasn't really happy," McMahon explained. "There were two people that I owe the rest of my BYU career to—one is Dr. Brent Pratley, who was our orthopedic surgeon at the time, and the other is my ex-wife, Nancy."

McMahon said that without their friendship and support, he would have gone elsewhere. He was BYU's rebel without a cause, unless that cause was winning games. McMahon's lifestyle didn't fit in with BYU's stringent honor code. "He spent more time in my office than I did," Edwards said of McMahon.

Fortunately for BYU, McMahon stayed in Provo. In his final two seasons, McMahon threw for 8,126 yards and 77 touchdowns and was a first-team All-American as a junior in 1980 and a consensus All-America selection in 1981. McMahon set 32 NCAA records in 1980, including single-season records for total offense (4,627 yards), passing yards (4,571), touchdown passes (47), and passing efficiency (176.9).

McMahon was the No. 5 overall pick of the Chicago Bears in the 1982 NFL Draft and, known as "the punky QB," helped lead the Bears to a Super Bowl title at the end of the 1985 season.

During his BYU Athletic Hall of Fame induction, McMahon expressed appreciation for his BYU teammates, saying, "I couldn't do everything myself. I had a great group of guys around me." At least one of those guys, Clay Brown—who caught the game-winning Hail Mary pass from McMahon to win the 1980 Holiday Bowl—attended the Hall of Fame ceremony. McMahon also thanked his former BYU coaches, including Doug Scovil and Ted Tollner, as well as Tom Holmoe, who now serves as BYU's athletic director.

He was also grateful to his teachers at BYU who helped him finish his last four classes to graduate, and his girlfriend, Laurie Navon, who helped push McMahon to finish his academic work.

He also mentioned his two daughters and two sons, who accompanied him on his return to Provo. "I think they understand now, after seeing stuff on the walls around here, that I was actually pretty good," McMahon said of his children. "I could actually play."

Finally, he paid homage to his parents. "Mom and Dad," McMahon said, "I did this for you."

Impressively, McMahon finished his degree while struggling with early onset dementia and depression, issues he believes were caused by the pounding he took playing football. Holmoe, a former teammate of McMahon's, did everything he could to ensure McMahon would graduate. "I've had tears since the day he said, 'I'm done,'" Holmoe said. "Jim is my favorite teammate I ever had from Pop Warner to the NFL. He was so much fun to be around. He was a serious dude, a field general, a smart student of the game who played it to perfection, and he had fun doing it. To go out to practice or play with Jim McMahon, it was like sandlot."

At halftime of the BYU–Utah State game in 2014, McMahon's No. 9 jersey was retired. A banner with McMahon's name and number were unveiled and will be permanently displayed on the press box at LaVell Edwards Stadium.

10 Dethroning No. 1 Miami

BYU fans have a longstanding reputation for being relatively staid when they attend football games at LaVell Edwards Stadium. But on September 8, 1990, at least for one night, that reputation was ruined. That's when BYU upset No. 1–ranked defending national champion Miami 28–21 on national television at what was then known as Cougar Stadium. Fans uncharacteristically showed up in droves well before kickoff, and not only did they stay through the entire game, they also celebrated raucously (in a stone-cold sober way) on the field after the Cougars' landmark victory.

It stands as the most memorable event in the history of the stadium and one of the biggest college football games in the history of the state of Utah. "I've never been in anything like that before," quarterback Ty Detmer said afterward of the spontaneous post-game party, which saw fans transform the field into a giant mosh pit. "I was just trying to high-five everybody. I took more hits going in [to the locker room] than I did the whole game."

Some fans wore blue Ty Detmer ties to promote the Cougars quarterback for the Heisman Trophy. As it turned out, Detmer stated his own case loud and clear. And he had plenty of backing from the then-record crowd of 66,235. "They were on their feet the whole night," Detmer said of the fans. "The student section right behind us really kept us going."

The game was billed as the state of Utah's version of the Game of the Century. BYU's sports information office issued 300 press credentials, including to media outlets such as *Sports Illustrated* (which did a story on the game in its next issue) and reporters from places such as New York, Chicago, Los Angeles, and Dallas. "Were you there?" then–BYU offensive coordinator Norm Chow asked a reporter a few years after the Miami game. "It was like electricity."

The BYU-Miami showdown was preceded by months of hype and buildup as Hurricanes players boasted that their quarterback, Craig Erickson, was better than Detmer. "He definitely isn't a great quarterback," Miami's Hurlie Brown said of Detmer. "Erickson is a great quarterback. Detmer is just good." That was one of many shots fired by the 'Canes. They said the Cougars' offensive line was slow and that the Miami offense would run over BYU's defense. Such disparaging comments didn't go unnoticed by BYU players and coaches.

32

The 'Canes were a 13.5-point favorite over the No. 16 Cougars, and all week leading up to the game, just about everybody predicted a Miami win. Legendary BYU coach LaVell Edwards, not one given to hyperbole, admitted that the game was huge. "It truly is a big event for us," he said. "What I think it is, is a tremendous opportunity, the kind of game you hope will come along for your program." Afterward, Edwards said, "It obviously has to be one of the biggest nights we've ever had, the biggest regular-season night we've had." So big that one Cougars player, defensive lineman Rich Kaufusi, later wrote an entire book, *Calming the Storm*, about that one game.

Not only did BYU dethrone the top-ranked team and defending national champs, but Detmer's Heisman Trophy–worthy performance grabbed the nation's attention. He ended up winning college football's top individual prize in December that year. Against Miami, Detmer completed 38 of 54 passes for 406 yards, one interception, and three touchdowns. Though Detmer was sacked a couple times, he was still able to elude the ferocious Miami rush and, like a magician, made big plays that baffled the Hurricanes defense.

"Ty Detmer, to me, is unbelievable," Miami coach Dennis Erickson said. "He made some great plays and throws with pressure in his face. Obviously, he's a great, great quarterback, and he showed it tonight."

At one point during the game, Detmer absorbed a hard hit as he completed a pass, resulting in a completion and a gash in Detmer's chin that required several stitches. But that was one of the rare times Miami actually got to Detmer. Another time, Detmer scrambled around in the backfield like he was playing tag in the backyard, escaping the grasp of a pair of Miami defenders, who ran into each other like a couple Keystone Kops. Then Detmer calmly threw a touchdown pass.

Though the Cougars coughed up five turnovers that almost marred the upset, Detmer almost overshadowed BYU's physical, opportunistic defense. The Cougars scored for the final time with three minutes left in the third quarter; then twice in the fourth quarter, the BYU defense came up with big stops. Alema Fitisemanu recovered a Miami fumble at the Cougars 15-yard line. Later, BYU fumbled at its own 37 and the 'Canes marched to the 13. On third-and-10, Cougars cornerback Ervin Lee intercepted an Erickson pass to turn Miami away. Finally, with less than two minutes left and the Hurricanes driving deep into BYU territory, the Cougars held again after an incompletion on fourth down on a ball was batted down by Lee.

BYU then ran out the clock, touching off a wild celebration in Provo as fans stormed the field with unbridled joy. It marked BYU's first—and only—victory over a No. 1–ranked opponent. Days later, the Cougars vaulted from No. 16 to No. 5 in the AP poll—their highest ranking since winning the 1984 national championship. Three voters were so impressed by BYU's win that they put the Cougars at No. 1 on their ballots. Fans in Provo talked about another national title.

Unfortunately for the Cougars, they lost a few weeks later at Oregon to spoil their undefeated season. BYU ended the 10–3 year with back-to-back blowout losses at Hawaii and against Texas A&M in the Holiday Bowl.

But on September 8, 1990, fans in Provo saw the top-ranked Hurricanes reduced to a mere breeze. Mighty Miami huffed and puffed, but it couldn't blow down the house that Edwards built. Provo had never seen a night quite like that, and it hasn't seen one since.

11 Beating Michigan for the National Championship

There may be more memorable touchdowns in BYU football history than the one Kelly Smith scored late in the 1984 Holiday Bowl. But he can lay claim to the one that ultimately lifted the Cougars to the national championship. His 13-yard TD catch from Robbie Bosco with 1:23 remaining beat Michigan and completed BYU's perfect 13–0 season. Prior to that game-winning touchdown, the top-ranked Cougars and unranked Wolverines were tied 17–17.

After suffering through a game that saw the Cougars turn the ball over six times and have a field-goal attempt blocked, BYU had one last chance to redeem itself. On third down, with the ball at the Michigan 13, the play call came into the huddle—69 halfback option. The primary receiver was Smith, a running back from Beaver, Utah, who had caught nine passes already that night. But on that play, Smith was double-teamed, and tight end David Mills, the second option, "got tackled," according to Smith.

"Robbie scrambled and we all went to different places. It was actually a broken play," said Smith. "I went down the sidelines, and Bosco found me in the back of the end zone. I wasn't supposed to be there." Bosco's pass to Smith gave the Cougars a 24–17 lead, which ended up being the final score.

BYU has never had more at stake in a game than it did on December 21, 1984, against Michigan. The Holiday Bowl pitted the No. 1 12–0 Cougars against a 6–5 Wolverines team. To win a national championship, the only thing the Cougars could control was beating Michigan and remaining unbeaten.

"The team goal was to go undefeated. By doing that, we would give ourselves a chance to win the national championship," said wide receiver Glen Kozlowski. "We just wanted to win every game. That's all we did. We talked about a national championship. But it wasn't that we would win it but that we would give ourselves a chance to win it if we went undefeated."

BYU wanted to play No. 2 Oklahoma in the Orange Bowl, but the Cougars were contractually obligated to play in the Holiday Bowl as the Western Athletic Conference champions. A loss to Michigan not only would have ruined any shot at a national championship but it would have justified the criticisms that the Cougars had absorbed from detractors around the country.

The Wolverines did everything they could to smash BYU's hopes of a national title. In the first quarter, Bosco dropped back and completed a pass to Kozlowski. At the end of the play, Michigan's Mike Hammerstein unloaded on Bosco, injuring his left leg. An official whistled Hammerstein for a late-hit penalty and Bosco was removed from the game as trainers and doctors attended to his left knee and left ankle. "I got hit down low," Bosco said. "My foot got stuck in the ground and [Hammerstein] rolled on it. He twisted it really bad. The most pain of the whole injury was my ankle."

Backup quarterback Blaine Fowler replaced Bosco, who was taken to the locker room. As it turned out, Bosco had sustained a partial medial collateral tear in the knee, and a Grade 2 ankle sprain. "I was thinking, *I can't believe I went the whole season without being injured*," Bosco said. "Now here's the biggest game of our careers, and I get injured."

As much as his leg hurt, not being able to play hurt even worse. Inside the locker room at Jack Murphy Stadium, Bosco could hear the muffled sounds of the crowd—and it was killing him. He approached quarterbacks coach Mike Holmgren and told him he wanted back into the game. "Are you sure?" Holmgren asked. Bosco was sure, and he returned early in the second quarter. But because of his physical limitations, the Cougars decided to employ the shotgun formation, something they hadn't done before during that season.

Somehow the Cougars made it work. A gimpy Bosco made plays when he needed to, completing 30 of 42 passes for 343 yards and two touchdowns. He also threw three interceptions. "Never have I seen a more courageous performance by a kid," LaVell Edwards said of Bosco after the game. "He was in pain. But as long as he could stand up, he wanted to play."

There was plenty to celebrate in the 1984 Holiday Bowl, including this fumble recovery in the second quarter of the game.

While BYU rolled up 483 total yards compared to 202 for Michigan, the Cougars' turnovers kept the game close. In fact, the Wolverines enjoyed a 17–10 advantage early in the fourth quarter. That only set the stage for another vintage Holiday Bowl finish.

The Cougars scored two touchdowns in the final 11 minutes, starting with a leaping grab in the back of the end zone by Kozlowski, who soared over a Michigan defender to tie the game at 17. As it had all night (and all season) long, BYU's defense came up big again to give the offense the ball back at its own 17-yard line with 4:36 remaining. Then came the Cougars' final drive that was capped by Smith's game winner.

BYU linebacker Marv Allen intercepted a Michigan pass with 44 seconds left to clinch the win. That was fitting, considering the key role BYU's defense played that night. "We had a lot of great players on that team. We as a defense were underrated by other people all year," said linebacker Leon White, a San Diego native who went on to play several seasons in the NFL. "When Robbie went down, it was big for the defense to step up. Without the defense that year, we wouldn't have been able to do what we did. You're not supposed to win games when you turn the ball over six times."

Two weeks later, on January 3, 1985, after the New Year's Day bowl games were completed, BYU was officially crowned national champions in the Associated Press and United Press International polls.

12 Jimmer Fredette

When James Taft Fredette was born, his mother, Kay, dubbed him Jimmer, and the name stuck like Velcro. "He was full of energy right from the start, and it fit him," Kay said. Her daughter Lindsay was nine when Jimmer was born, and initially she refused to use that moniker for her brother. "She didn't realize there was a method to my madness," Kay explained. "I knew people would one day remember that name." Mom was right. Now everybody knows his name . . . and his game.

During his four years playing basketball at BYU, Fredette became known all over the country. And it seems everyone knows the prolific-scoring guard with the boy-next-door persona and aw-shucks smile simply as Jimmer.

Fredette's meteoric rise to national prominence began with natural talent, a competitive spirit, and a loving family—including an older brother who wouldn't let him settle for anything less than greatness. Jimmer honed his unconventional game in unconventional ways and unconventional places, and at BYU the Cougars guard made the amazing happen on a regular basis. In 2010 Jimmer scored 37 points while leading the Cougars to a double-overtime win over Florida for their first NCAA Tournament victory in 17 years. A year later, the senior guided BYU to its first Sweet 16 appearance in 30 years.

Along the way, Jimmer became a recognizable word in college basketball vernacular, as in "You got Jimmered," chanted after he would unleash a flood of points on an opponent. He inspired countless musical, Internet, and cardboard tributes. His relentless will to score produced highlights that live on in perpetuity on YouTube. He single-handedly spawned legions of Cougars fans in his hometown and wound up as the best BYU basketball player since the legendary Danny Ainge. In the end, Jimmer Fredette became BYU's first consensus All-American since Ainge.

Jimmer freely admits he wouldn't be the basketball player he is without his older brother, TJ, who loved Jimmer but didn't coddle him. As Jimmer excelled in high school, TJ knew his brother's goal was to play in the NBA. So TJ drew up a contract. Jimmer signed the piece of paper and hung it in the room he and TJ shared in Glens Falls, New York. He read the contract every day.

Though he was largely unknown, especially in the West, it didn't take long for Jimmer to establish a national reputation in college. As a sophomore, Fredette started in 32 of 33 games, was the Cougars' second-leading scorer, and was named an All–Mountain West Conference player. He began to attract attention in earnest early in his junior season when he poured in 49 points at Arizona—shattering a 48-year-old BYU scoring record of 47 points in a game. "The improvement he made from his sophomore to junior year catapulted him into an arena where he received national attention," said head coach Dave Rose.

Jimmer's unlimited range was so dangerous that he scored from almost anywhere on the court, and in a variety of ways. He owned a vast repertoire of shots, such as his patented crossover three-pointers, windmill reverse layups, off-balance jumpers, and floaters in the lane that made opposing defenses shake their heads in capitulation. Few foes found a way to slow him down, let alone stop him, despite devising a multitude of defensive schemes for that purpose.

In January 2011 Jimmermania shifted into high gear. First there was his 47-point outburst at Utah, including a 40-foot shot at the buzzer to cap a 32-point first-half effort. It was so impressive that even some Utes fans rose to their feet. That was followed by a 42-point explosion at Colorado State. Then on January 26, in perhaps the biggest game ever played at the Marriott Center, No. 9 BYU downed No. 4 San Diego State as Fredette dumped 43 points

Jackson Emery Steals Record

During much of his basketball career at BYU, guard Jackson Emery was overshadowed by superstar consensus All-American Jimmer Fredette. But Emery was a huge part of the Cougars' success during those seasons, and he's considered one of the best defensive players in school history. BYU played mostly zone defense, relying on Emery to do much of the heavy lifting on the defensive end of the court.

It was fitting that on the day Emery broke Danny Ainge's record of 195 career steals, it came on the same night that Fredette dropped 47 points, including six three-pointers (one of those was the half-court shot at the halftime buzzer) in a 104–79 rout at Utah. Emery finished with 249 career steals.

Emery joined the program in 2005–06, which was also Coach Dave Rose's first season at the helm. At the time, BYU was coming off a 9–21 campaign. Emery finished his career having helped lead the Cougars to a 32–5 record and their first trip to the Sweet 16 since 1981.

on the Aztecs—in front of a sellout crowd of nearly 23,000, including 24 NBA scouts.

By that night, the Jimmer story had gone viral. There was ubiquitous coverage—in tweets, blogs, and newspapers as well as national television and radio. It was all Jimmer all the time on the ESPN family of networks. After the San Diego State game, NBA star Kevin Durant, who had scored 47 points himself that evening, tweeted, "Jimmer Fredette is the best scorer in the world!!"

During Jimmer's senior year, the Cougars won a school-record 32 games, claimed a share of the MWC regular-season championship, earned their first trip to the Sweet 16 since 1981, and spent numerous weeks ranked in the top 10, peaking at No. 3.

Jimmer Fredette achieved his goal of playing in the NBA. He was drafted in the first round, No. 10 overall, in the 2011 NBA Draft before bouncing around the league with the Sacramento Kings, Chicago Bulls, New Orleans Pelicans, and New York Knicks. His defense and foot speed were considered liabilities in the NBA. But when he signed with the Shanghai Sharks in August 2016, Jimmer started doing Jimmer things again, sinking long three-pointers just like he did at BYU.

Years after leaving Provo, Jimmermania swept China. By the end of the 2016 season, Fredette was named International MVP of the Chinese Basketball Association. He averaged 37.4 points, 8 rebounds, and 4.3 assists while shooting 40 percent from three-point range. During that season, he poured in 73 points in a single game.

Chinese basketball fans know Jimmer by the titles Lonely God and Loneliness Master because his play is at such a high level, nobody compares to him.

13 Answered Prayer

As the sun was setting that brisk, late November afternoon in Salt Lake City, the sun was also setting on John Beck's mercurial college career. The senior quarterback trotted onto the field at Rice-Eccles Stadium with his team trailing Utah 31–27 with 1:09 remaining. The ball rested on BYU's own 25-yard line, and the red-clad Utes fans were intoxicated with joy, reveling in anticipation of a big upset of a ranked team and spoiling the Cougars' season—again.

Meanwhile, Beck's legacy as a BYU quarterback hung in the balance. Despite all he had accomplished during the 2006 season (ascending to No. 2 all-time in passing in school history and becoming only the second returned missionary quarterback to lead the Cougars to a conference championship), the way BYU fans would remember him—fair or not—would be determined by the outcome of this series. Besides that, he was confronting demons from his past: that he couldn't win a close game and couldn't beat the archrival Utes.

Sure, the Cougars had already clinched an outright Mountain West Conference championship and had accepted a bid to play in the Las Vegas Bowl. But the season would not be complete without a win over Utah. BYU had lost four straight games to the Utes. The Cougars knew they still had some unfinished business. For them, could any success compensate for failure against Utah?

Due to a blocked extra point earlier in the quarter, a field goal wouldn't be enough on this drive. It was touchdown or bust. Despite the weight of the hopes and dreams of Cougars fans saddled on his shoulder pads, Beck was unflappable. "He came in the huddle and said, 'We're going to get this done. We're going to score,'" said tight end Daniel Coats. "He was just cool, calm, and collected."

On the sideline, Beck's teammates were confident, but even they couldn't have predicted what was about to unfold. As he had done throughout the season, Beck methodically marched the Cougars down the field to the Utah 11-yard line, which included converting on a clutch fourth-and-4 pass to tight end Jonny Harline with 27 seconds remaining. That eventually set up a third-and-10 situation with 3.2 seconds left. BYU took a timeout to devise a final play.

Offensive coordinator Robert Anae called 59, with the first option a fade throw to Harline on the right side of the end zone. "I got to the line and signaled the play," Beck recalled. "I just took a deep breath. I reminded myself how many times in my career plays didn't go our way. Those were tough on me, because I wanted to make the play. When I took that deep breath, it reminded me of all those times I promised myself that when I had a chance to make the play, I would make it."

What happened next was nothing like the way 59 is drawn up. That's because Utah's defense opted to drop eight players into zone

Voices of the Cougars

Since 1965 there have been only two Voices of the Cougars—Paul James and Greg Wrubell.

James, an Ogden native, started his play-by-play career calling University of Utah football and basketball games, but when the radio station that employed him, KDYL, lost the broadcast rights to Utes games, he accepted a job offer from KSL Radio, the 50,000-watt Clear Channel Radio (now iHeartMedia) station and longtime flagship of BYU athletics. James also served as sports director at KSL-TV until 1991, teaming up with anchorman Dick Nourse and weatherman Bob Welti, the longest-running nightly news team in the country at that time. James stopped calling BYU basketball games in 1996 and was replaced by Wrubell, though he would continue to call football games.

In the press box at Utah's Rice-Eccles Stadium before kickoff of the BYU-Utah game in 1996, James was treated for a heart ailment. Paramedics had him sign a release before he broadcasted that game. Afterward, James drove himself to the hospital and underwent a sextuple-bypass heart surgery (that's six, folks).

Before the 2000 season, legendary coach LaVell Edwards announced his retirement at the end of that year, and James, as he had previously promised, decided to retire as well. James, who was the Voice of the Cougars for 35 years, was inducted into the BYU Athletics Hall of Fame in 2005.

Wrubell became the new Voice of the Cougars for football at the beginning of the 2001 season, the same year Gary Crowton replaced Edwards. Before taking over play-by-play duties, Wrubell had been the sideline reporter for KSL since 1992.

A native of Canada, Wrubell enrolled at BYU in 1984. "My freshman year, BYU happened to win a national championship, so I just figured that was the way that it went," Wrubell recalled. "I learned about BYU in a hurry. It was a great year to start getting immersed in the tradition."

In 2016 Wrubell left KSL to become BYU's director of broadcast media, and remained on board as the Voice of the Cougars and part of the IMG Network.

coverage. Beck and the Cougars would have to improvise and resort to playground tactics.

When the ball was snapped, Harline sprinted into the right side of the end zone then dragged all the way to the left side of the end zone, covering some 40 yards. While the rest of the Cougars receivers drifted to the right side, the Utes defenders followed. That left Harline all by himself. Beck danced to his left then scrambled to his right, surveying the field, directing traffic, and searching for an open receiver. The strong-armed Beck was hit, then he jumped into the air and threw across his body to the opposite side of the field. Beck's wing-and-a-prayer found Harline, fittingly, on his knees as he slid to cradle the ball in his arms just inside the goal line. Touchdown. BYU 33, Utah 31. In real time, the play lasted 12 seconds, the same number that was on Beck's jersey. "After a while the play just kind of broke up," Harline said later. "I just ran to where I thought I'd be open."

That final play capped perhaps the greatest game in the long history of the rivalry and served as the perfect culmination of a magical regular season. "It's a play I dreamed [of] being a part of since I was little," Beck said. "I grew up watching highlights of Jim McMahon in the Miracle Bowl, Steve Young against Missouri when they threw it back to him, and so many of Ty Detmer's amazing plays. To be able to be here at BYU, wearing that same *Y* on my helmet, to be able to be a part of a play like that, means a lot to me."

Beck completed 28 of 43 passes for 375 yards and four touchdowns. He led three touchdown drives in the fourth quarter, all with BYU trailing. The lead changed hands three times in the game's final three and a half minutes.

For Beck, it was sweet redemption, and erased memories of his past failings in clutch situations. One year earlier, in overtime, he had tossed an incompletion in the end zone that thwarted his team's shot at a victory over the Utes. Beck proved he had learned from past mistakes. "This is what we prepared for," Beck said. "All those times the last two years where we've come so close have been preparing me for this. I've gone over plays in my head, and those losses prepared me for moments like this, when a play needs to be made. Just be calm and make a play."

14 BYU's Declaration of Independence

In the wake a major conference shakeup during the summer of 2010, BYU found itself standing at a crossroads, as part of the changes that occurred saw archrival Utah bolt from the Mountain West Conference to become part of the new Pac-12 in June. Left behind, and frustrated by aspects of the Mountain West, BYU needed to evaluate its position in the college football world.

In July Coach Bronco Mendenhall told reporters convened at Media Day in Las Vegas that his program was "prepared to go it alone, if that is what it comes down to" in order to remain competitive among the top echelon of college football. About one month later, Mendenhall's words proved prophetic, as BYU announced on August 31, 2010, that it would be leaving the MW and becoming a football independent, starting with the 2011 season.

While the Cougars' move raised eyebrows around the country as it transitioned to an independent, it was clear that they weren't completely alone. In addition to the plan to navigate the largely uncharted waters of independence, athletic director Tom Holmoe also announced that the school had signed an eight-year contract with ESPN to broadcast home games on the network. It was also a significant financial upgrade from being in the Mountain West. "This is the pathway we chose to go for," Holmoe said that day.

Attend a Road Game in Four Different Time Zones

As an independent football program, BYU plays games from coast to coast. Whether it's at Boston College or Georgia Tech or UCLA or Texas, BYU fans show up in droves. They even turn out at remote places such as Las Cruces, New Mexico. BYU's coaches frequently express gratitude toward the fans who attend road games in droves.

Former BYU athletic director Glen Tuckett believed the Cougars could increase exposure for the Church of Jesus Christ of Latter-day Saints by playing in various areas of the country, providing church members with chances to see BYU in action. "We always wanted to get the team where the saints could see us," Tuckett said. Current athletic director Tom Holmoe shares a similar belief, having scheduled games all over the country.

Since going independent, BYU has played games against a variety of opponents from all five Power 5 conferences as well as the Group of 5 leagues. The Cougars have played the following programs either on the road or at neutral sites: Ole Miss, Texas, Oregon State, Hawaii, Boise State, Notre Dame, Georgia Tech, New Mexico State, Virginia, Houston, Wisconsin, Nevada, Connecticut, Central Florida, Middle Tennessee, California, Nebraska, UCLA, Michigan, Missouri, San Jose State, Arizona, West Virginia, Cincinnati, and Michigan State. In all, since becoming an independent, the Cougars have played road games in nearly 20 different states.

In the coming years, BYU has games scheduled against Louisiana State, Mississippi State, East Carolina, Fresno State, Washington, Toledo, Washington State, Massachusetts, Arizona State, Northern Illinois, Stanford, Minnesota, South Florida, USC, Baylor, Oregon, and Tennessee.

For many BYU fans, including those who live outside Utah, the road schedule is the highlight of being independent. "I'm so glad BYU has gone independent and that they are willing to travel all over the country," said Dan Vawdrey from Norfolk, Virginia. "For the fans that live outside Utah, it gives us a chance to go see the Cougars, and sometimes not have to travel far to do it."

BYU wanted to capitalize on its national brand and have its games televised by ESPN in order to gain exposure for itself and its sponsoring institution, the Church of Jesus Christ of Latter-day Saints.

Holmoe also unveiled the plans to put together a diverse and difficult schedule. "Our vision is to play football games across the country against many of the storied football programs in their legendary stadiums and to have those same highly regarded programs return to Provo to play in LaVell Edwards Stadium," Holmoe said. "One of the challenges of being an independent in football is that of scheduling games. With the success of our football and basketball programs, it hasn't been easy to get teams to come to LaVell Edwards Stadium and the Marriott Center. There's another area where our new partnership with ESPN will benefit us. The top matchmaker in college sports."

"This is just a tremendous day for ESPN to be back in business with BYU in a formal basis," Dave Brown, ESPN vice president of programming and acquisition, told reporters. "It's a tremendous addition to our college football schedule."

Legendary former BYU coach LaVell Edwards, who attended the news conference, said the relationship with ESPN began three decades before. ESPN's first live regular-season college football game, in 1984, featured BYU knocking off Pittsburgh. "We had a lot of exciting games. We started throwing the football before anybody else did, and so that right away created a lot of excitement," Edwards said. "ESPN was a new company and we were kind of the new kids on the block. We just kind of grew up together that way."

Holmoe said the decision to go independent was years in the making. "We have studied this long and hard. We felt a responsibility to do the right thing." He described the previous two weeks in this process of going independent as everything from "terrible" to "exhilarating." Added Holmoe, "We knew we could not let this window of opportunity pass us by."

During its stint as an independent, questions have arisen about the sustainability of independence in a landscape that features an increasingly wider financial gulf between the haves and the have-nots in college football. As an independent, BYU sits in a college football no-man's-land of sorts—not really part of the Power 5 conferences, not really part of the Group of 5 conferences.

Six years after going independent, Holmoe addressed BYU fans in a video message, assuring them the reasons for going independent remained valid. "Six seasons later, our stated goals in going independent have been reached and surpassed to levels we never expected," Holmoe said. "We are averaging 10 football and 14 men's basketball games a year on ABC or ESPN. Our partnership with ESPN is strong. It's unique. It gives us an opportunity to play some of the nation's best competition in front of a national audience."

In the six years since going independent, 47 of BYU's football games have been broadcast on one of the major national TV networks.

15 The Hawaiian Leap

It's regarded as the single-greatest defensive play in BYU football history, and one of the best in college football history. On September 22, 1984, in Honolulu, Hawaii, Cougars safety Kyle Morrell's timed leap over the line of scrimmage to tackle Hawaii quarterback Raphel Cherry just short of the goal line helped preserve a hard-fought 18–13 win and, as it turned out, played a key role in BYU's eventual national championship.

"Whenever I go anywhere, like the golf course or a movie, there's always somebody who introduces me as that guy who jumped over the line at Hawaii," Morrell said years later. "They don't remember my name. They just remember that play. It's kind of funny. I've gotten a lot of recognition for it, which is nice. But I'm just an average guy who was put in a position to make a play, and fortunately, it worked out."

As great as that play was, is it frustrating to be remembered for only one? "That's the thing. I remember a lot of other plays I made," said Morrell, who ended up playing in the NFL. "The coaches have told me, 'That play won the national championship, but you made so many other great plays.' A lot of the coaches remember me as a kid who was willing to fly around on the football field and sacrifice his body."

Vai Sikahema, who starred on that '84 team, said this about Morrell's play: "It's arguable, but the greatest single play in BYU sports was Kyle Morrell's leap over the line at Hawaii. That play, to me, kept us on course that season. That one play, to me, epitomized an entire season. It was a microcosm of the entire season. Guys on our team did that—left their assignments for the greater good of the team, to make a play."

In October No. 6–ranked, 3–0 BYU was in the Islands facing a fired-up Hawaii squad. At the end of three quarters, the score was BYU 12, Hawaii 10. In the fourth quarter, Cherry led his team on a 10-minute, 84-yard drive down to the BYU 2-yard line, first-and-goal. On first and second downs, Cherry tried a quarterback sneak, but both times he was stopped after minimal gains by linebacker Marv Allen. That brought third-and-inches. Morrell decided on his own to line up across the line of scrimmage from Cherry as if he were the middle linebacker.

Just as Cherry took the snap, Morrell, with flawless timing, ran toward the line of scrimmage, launched himself over the center, collared Cherry by the shoulder pads, and made a complete flip in the air. On his way down to the Aloha Bowl turf, his teammates smothered Cherry. Hawaii had to settle for the field goal, giving them a 13–12 lead.

"Throughout the game, I really got to know their cadences," Morrell explained. "We were trying to disguise our coverages all night. I always tried to keep myself in position. I just thought, *You've got to make something happen.* It was an instinctive thing. I'll never forget Raphel Cherry. I remember I could see his eyes as I went over the line. They were as big as saucers."

"I had no idea whatsoever that Kyle was going to do something like that. Honestly, even at the time, I didn't really know what happened," said defensive lineman Jim Herrmann. "It wasn't until I got back from Hawaii, after seeing the replay, that I realized what had happened. He timed it perfectly. It honestly was one of the top five plays in college football history. When you look at the net effect of an undefeated season and what he did, it was a big play for sure."

At the time, Morrell didn't think of his heady play as a big deal. But over the course of the next week, the play was being shown all across the nation, including on *Late Night with David Letterman.*

While die-hard Cougars fans remember Morrell's improvisational play, it's not so well-known nationally. "That may be one of the single-most outstanding plays that I've ever seen a guy make," Coach LaVell Edwards recalled. "It's a shame it didn't happen today, because it would have been on ESPN and all of the other [highlight shows], because that play never got the [media attention] it should have. It was special."

"I'm a college football analyst for ESPN now, and I see a lot of plays. I still haven't seen a play that tops that, in terms of timing and importance," said offensive lineman Trevor Matich.

After Hawaii's field goal, BYU retook the lead by scoring on the Cougars' next possession, a drive capped by a touchdown pass from Robbie Bosco to Glen Kozlowski on third-and-21 with a little more than five minutes left. Still, the drama wasn't over.

Hawaii punted on their ensuing possession, but BYU failed to move the ball and also had to punt. Johnson's punt was blocked by Al Noga, giving Hawaii the ball at the Cougars 16-yard line. Once again, BYU's defense kept Hawaii out of the end zone. Then, with 40 seconds remaining, Hawaii receiver Walter Murray dropped a pass that hit his hands in the end zone.

The Cougars escaped Honolulu that night with their perfect season still intact—barely.

16 Tom Holmoe

Knowing LaVell Edwards was entering the twilight of his coaching career, observers everywhere saw Tom Holmoe near the top of the list of potential replacements for the legend. Holmoe played for Edwards, and he played in the NFL for many years, winning four Super Bowl rings with the San Francisco 49ers. He also played for, and coached with, one of the greatest NFL coaches: Bill Walsh. He was an assistant at Stanford and became the head coach at Cal. Little did anyone know at the time, Holmoe's impact at BYU would be in an administrative role as opposed to as a head coach. But that was really no surprise to Holmoe, who had had his sights set on athletic administration earlier in his career.

In 1990, after retiring from a seven-year National Football League career, Holmoe was ready to enroll at Ohio State to study athletic administration. That summer, Edwards called Holmoe and asked if he would like to be a graduate assistant coach on BYU's staff. Holmoe said yes, and that launched a 12-year coaching career.

In the back of his mind, though, Holmoe—who was a Cougars defensive back from 1979 to 1982—knew he wanted to be an administrator someday. He ended up earning a master's degree from BYU in athletic administration in 1995. Yet he continued down his coaching path.

When Holmoe left the head coaching spot at Cal at the end of the 2001 season, following a 1–10 record in his final campaign, BYU athletic director Val Hale called him to discuss a possible return to Provo. Holmoe took some time off to be with his family to think about his next step. He contemplated going back to the NFL as an assistant coach and returning to college coaching. Hale offered him a different challenge in 2002 as BYU's associate athletic director for development. His main responsibility was overseeing fund-raising efforts for the men's and women's athletic departments.

"I knew if I was to make this step into athletic administration, this was the right time," Holmoe then said. "As a coach, I've been in a competitive mode, chasing a carrot. You have to be careful not to be addicted to the game, doing anything to succeed. I've been doing that a long time, and I needed to make a change. I did what was best for me. I've got no five-year plan. I'll be here as long as they need me. I'll be a role player. I was a nickelback with the 49ers, doing whatever needed to be done. In this case, that's what I'm doing at BYU. My No. 1 assignment is fund-raising. My job is to raise money and increase support for BYU athletics. It's special to be able to give something back to BYU."

In 2005 Holmoe was hired as BYU's athletic director at a time when the football team had suffered three straight losing seasons and the basketball team was coming off a 9–21 campaign. Holmoe was instrumental in the hiring of Bronco Mendenhall and Dave Rose, who helped return the football and basketball programs, respectively, to national prominence, and winning conference championships.

During his tenure, all the athletic programs at BYU have competed at the highest levels. The Cougars are ranked 39th nationally in the NACDA Directors' Cup rankings—emblematic of overall athletic department success—over the past 10 years.

He oversaw BYU's move from the Mountain West Conference to independence in football and the move from the MW to the West Coast Conference in basketball and most other sports.

But for Holmoe, his favorite part of being athletic director is the relationships he forms with the athletes, noting that they are the ones who make the difference between winning and losing in any sport. "The secret sauce is our kids. We can't do anything without those kids," he said. "It's really all predicated upon how much they come together. Whether we're better, or our very best, depends on a lot of intangibles. A lot of those intangibles have to do with chemistry and whether the players love each other. I played on many successful teams in my career, and the best teams are the ones where the players care about each other."

17 Stan Watts

What LaVell Edwards was to BYU football, Stan Watts was to BYU basketball. While Edwards incorporated the forward pass, Watts incorporated a fast-break offense. "I think Stan put BYU on the map athletically, when football wasn't what it is today," said Pete Witbeck, one of Watts' former assistant coaches.

Thanks to Watts, the Cougars won championships, and his success was the impetus behind the construction of both the George Albert Smith Fieldhouse and the Marriott Center. Some still refer to the Marriott Center as the House That Stan Watts Built.

Watts built quite a basketball program too. His name is synonymous with Cougars hoops greatness. He was considered one of the preeminent and most respected coaches in NCAA history. During his 23 years at the helm of BYU basketball (1949–72), Watts won a pair of NIT championships in 1951 and 1966, posted an overall record of 371–254, won Western Athletic Conference championships in 1965, 1967, 1969, 1971, and 1972, and earned the respect of the basketball world. "You have to rank Stan Watts with the Adolph Rupps, Henry Ibas, and John Woodens," said Witbeck.

Watts' list of accomplishments also includes serving on the NCAA's rules committee, being named the president of the National Association of Basketball Coaches, and chairing the U.S. Olympic basketball committee in 1976. Watts even spent six years as BYU's athletic director and was for a time a defensive backs coach for the football team.

Watts was widely known for his integrity and resilience. "Stan Watts was bigger than life in Provo," someone once wrote of Watts. "Not just because he was a great coach, but because he was a nice man. A true gentleman."

Even rivals respected and adored Watts. In 1971 Fresno State coach Jerry Tarkanian arrived at the Smith Fieldhouse to play BYU. It was Watts' final game before he was to undergo surgery to remove a cancerous tumor in his prostate gland. "I was crying like a baby in front of 14,000 fans," Tarkanian recalled.

Watts endured a 14-hour surgery, and many wondered if he'd survive. It was only the fourth case of this type of cancer in medical history, and the three others who had contracted the disease died. But Watts beat it, just like he beat opposing teams on the basketball court. He spent 17 days in intensive care and remained in the hospital for two months. Wouldn't you know it—by the next season, in 1971, he led BYU to a Western Athletic Conference championship in the brand-new Marriott Center.

"His won-loss record speaks very well for the kind of coach he was," said former player Harold Christensen, who played for Watts on the 1951 championship team. "His reputation among his fellow coaches suggests how much they respected him. He still has that, and is still honored in the community in which he coached."

During his time at BYU, Watts' teams played a fast-break style of play that he believed could fill up the 22,000-seat Marriott Center on cold winter nights. "It has always been our contention that the average basketball fan likes to see fast-scoring, speedy, exciting basketball," Watts once wrote. Playing an entertaining, up-tempo style, Watts' basketball teams averaged nearly 100 points per game most seasons.

"He was the master of fast break, high-scoring basketball," remembered former BYU sports information director Dave Schulthess. "He also loved to bring the big teams to campus. He was responsible for San Francisco and Bill Russell playing in Provo. He also took his teams abroad, to South America and Asia. He just had a remarkable career."

The year Watts retired from BYU was the same year Edwards was hired as the school's football coach. Confined to a wheelchair after he lost the use of his legs, Watts tried to attend as many games as he could.

"He was the finest man I ever met," Witbeck said. "He was one of the great men in the world and one of the greatest coaches basketball ever had. He was just revered.... The greatest tribute I can pay to Stan Watts is [to say] he's truly a man of God. He's always been a gentleman and great man. You don't see that very often."

Watts became the first Cougars coach inducted into the Basketball Hall of Fame in Springfield, Massachusetts, on March 6, 1986. He died on April 6, 2000, at the age of 88.

18 Ty Detmer

Considering his slight build, ebullient smile, and soothing Texas drawl, you'd never guess by looking at him that Ty Detmer was one of the most feared quarterbacks in college football history.

The first time LaVell Edwards met Detmer, while trying to learn more about the kid out of San Antonio, Texas, he wasn't impressed. "I'd heard of his numbers [8,005 yards in his high school career], of course, but we hadn't really recruited him," Edwards said. "So I'm thinking John Elway, and in walks Pee-wee Herman."

But Detmer's physical attributes belied his competitiveness, toughness, and heart. Among many other things, he was known for running into the end zone and head-butting teammates after touchdown passes. Why? "Well, sir," Detmer explained, "you can knock them down if you hit 'em just right."

And the 1990 Heisman Trophy winner had plenty of opportunities to celebrate touchdowns at BYU. Detmer finished his career having collected 59 NCAA records and tying three others. He ended up with a then–NCAA record 15,031 yards passing and 14,665 career yards in total offense. He threw 121 touchdown passes and made 958 completions, and had a career pass efficiency rating of 162.74. Detmer had 5 500-yard passing games, 14 400-yard passing games, and 36 300-yard passing games.

Still, those jaw-dropping numbers can't convey what it was like to watch Detmer play. "He just had an innate feel for the game," Edwards said. It was the way he'd hold on to the ball until the very last nanosecond and deliver a perfect strike to a receiver, or the way he could dodge a pass rush, rendering opposing defenders helpless.

"Ty is a fearless, confident, and composed competitor. The players follow him and respect him, not only for his athletic ability but even more for his character," said longtime assistant coach Lance Reynolds. "Ty told one of our receivers, who was supposed to run a route over the middle, 'If you're scared, don't play!' That's Ty Detmer."

The Detmer legend began when he was a freshman, in 1988. He came off the bench to guide BYU to a 20–17 Freedom Bowl triumph over the Colorado Buffaloes, who would go on to win the national championship two years later.

After being the first Cougars player to be voted a captain as a sophomore, Detmer set an NCAA record for passing as a sophomore, with 4,560 yards. Then came his Heisman Trophy season that saw him enjoy one of the best seasons in college football history, passing for 5,188 yards and 41 touchdowns.

As a senior, most of Detmer's supporting cast had graduated, leaving him surrounded by inexperienced players. Plus the Cougars were facing an arduous early-season schedule against Florida State, UCLA, and Penn State. BYU lost all three games to start 0–3. But

BYU's All-America Tight Ends

Clay Brown	1980
Gordon Hudson	1982
Gordon Hudson	1983
David Mills	1984
Trevor Molini	1985
Chris Smith	1989
Chris Smith	1990
Byron Rex	1992
Chad Lewis	1996
Itula Mili	1996
Jonny Harline	2006
Dennis Pitta	2008
Dennis Pitta	2009

Detmer showed his leadership by not letting his team continue to spiral downward. In fact, the Cougars didn't lose again that season. BYU won seven games in a row before leading an epic comeback against San Diego State. The Cougars trailed 45–17 in the second half and eventually pulled even with the Aztecs at the end, 52–52—the highest-scoring tie in NCAA history. For BYU, this tie engineered by Ty felt like a win because it clinched yet another Western Athletic Conference championship.

Detmer was selected in the ninth round of the 1992 NFL Draft and ended up playing 14 years for six different teams, mostly as a backup to stars such as Brett Favre and Steve Young. With his knowledge of the game, he was like another assistant coach. He later became the coach at St. Andrews Episcopal School in the Austin, Texas, area.

In December 2015, Detmer returned home when he accepted the offensive coordinator position on BYU's staff under new head coach Kalani Sitake. He was looking forward to making his mark on Cougars football as a coach. "My family and I are extremely excited to be part of the football program at BYU again," Detmer said. "I feel it is the right time to make a move and jump in head-first. I couldn't be more excited."

It wasn't an easy transition from Provo celebrity to college coach. After the spring game in 2016, Detmer was mobbed by fans wanting to talk to him and pose for pictures with him. But he'll always be remembered as the record-setting, Heisman Trophy–winning quarterback with a skinny frame and enormous competitive spirit. "He is the best quarterback in the country. I know that is a lot to say, but I firmly believe that," Edwards said after Detmer's sophomore season. "He's as good at executing, reading, and knowing what to do as anybody I've seen. He just makes good decision. You couldn't make a mold and have a guy turn out any better than Ty."

19 LaVell's Quips

Legendary BYU coach LaVell Edwards was one of the most universally liked and respected coaches in college football history. One of the reasons for his likability was his keen sense of humor. His dry wit came out often during interviews with the media. If LaVell hadn't been such a great coach, he probably could have made a living as a stand-up comedian.

Here are some of his funniest one-liners:

"I guess we have maybe five or so excellent receivers, really good, and we substitute freely to keep them fresh. Then, of course, our running backs are always ready to catch passes. You know how it goes: the center snaps the ball, our quarterback fades back—and I've been accused of sending the entire Tabernacle Choir out for the pass."

"If we don't win a bowl game before I die, I'm afraid my epitaph will read: 'He won a thousand games but couldn't win a bowl game.'" —Prior to the 1980 Holiday Bowl win

"It obviously was one of the all-time great robberies because we no more deserved to win that game than fly to the moon." —After the 1980 Holiday Bowl

"If we don't win our first few games, we might start looking for some hell-raisers." —In 1976, when 20 missionaries joined the team after two-year missionary service

"I'd rather lose and live in Provo than win and live in Laramie." —After a 33–20 loss in a blinding snowstorm at Wyoming in 1981

There is no bigger name in BYU sports history than LaVell Edwards.

"Someone once asked me the difference between Don Coryell and myself. The first thing I though of was about $200,000 a year."

"Before the season, *Playboy* magazine picked us third or fourth in our conference. But that's okay; they don't have much of a circulation in Provo."

"I like them to have both, but if they had both, they'd be at Southern California." —On whether he prefers speed or quickness in his receivers

"You might as well join me. Don't worry about being in the way. I just stand around and do nothing anyway." —Talking to golf legend Arnold Palmer, whom he invited to be on BYU's sideline for the 1985 Citrus Bowl

"We don't have toll booths in Provo. We just got the street paved last year." —Explaining why he arrived late for a press conference before the 1985 Kickoff Classic in East Rutherford, New Jersey

"Talk about cruel irony. It was bad enough to lose, but by that score again?" —In 1994, after suffering back-to-back 34–31 losses to archrival Utah

"There are 10 other bowl games out there that would pay a million bucks for a game as good as one of our four Holiday Bowls." —After BYU's 38–36 win over Washington State in the 1981 Holiday Bowl

"Thinking back to when I first came here, to when we were playing games where the Richards PE Building is, with the likes of Western Michigan—who beat us—and other teams like that. Now after all these years we're playing teams like Florida State."

"They used to say when we went to the Holiday Bowl that BYU fans would bring a $50 bill and the 10 Commandments and never break either one of them."

Finally, in 1997, after undergoing surgery to repair blocked carotid arteries in his neck, days after a frustrating loss to in-state rival Utah, Edwards joked that the reason his team passed the ball only 16 times was a lack of oxygen to his brain.

20 Missionary Program

NCAA rules state that players who participate in church or military service have seven years to play four. At BYU, which is owned and operated by the Church of Jesus Christ of Latter-day Saints, many athletes embark on two-year missions, interrupting their football careers. They are assigned to serve in one of 418 missions throughout the world in 150 nations speaking more than 160 languages. Missionaries must pay their own expenses for this two-year period. BYU's 2016 football team had 84 players who had served missions and another 27 who were currently serving.

Missions may be one of the most misunderstood aspects of BYU sports. Critics say they give BYU an unfair advantage of men playing against boys. When things are going well in Provo, the players' maturity and experience are often brought up as reasons for the success. When things aren't going well, like during the three straight losing seasons in football from 2002 to 2004, some blame it on all the returned missionaries in the program, saying they're too old and lack a killer instinct.

"They used to say we couldn't win because of missionaries," Coach LaVell Edwards told *Time* magazine in 1984. "Now they're saying we win because of missionaries. I wonder where all those people were when we were losing."

Edwards' son, Jim, served a mission to Sweden. "The coach never urged even the best players not to go," Jim said. "And when you found out that he thought spirituality was more important than football, that's when you got perspective."

So are missions an unfair advantage? Coaches who make sure claims in the affirmative need a no-expense-paid tour of the mission field. Would they send their prized prospects to some far-flung area of the world for two years, facing a variety of deprivations and hardships? Missionaries are allowed to exercise for only an hour a day while spending 10 hours a day for 24 months sharing messages about the gospel of Jesus Christ and helping others gain a knowledge of their purpose on Earth. They are allowed to call home twice a year and send a weekly email.

But those unfamiliar with the missionary program are quick to turn it into a punch line. During fall camp in 2016, for example, fifth-year senior quarterback Taysom Hill, who served a mission in Australia, turned 26, and some pointed to that as being unfair.

In the fall of 2001, when the Cougars were undefeated, *Sports Illustrated* columnist Rick Reilly offered his opinion in a column titled "Brigham Young? I Don't Think So." Reilly quoted Wyoming coach Vic Koenning, who said of the Cougars, "I look in their locker room and see guys with receding hairlines. I look out and see a lot of my guys still wearing their high school letter jacket[s]." Reilly also referred to BYU as "Brigham Old."

Every time the Cougars make a national splash, it seems, some people make an issue of the missionary program. "I think that argument is old and outdated," then–athletic director Val Hale said in response to Reilly's column. "Anyone who makes that argument is misinformed. Speaking strictly from an athletic standpoint, BYU would be better off without the missionary program. But we realize the benefits that come to young men when they serve missions. Those benefits are spiritual, emotional, and the discipline they learn. Missions make them better students and better prepared for life. We know they'll be better students and citizens in the long run, not better athletes."

During the 1950s and 1960s, the missionary program didn't have much of an impact on BYU football. Players were discouraged from serving, and those who did were forgotten. But when Edwards took the helm of the program in 1972, the issue weighed on him, and after much consideration, he eventually decided to change BYU's approach by reserving scholarships for those who served missions. At that time, few believed that an athlete could take a two-year break from playing football and be successful in the sport after returning.

Meanwhile, around that same time, LDS Church president Spencer W. Kimball announced that every worthy male should serve a mission. Over time, BYU proved that returned missionaries could play football at a high level after their service.

Certainly, Edwards' philosophy about missionaries helped carry the Cougars to national prominence. He had changed what had been perceived as a weakness and turned it into a strength of the program. It isn't easy, however, as coaches have to juggle their rosters with the many missionaries coming and going.

Current coach Kalani Sitake, who served a mission in Oakland, California, sees the missionary program as an advantage. "We're going to draw on their strengths and things they've already accomplished in life and transfer that to the football field. I think we'll have a great outcome. I've said it before—our team has more guys that have sacrificed more than anybody else in the country when it comes to life. In the prime time of their lives, they spent two years away from their families, paid their own way to go serve the Lord. Not a lot of people are doing that these days, and we have a team full of them. We're going to draw upon those experiences and that maturity."

During ESPN's *Coaches Film Room*, aired during the 2017 National Championship Game, Sitake joined five other coaches to break down the game and discuss issues facing college football. At one point, Syracuse coach Dino Babers good-naturedly referred to BYU's older players who had served missions. "Hey, they don't go on a mission to Gold's Gym, I'll tell you that," Sitake responded. "Those guys are riding bicycles and eating ramen noodles for two years. If it were a great system to develop your athletes, Alabama would be doing it."

21 Ezekiel "Ziggy" Ansah

If you would have told someone in 2010 that BYU's roster that season featured a future first-round National Football League draft pick, that wouldn't necessarily have surprised anybody. After all, BYU had a freshman quarterback who was widely regarded as the top high school QB in the nation the previous year.

But nobody would have guessed the future first-round pick would be linebacker Ezekiel Ansah, a walk-on from Accra, Ghana, who, when he arrived in Provo in 2008, had never even seen a football game let alone played in one. The 6'6" Ansah was an untapped talent who would end up tying Jim McMahon as the highest draft pick in BYU history—taken No. 5 overall in the 2013 NFL Draft.

Ansah was baptized into the LDS faith in Accra and arrived at BYU to attend school. His ultimate goal was to play in the NBA. Despite a 39-inch vertical leap, he was cut from the Cougars basketball team twice. Then Ansah tried track-and-field. When Ansah walked into Coach Leonard Myles-Mills' office, the track-and-field coach saw potential in the imposing, soft-spoken stranger standing before him. Myles-Mills' first impression of Ansah? "I looked at him, and I said, 'Holy smokes!'"

Ansah introduced himself and told him he was from Accra, Ghana, and Myles-Mills could relate. Myles-Mills is also a native of Ghana, having arrived at BYU on a track scholarship in the mid-1990s. During their conversation, Ansah told him he would like to try out for the track team. Myles-Mills figured that would be a good idea, and it didn't take long for him to notice Ansah's speed, strength, and athleticism.

Myles-Mills hadn't seen someone with Ansah's size run like he could—clocking 21.9 seconds in the 200 meters. But he was unpolished. "I told him, 'As much as I'd like to help you, you need to play football.' I literally held his hand and walked him up there to the [BYU] football office and dropped him off like a child being left at a day care," Myles-Mills said.

In the football office that day was assistant coach Paul Tidwell, who oversaw the walk-on program. Tidwell immediately recognized that Ansah looked like a football player straight out of central casting. "Obviously my eyes were big and I welcomed him," Tidwell said. "I sat down with him, mapped out the plan, how it works, and what he needed to do. Man, he's become a diamond in the rough."

Back in Ghana, a third-world nation located in West Africa, the naturally gifted Ansah had played basketball and soccer. On that first day at BYU football practices in 2010, Ansah didn't know how to put on his pads. "I remember the first time I put on the helmet, somebody smacked me right away," Ansah remembered. "I was like, 'Oh, man, this is going to be miserable.' My teammates helped me put on my stuff, and I just went out there."

BYU linebacker Kyle Van Noy described Ansah's first few practices. "The first time he lined up, he looked like a crouching frog. He was just raw. He still is raw. But the potential he has is more than anyone I've ever seen play a sport."

Ansah started out on special teams, and then learned how to play with the defense. "I thought he could become something special," said Tidwell. "There were times when you'd see bits and pieces and say, 'Wow.' On kickoff cover, for example, he could not be blocked. He's run over two or three people getting downfield. He didn't always make the play, but he was fast and physical and tough, and nobody could block him. Then you put him in the game and he'd make a mistake. Then other times you'd think, *This kid is going to be special.* It was a growing period."

The NFL certainly saw Ansah's potential. The night he was supposed to graduate from BYU coincided with the NFL Draft. Ansah wasn't just your average jock. He graduated from BYU with a degree in actuarial science and a minor in math. Initially, Ansah declined an invitation to be in the green room at Radio City Music Hall in New York City because he wanted to graduate. Then he was told he could still receive his diploma without being in Provo. BYU officials joined Ansah in New York and, hours before the draft, had him dress in a cap and gown and "graduate."

Legendary Dallas Cowboys executive Gil Brandt has seen, and drafted, some of the greatest athletes in NFL history. "He's absolutely the most incredible athlete I've ever seen," Brandt said before the draft. "I tell you, he's absolutely amazing, running around out here. He's got the biggest fingers and hands. And the guy is all

Top BYU Football Nicknames

Nick "the Bear" Eyre
James "You Punt, You" Dye
Omarr "the Blanket" Morgan
Gifford "the Mormon Rifle" Nielsen
Cameron "the General" Jensen
Eldon "the Phantom" Fortie
Chris "the Galloping Greek" Farasopoulos
Keith "Mad Dog" Rivera
Dustin "Moose" Johnston
Rob "Freight Train" Morris
Joe "the Toe" Liljenquist
Virgil "the Blue Darter" Carter
Brian "Lunchroom" Sanders
Roger "the Creature" French
Dewey "the Swamp Rat" Warren

muscle. Out here, he made a one-handed interception. He's like a wide receiver. He's unbelievable."

Less than an hour into the draft, former Lions legendary running back and Pro Football Hall of Fame member Barry Sanders stood at the podium and announced that the Detroit franchise had selected Ansah, who strode onstage wearing 3-D glasses without lenses.

Since joining the Lions, he's been a force and is regarded as one of the top pass rushers in the NFL. After the 2015 season, he recorded a team-high 14.5 sacks and earned a spot in the Pro Bowl.

Though Ansah picked up football relatively quickly, he didn't start at BYU until his senior year, halfway through the season—and that was because a starter ahead of him got injured. In just a few short years, Ziggy Ansah went from a football novice to scholarship player to an NFL Draft prospect. Based on his background, Ansah is the unlikeliest of stars BYU has produced. "Ziggy's a remarkable story," Coach Bronco Mendenhall said. "You could make a movie about it at some point."

22 Shawn Bradley

Shawn Bradley was born in Germany (he was 19.5 inches long and weighed 10 pounds at birth), was raised in the small Utah town of Castle Dale (he was seven feet tall in ninth grade), attended BYU for two semesters (where he played as a 7'6" center), and served a mission to Sydney, Australia, for two years (he added 40 pounds and a layer of thick skin to his thin frame). Nobody had ever seen a player quite like Bradley, who was one of the most highly recruited athletes to attend BYU.

1–25

Going into the 1996–97 basketball season, it was clear BYU coach Roger Reid could be in trouble, despite having guided the Cougars to seven winning seasons. He had lost Bryon Ruffner, who averaged 18.8 points per game as a junior, due to a felony charge in October. In November Reid, who had spent years recruiting highly touted LDS big man Chris Burgess, found out that Burgess had chosen to sign with Duke. Reid told Burgess that by not enrolling at BYU he was "letting down nine million Mormons." That comment became a public relations nightmare.

On the court, the Cougars were counting on eight freshmen, and they opened the season with a 1–6 record. Not long after BYU lost its sixth game, before a crowd of 3,418 at the Marriott Center, and eight days before Christmas, Reid was fired. That left assistant Tony Ingle as the interim head coach, which was tantamount to being named interim captain on the *Titanic*. The Cougars finished with their worst record in school history: 1–25. The lone win came at home against Utah State.

In March 1997 BYU hired Steve Cleveland from Fresno City College. Cleveland, who had never coached at the Division I level, came with a huge rebuilding job to do. One of the players who helped Cleveland dig the Cougars out of a dismal situation was Provo High's Mekeli Wesley, who was part of the recruiting class BYU was hoping would include Burgess.

BYU won the Mountain West Conference tournament championship in 2001—Wesley's senior year—and returned to the NCAA Tournament for the first time since 1995. Wesley ended up scoring 1,740 points in his career.

Under Cleveland, the Cougars won two regular-season Mountain West titles and earned two more NCAA Tournament appearances. When Cleveland left BYU in 2005 to take over at Fresno State, BYU hired Cleveland's longtime assistant, Dave Rose. From the ashes of a 1–25 season, the Cougars rose again to national prominence and reached the Sweet 16 of the 2011 NCAA Tournament.

This story had a positive ending for Tony Ingle too. He led Kennesaw State to a NCAA Division II national title in 2004, guided Dalton State to an NAIA national championship in 2015, and was named NAIA Coach of the year in 2017.

Reid, meanwhile, went on to be an assistant coach with the NBA's Phoenix Suns, serving as an assistant under a player he coached at BYU, Danny Ainge. He also coached in China before spending stints as the head coach at Snow Junior College and Southern Utah University.

Alas, Bradley played only one season for the Cougars, in 1990–91, but he made a lasting impact. He set NCAA freshman records with 177 blocks (currently third) and 5.2 blocks per game (currently fourth). He tied the NCAA single-game record with 14 blocks against Eastern Kentucky (currently tied for second). He averaged 14.8 points and 7.7 rebounds for BYU and recorded a career-high 29 points against Eastern Kentucky. He was named to the Basketball Times All-Freshman Team, was an Associated Press honorable mention All-American, was named the WAC Freshman of the Year, and earned All-WAC defensive team honors.

Based on that freshman performance, Cougars fans couldn't wait for his encore as a sophomore. They had visions of Final Fours dancing in their heads. But they would have to wait until after Bradley's two-year LDS mission to Australia. During his absence, many—including ESPN's Dick Vitale—could see the Cougars contending for a national championship, especially considering the talent that then-coach Roger Reid had recruited to surround him. But it wasn't to be.

Not long before returning home from his mission, Bradley announced through his family that he would bypass his collegiate eligibility to enter the NBA Draft. It was one of the most crushing departures in BYU history. "I can't say I was devastated, really. I thought this might happen," Reid said. "When you've got a guy in his situation, with all the money involved, how can you not expect a man to go for that? How can I as a basketball coach tell him not to? The thing I feel bad about personally is we thought we'd get him for at least a year. That's what we understood. I thought of the recruiting, about all the excitement involved in that. I thought about our fans already having us in the Final Four the next year. And now, it's like they said on ESPN, we go from a top 10 team to out of the picture."

In June 1993 Bradley became the highest draft pick in BYU sports history, going No. 2 overall to the Philadelphia 76ers in the NBA Draft.

Nobody had seen the combination of size and athleticism Bradley possessed. Bradley could water-ski and was a great golfer. He batted .407 in high school baseball. He could dribble, run a fast break, and hit the outside jumper. As they say, you can't coach height. Golden State coach Don Nelson said of Bradley, "When he sits down, his ears pop."

Meanwhile, Bradley had enormous pressure on that 7'6" frame. When he signed an eight-year, $44.2 million contract, 76ers owner Harold Katz admitted the signing was "the biggest gamble [he'd] ever taken by far." Some of the brightest minds in basketball believed Bradley would revolutionize the game.

"I'm just a 7'6" kid who loves to have fun," Bradley said on draft night. "I want to be the best I can be in anything. My mission prepared me for life. Even though I love basketball with all my heart, my missionary work is something I'll never regret."

Following the decision to enter the NBA Draft, Reiner Bradley, Shawn's father, said his son received two to three dozen pieces of hate mail from outraged Cougars fans. "I know there will be some people who will think I'm wonderful and some people who will think I'm the biggest idiot in the world," Shawn said. "In fact, there are some people who already think I'm the biggest idiot in the world."

One of his supporters was none other than former Cougars star Danny Ainge, who would go on to become both an NBA coach and general manager. "I don't think Shawn would have gotten the money he's getting now had he gone back to college," Ainge said. "I'm not sure how much you improve playing college basketball."

In 1994, at the start of his second NBA season, the Philadelphia 76ers and Minnesota Timberwolves held a preseason game at the Marriott Center. About 10,000 fans showed up to watch Bradley's return. It lasted only 31 seconds, as Bradley sustained a knee injury while trying to block a shot.

During his 12-year NBA career, he ranked among the top shot blockers in league history. While he drew a lot of criticism for not living up to impossible expectations, Bradley will be remembered for his unusual mixture of height and athleticism—and, for BYU fans, what might have been had he remained at BYU for at least one more season.

23 Attend a BYU-Utah Football Game

It's a fervent in-state rivalry that divides families for at least one week per year. It's red vs. blue. It's "Utah Man" vs. "Rise and Shout." It's north vs. south. It's public school vs. private school. And when the two teams meet in football, it's usually an amazing experience.

With every game, another fascinating chapter is added as the football field turns into a stage featuring unforgettable moments, intriguing subplots, surprises, drama, emotion, heroes, and goats.

Over the years, some games have had more national impact than others. For example, BYU's 1984 win over Utah propelled the Cougars to No. 1 in the national polls for the first time. And Utah's 2004 victory over BYU sent the Utes to the Fiesta Bowl for the first time.

Still, the series has been marked by long stretches of domination by one side or the other. When BYU football began in 1922, Utah crushed the Cougars 49–0. That set the tone for the next 20 years. From 1923 to 1938, Utah outscored BYU 416–39 in those 15 games and shut out the Cougars 10 times. Over the first

48 games played between BYU and Utah, the Cougars posted a 6–39–3 record against the Utes. It wasn't until 1942 that BYU finally recorded a win over Utah. BYU blocked a punt at the Utah 10-yard line, and on fourth down, Herman Longhurst scored on a four-yard run to lift the Cougars to a 12–7 victory in Salt Lake City. BYU fans ripped down the goal posts and sawed them up for souvenirs.

Because of World War II, the teams didn't meet again until 1946, but not much changed after the long layoff. Utah continued thrashing BYU, with rare exceptions. The turning point came, of course, in 1972, when LaVell Edwards took the helm at BYU. At the time, the Utes held a 38–5–4 advantage in the series. Then Edwards' teams won 18 of the next 20 contests. In 1989 BYU avenged a rare loss to Utah the previous year by taking a 49–0 lead at halftime before earning a 70–31 thrashing of the Utes.

In the 1990s the Utes, under coach Ron McBride, made the rivalry competitive on a yearly basis for the first time. In 1993 the Utes stunned the Cougars 34–31 when kicker Chris Yergensen booted a 55-yard field goal with 25 seconds remaining to give Utah its first win in Provo since 1971.

The Utes tried to tear down the goal posts, which BYU players stopped. But defensive lineman Lenny Gomes' quote lives on: "All those [Utes] think that's all there is to life. But when I'm making $50,000 to $60,000 a year, they'll be pumping my gas. They're low-class losers."

The following year, the Utes won again, 34-31, inspiring TV commercials and bumper stickers seen across the state. Since 1993 18 contests between the two schools have been decided by a touch-down or less.

From 2014 to 2015 the series took a two-year hiatus. Utah, which had recently joined the Pac-12, wanted to take a break in the rivalry, explaining it was looking for balance in its schedule. It was the first interruption of the series since World War II.

But as fate would have it, the hiatus didn't last as long as expected. The Cougars and Utes ended up playing in the 2015 Las Vegas Bowl, in which Utah won 35–28. The two schools resumed the series in 2016 in Salt Lake City. The Utes won their sixth straight over the Cougars with a 20–19 victory.

Aside from the games, the climate surrounding this rivalry is unique. "It's more than a rivalry," BYU coach Bronco Mendenhall once said. "Any time religion or politics are part of a rivalry, there's a personal element that starts to take shape. So not only is it school against school, it's person against person. Then it starts touching hearts and minds of people and makes them do things they wouldn't normally do. It's an amazing experience—not always fun, based on the outcome."

Just when no one thought the rivalry could get any more intense, or personal, it did. In December 2004, for example, BYU's Gary Crowton had stepped down as coach, and Utah had lost Coach Urban Meyer to Florida. With both schools simultaneously searching for new coaches, both targeted Kyle Whittingham, a former Cougars linebacker and longtime Utes defensive coordinator. Ultimately, Whittingham decided to stick with Utah. And BYU elevated its own defensive coordinator, Mendenhall, to head coach. For more than a decade, Mendenhall and Whittingham led their respective teams in epic BYU-Utah games. In 2005, 2006, 2007, 2009, 2010, and 2012 the outcome was decided on the final play.

BYU coach Kalani Sitake, a former Cougars fullback who spent a decade on Whittingham's staff at Utah, would love nothing more than to help BYU end its six-game losing streak to the Utes. He has a different view of the heated rivalry than the majority of fans. Add to that his strong friendship with Whittingham, and perhaps it signals a kinder, gentler approach to the rivalry.

24 Polynesian Pipeline

In the mid-1990s, a reporter entered former longtime offensive coordinator Norm Chow's office with questions about why BYU had attracted hundreds of Polynesian players to the program over the years. As Chow talked, a sound—barely audible—emanated from the stereo in his office. It wasn't the kind of music associated with football.

Chow, a native of Honolulu, Hawaii, was oblivious to the muffled noise until he was asked about it. Then a broad smile broke out over his face. He reached down and turned the volume up a notch or two. "All I listen to," he said matter-of-factly, "is Hawaiian music." There you have it. BYU's intricate, high-flying offensive scheme in the 1980s and 1990s had a soundtrack, and it was filled with ukuleles.

Some 20 yards away that day, in the lobby of the BYU football office, more distinct sounds were heard. Plopped down on couches that afternoon was a group of Polynesian players wearing flip-flops, shorts, and T-shirts. They were laughing and speaking a variety of languages: Samoan, Tongan, and pidgin English. "The football office is the gathering place," said BYU linebacker Donny Atuaia. "We love to go there and talk stories."

Explained Cougars fullback Kalani Sitake: "You can take the boy away from the island, but you can't take the island away from the boy." Of course, not all Polynesian players arrive directly from an island. But no matter where they're from, all trace their genealogy to some tiny island in the South Pacific.

Polynesian players have been staple imports in Provo for decades. "They've made a major impact," said then–Cougars coach LaVell Edwards. "We've never had a team without key Polynesian

Vai Sikahema, one of the many Polynesian Pipeline players, went on to a productive NFL career.

players." BYU was one of the first schools to recruit Polynesian players, a trend that has taken hold at many schools around the country since. It was fitting that in 2015 BYU hired the first Tongan head coach in the FBS—Sitake.

In 1951 Harry Bray of Hilo, Hawaii, transferred from Weber College to play for BYU, opening the Polynesian Pipeline to Provo. The Cougars had had Polynesian players trickle into the program in previous seasons—many via what was then Weber State College— but coach Tally Stevens decided to actively tap the resource in the late 1950s. Stevens hired Chris Apostol in 1959 as an assistant and subsequently issued him an edict to recruit in Hawaii. So Apostol began panning for talent there.

During the 1960s Chris Apostol felt as if he had discovered gold. For 11 years he traveled to the islands a couple times a year to scour the playing fields for athletes. Basically, he had the place to himself. "There was virtually no competition," recalled Apostol, who was considered the unofficial godfather of the Polynesian Pipeline.

Perhaps partially due to the BYU-Hawaii campus in Laie and the influence of the LDS Church, BYU "always had a presence there," said Apostol. "It was the mystique of coming to the mainland for the kids."

Apparently Stevens found the right man for the job in Apostol. "He related to those guys very well, and he was very successful," said Edwards. During Apostol's tenure, BYU didn't offer a lot of scholarships to players from Hawaii, but enough came that by the late 1960s and early 1970s other programs began taking notice. "After we had some success, Arizona State started coming, then USC and Michigan State," said Apostol.

Making Polynesian players feel comfortable in Provo was not a problem. "On campus visits," Apostol said, "I would call the Polynesian Club and 200 kids would show up to meet the prospects. And 20 of them would be relatives."

When Edwards became head coach, the Cougars began scheduling games against the University of Hawaii on a regular basis, increasing BYU's exposure on the islands, and then Hawaii joined the Western Athletic Conference, ensuring regular meetings between the two schools. As a result, Hawaii became a recruiting stronghold for the Cougars.

BYU running back Hema Heimuli remembered Edwards arriving at the family's home to recruit his older brother, Lakei. "My brother was [among] the first wave of Polynesians that came to BYU. LaVell understood the Polynesian culture," Heimuli said. "He knew how to recruit Polynesians. He came to our humble house in Hawaii and he told my dad, 'I will make sure your son

Vai Sikahema

At BYU Vai Sikahema became the school's all-time leader in punt returns (153) and punt-return yards (1,312). He returned three punts for touchdowns, behind only James Dye and Golden Richards, who each had four. And he had an 89-yard punt return, the fourth-longest in Cougars history.

Sikahema went on to a successful NFL career. At the time he retired, after the 1993 season, he had returned more punts—292—than any other player in the history of the NFL, and he was in second place on the all-time list for most punt-return yards with 3,169, just 148 shy of the mark set by Billy "White Shoes" Johnson.

Sikahema, the first Tongan to play in the NFL, could have sleepwalked his way to the record in 1994. However, instead of returning for a surefire chance to eclipse Johnson's feat, Sikahema retired to become a full-time, five-days-a-week sportscaster at WCAU-TV in Philadelphia. He is currently a morning news anchor at NBC 10 in the City of Brotherly Love.

Yet Sikahema's chosen post-football profession isn't unusual for a former BYU athlete. Johnny Miller, Trevor Matich, Todd Christensen, Gifford Nielsen, Glen Kozlowski, Danny Ainge, Michael Smith, Bobby Clampett, Marc Lyons, Blaine Fowler, Mark Durrant, Hans Olsen, Steve Eager, David Nixon, and Brian Logan are among the many Cougars who have made the transition from athlete to commentator.

Does coincidence explain this BYU sportscasting phenomenon? "No, it's not coincidence," Sikahema said. "Many athletes come out of BYU as returned missionaries. They're married too, and have a maturity level beyond their years. We don't have to cultivate our abilities. Coming out of BYU, we already have them."

graduates.' That's all my dad needed to hear. That's the reason why most Polynesians came to America, to get an education. He was way ahead of his time. He saw the potential of Polynesians in football and he went after them. He knew what we valued most."

Since 1951 hundreds of Polynesians have played for the Cougars, from places throughout the Pacific including Samoa, Tonga, Fiji, and Hawaii. Among the best include Vai Sikahema, the NCAA career leader in punt returns; All-America tight end

Itula Mili; and two of BYU's top all-time leading rushers, Harvey Unga and Lakei Heimuli. Safeties Aaron Francisco and Kai Nacua were two of the best to play that position at BYU. Other Polynesian stars included K. O. Kealaluhi, Mark Atuaia, Eathyn Manumaeuna, Travis Tuiloma, Bronson Kaufusi, Peter Tuipulotu, Harvey Langi, Alema Fitisemanu, Kaipo McGuire, and Tevita Ofahengaue.

And Polynesians are well-represented on the Cougars' current coaching staff. Head coach Sitake naturally welcomes Polynesians to his program with open arms. "If your name is hard to pronounce," he said, "we want you here."

25 Jamaal Williams

Running back Jamaal Williams, an African American and a nonmember of the LDS Church, signed with BYU at the tender age of 16. When he enrolled at age 17, it required a leap of faith for the Fontana, California, native to choose the Cougars over a host of other schools vying for his services out of high school.

"Jamaal had to trust us to come to BYU," said Coach Bronco Mendenhall. "There are a lot of things in the typical stereotype of a BYU player that Jamaal doesn't fit. But he trusted us. I think that's endeared him to us, and vice versa."

During his career, Williams certainly endeared himself to Cougars Nation, and left quite a legacy in the record books. For starters, he became the school's all-time leading rusher, finishing with 3,901 yards to surpass the previous record holder, Harvey Unga. He achieved this feat against Mississippi State on October 14, 2016. Weeks earlier, on September 30, he had broken the school's single-game rushing record against Toledo, picking up 287 yards on 30 carries. That eclipsed the mark set by Eldon Fortie, who ran for 272 yards against George Washington on September 29, 1962, almost 54 years earlier to the day. Williams also ran for five touchdowns on that September night, tying another school record. Just as impressive is that during his BYU career, he fumbled five times and lost only two. In his final game as a Cougar, Williams turned in a 210-yard performance in a 24–21 Poinsettia Bowl win over Wyoming. That night, Williams recorded his 16th 100-yard rushing game, the most at BYU, and his third 200-yard rushing games, also No. 1 in school history.

What made his senior season even more special was that just one month before the 2015 campaign, he withdrew from school due to an honor code violation and moved back home to California. During that time away from Provo, Williams prepared for his final year.

One of the reasons for returning as a 21-year-old senior, aside from finishing what he had started, was becoming BYU's all-time leading rusher. "It's always in the back of my head. I've always been working towards it. I do want the record," Williams said before the season. "At the same time, I want our team to do great too. Honestly, it comes by me working hard. We have a whole bunch of great players on this team. I'm working hard, getting ready for them, and I won't let them down this year."

While Williams matured during his time at BYU, he never lost his fun-loving demeanor. He enjoyed teasing teammates, coaches, and media members, and on occasion doing some impromptu dancing. Before games, he would walk around the field and play catch with fans in the stands.

Williams, also known by his Twitter handle @jswagdaddy, did a lot of things differently than most BYU athletes. For example, after the first practice before the 2014 season, Williams met with the media and was, as always, candid. He had spent the afternoon practice session working with the second team rather than the starters. Then, in front of an army of reporters, he confirmed a rumor that had been swirling for a couple weeks—that the junior running back would miss the season opener at UConn due to an honor code–related suspension. It may have been the first time in BYU football history that a player announced his own suspension.

From the beginning of her son's recruitment to BYU, Williams' mom, Nicolle, loved what the school stands for and its honor code. "The person Jamaal is now, that wasn't Jamaal. He wouldn't talk. It was just video games and spending time at home," Nicolle said. "The atmosphere, and the school itself, is helping him grow. That atmosphere is molding him into a respectable, admirable young man. I'm very proud that he made the decision to go to BYU. He used to wear an earring, but he doesn't wear that anymore. He can always wear an earring later on. There were certain things that he accepted, and things that he is able to do. It will help him in the real world."

Despite sitting out the 2015 season, Williams was confident he could accomplish big things as a senior, saying, "I worked hard for it. I did everything right. I worked hard, I believed, I prayed. When you're going through your struggles, all you've got to do is pray to God, do it the right way, stay loyal, stay faithful. If you have a good support staff behind you, family members and everything, keep them close, because those are the ones who believe in you from the beginning."

The man who previously held the all-time rushing record, Harvey Unga, served as a graduate assistant during Williams' final season. "To see everything that he's gone through and to come out and have the success he's having this year, it's awesome," said Unga. "That time he spent away from here, he came back and didn't skip a beat. That's a testament to his work ethic, his drive, his passion for the game."

In the spring of 2017, Williams was drafted by the Green Bay Packers.

26 Watch a Game at LaVell Edwards Stadium

Frequently, when first-time visitors arrive on BYU's campus for a football game, they are mesmerized by the spectacular mountain view LaVell Edwards Stadium furnishes. ESPN's Chris Fowler listed his five best settings for college football in 1995 and had Edwards Stadium at No. 3, with this explanation: "Wasatch Mountains a breathtaking backdrop."

The stadium, and natural grass field, have been home to numerous memorable moments through the years. In 1964 the stadium, then known as Cougar Stadium, was built on the north end of campus with a capacity of just fewer than 30,000 seats. As BYU football gradually became a national power, seating was increased to 35,000, followed by temporary bleachers installed at the back of the end zones that made it a 45,000-seat facility. Before stadium expansion, BYU hosted the NCAA track-and-field championships in 1967 and 1975. The track was removed from the stadium when it was expanded.

Then in 1982, two years before BYU won the national championship, seating was expanded again, to 65,000. The Cougars' first home game that season, against Air Force on September 25, produced a crowd of 64,253, which was reported at the time as "the largest gathering ever in Utah history." Since 1982 the stadium has consistently ranked among the nation's top 25 in attendance.

The largest crowd to attend a BYU home football game took place on October 16, 1993, when the Cougars hosted Notre Dame, as a crowd of 66,247 looked on. On September 8, 1990, a crowd of 66,235 watched BYU beat No. 1 Miami.

In 2003 BYU added luxury "club seating" to the east stands, which lowered the stadium capacity to 64,045. Due to more

Go to a Pregame Tailgate Party

There was a time at BYU when tailgating had nothing to do with pregame festivities but rather was defined as "driving too close to a preceding car in traffic down University Parkway." But after the 2011 season opener at Ole Miss—BYU's first game as an independent— Cougars fans who attended that game in Oxford, Mississippi, witnessed a tradition they wanted to bring back to Provo.

The Ole Miss Rebels practically invented tailgating. *Sports Illustrated* has named Ole Miss the nation's No. 1 tailgating school, and the *Sporting News* has called the Grove, the Rebels' famed tailgating area, "the Holy Grail of tailgating sites." The *New York Times* has called it "the mother and mistress of outdoor ritual mayhem," while *Sports Illustrated* has raved, "in Oxford lies the most magical place on all of God's green, football-playing Earth: the Grove."

The Grove features 10 acres of lush, green grass, lined by oak trees, in the middle of campus. Every game day, the place is "transformed from a tranquil picnic spot into tailgating paradise when thousands of football fans crowd into every corner of the land," according to the Ole Miss media guide.

Well, BYU's campus doesn't have such a place near LaVell Edwards Stadium. However, fans worked with the school's administration to start creating their own tailgating tradition. In 2014 BYU announced revised tailgating plans to improve the tailgating experience at BYU by combining the RV lot with regular tailgate parking (Lot 20) located north of the BYU Broadcasting building. "The goal is to create a centralized location that gives Cougars Nation more space to enjoy the pregame tailgating experience with friends and family," athletic director Tom Holmoe said at the time. "It's part of our continued effort to improve the game day experience at BYU."

There is an additional parking lot for late-arriving RVs and oversized vehicles that do not arrive at least three hours before the game. This lot is located at 2230 N. 150 East (Canyon Road), approximately three blocks north of LaVell Edwards Stadium. The lot is for parking only and is not meant for tailgating.

There are restrictions, such as no alcohol allowed. It's not exactly like Ole Miss, but it's a new tradition that's building momentum in Provo.

renovations, capacity of Edwards Stadium is 63,470. In 2012 BYU replaced the video walls and scoreboards at LaVell Edwards Stadium and replaced those with state-of-the-art LED video walls in the north and south end zones, as well as LED ribbon boards across the top of both end zones.

Prior to kickoff in legendary coach LaVell Edwards' final home game on November 18, 2000, LDS Church president Gordon B. Hinckley announced the renaming of Cougar Stadium as LaVell Edwards Stadium. BYU beat New Mexico 37–13 that day.

When asked which memory stands out about playing at this stadium, Coach Kalani Sitake said, "All of it. Obviously I remember my last game because it was LaVell's last one here. They changed the name to LaVell Edwards Stadium. That was awesome. Every time I drive by this stadium, it gets me going. That's just how it is for me. It's always a good feeling being in this stadium."

Up until 2005 part of the largest collection of Jurassic period fossils in North America was stored underneath the east bleachers of the stadium. They are now on display at BYU's Museum of Paleontology.

The press box at Edwards Stadium has been referred to as the Provo Marriott by members of the media who cover BYU football. Standing more than 10 stories high, the four-level press box runs the entire length of the stands. In 1982, 1988, and 1997 the Football Writers Association of America praised BYU for its "outstanding press box working area."

A new stadium pregame tradition started in 2013 with the introduction of the Cougar Walk. Fans gather to watch the team get off buses at the northeast corner of the stadium and walk along the east side to the southeast gate near the BYU locker room. The BYU marching band, the Power of the Wasatch, leads the Cougar Walk, followed by the cheerleaders. Coaches and players come next, providing fans the opportunity to see and cheer them on a few hours before kickoff.

Every Fourth of July since 1980, Edwards Stadium has hosted the Stadium of Fire, which is held in conjunction with America's Freedom Festival. Those who have performed at Stadium of Fire include the Osmonds, Bob Hope, the Beach Boys, the Mormon Tabernacle Choir, Natalie Cole, Barbara Mandrell, Jay Leno, the Jets, Alabama, Martina McBride, Lonestar, Carrie Underwood, Miley Cyrus, the Jonas Brothers, David Archuleta, Kelly Clarkson, Journey, and Tim McGraw.

Fire the George Q. Cannon

Sitting at the east side of the east corner of the north end zone at LaVell Edwards Stadium during football games is a World War II vintage M120 75mm howitzer, painted blue and dubbed George Q.

The name is inspired by George Q. Cannon, an early member of the Quorum of the Twelve Apostles of the Church of Jesus Christ of Latter-day Saints. He was a five-time territorial delegate to the US Congress and was the church's chief political strategist. After the Cougars score a touchdown or field goal, the Cougars Battalion, made up of five to seven ROTC cadets and one ROTC instructor, fires the cannon in celebration. Also, the Q Cannon Crew does push-ups for every point the team has scored. Cadets involved are chosen based upon their push-up score from their last Army Physical Test. An honorary cannon crew member is selected to fire the first round. The honorary crew member receives a free T-shirt from the BYU Army ROTC.

In 2015 BYU running back Algernon Brown collided with the George Q. after scoring a 37-yard touchdown against Wagner. As he went into the end zone, Brown was pushed, and his cleats slipped on the concrete pathway and he smacked into the vintage artillery. Brown suffered a bruise, scrape, and laceration. "I'm glad he didn't hurt the cannon," offensive coordinator Robert Anae said later. "I'm all for the cannon. For all of the hoopla and how he got beat up by the George Q. Cannon, he's back and seems to be the healthiest guy."

1981: Elite Eight

BYU's basketball team ended the 1981 regular season with a 22–6 record and finished second in the WAC behind Utah. However, in the regular season finale in Provo, and Danny Ainge's final game at the Marriott Center, the Cougars blasted the No. 7 Utes by 19 points. That set the tone for what was to come.

BYU was sent to the NCAA East Regionals in Providence, Rhode Island. At the time, the NCAA Tournament featured 48 teams and the higher-seeded teams drew byes for the first round. The Cougars' first-round matchup was against Princeton.

Ainge, who had been spending his summers playing baseball for the Toronto Blue Jays, almost missed the game because of back spasms. He played anyway. "I decided no painkillers," Ainge said after the 60–51 win. "If I couldn't play without them, I couldn't play." Ainge scored 21 points.

Next up was UCLA, which was ranked No. 10 in the national rankings. Ainge outscored the Bruins by himself in the first half and finished with 37 points in a 78–53 victory over the school where BYU coach Frank Arnold had once coached under the legendary John Wooden.

Then in the regional semifinals, the Sweet 16, BYU squared off against Notre Dame at the Omni in Atlanta. It was the Cougars' first meeting with the Fighting Irish in either basketball or football. With 10 seconds left in the game, forward Kelly Tripucka nailed a 16-foot jumper to give Notre Dame a 50–49 lead. With eight seconds left, BYU called timeout.

Ainge wanted the ball. "I remember Arnold trying to explain the play," recalled Cougars forward Steve Trumbo. "I was looking around, and the play wasn't the one designed. Danny took matters in to his own hands." Ainge took the inbounds pass, deftly dribbled the length of the court (going behind his back around a defender at midcourt), raced into the key, and softly floated the ball over the outstretched fingertips of Notre Dame center Orlando Woolridge. By the time the Irish could inbound the ball, time had expired. As BYU players celebrated on the court, Tripucka sat on the floor, agonizing and staring at the scoreboard in disbelief.

"I had two things on my mind as I dribbled upcourt," Ainge said. "I made up my mind to either dribble straight for the hoop or, if covered, to stop and take the jumper and possibly draw the foul. I dribbled between two guys at half court and saw the clock ticking away. I just went to the hole. I was just gonna keep going until they made me stop. That was the plan. I figured that, in that situation, nobody would have the guts to step in front of me and take the charge. That was the only thing that was going to stop me."

"After Tripucka made that shot, I went over and sat down on the bench," Trumbo said. "I had a calm feeling. I felt like we were going to win. When I looked up and saw Danny dribble the ball behind his back, I thought, *Oh, heavens.* Orlando came within an inch of blocking Danny's shot."

Ainge's heroics made front-page news the next day in several major newspapers, including the *Atlanta Journal-Constitution* and the *New York Daily News*, with prominent photos of the Cougars bench erupting after Ainge's shot settled into the net. "In its quest for territorial supremacy of the Holy Eastern Empire, Brigham Young, the Mormon all-white group from Provo, has captured a few fans on novelty alone, particularly in the win over the Irish Catholics of Notre Dame on Thursday," proclaimed the *Atlanta Journal-Constitution.*

That win propelled the Cougars to the Elite Eight for the first—and only—time in program history. Two days later, BYU saw its Cinderella season end courtesy of 7'4" Ralph Sampson and Virginia. And the Cougars' dream of reaching the Final Four

Danny Ainge maneuvers past a Bruins defender in the 1981 NCAA Tournament.

for the first time fell short. Legendary coach and broadcaster Al McGuire said, "BYU is an outstanding team that hasn't got any recognition because it's in the wrong time zone."

Today BYU holds a dubious record: the most NCAA Tournament appearances—29 and counting—without a Final Four appearance.

28 Upset at Jerry World

Almost 25 years ago to the day after BYU upset No. 3 Pittsburgh on the road in its 1984 season opener, the No. 20 Cougars managed the feat again in 2009, shocking No. 3 Oklahoma 14–13 before a crowd of 75,437 at Cowboys Stadium. It was the first college game played at the Dallas Cowboys' new $1.3 billion 111,000-seat facility built by owner Jerry Jones, known as Jerry World.

It also marked BYU's first triumph over a nonconference team ranked in the top 10 since a 28–21 win over Miami in 1990 in Provo. "It's one of the greatest wins in BYU history," said wide receiver McKay Jacobson, who caught the game-winning seven-yard touchdown pass from Max Hall with 3:03 remaining.

"BYU fans will look back on it forever," said defensive lineman Brett Denney. "A lot of people thought it was impossible for us to win this game. But our coaches helped us realize that it wasn't impossible."

BYU's stunning victory all but ended Oklahoma's plans for an eighth national championship. The Cougars, who were three-touchdown underdogs, outplayed the heralded Sooners, outgaining them 357 yards to 265. BYU, which staged a memorable goal-line stand, also limited OU to 2-for-11 on third-down conversions and held a team that averaged more than 50 points the previous season to a mere 13.

With injuries to star offensive players for both teams, including BYU running back Harvey Unga, did not play due to a hamstring injury, who the game became a surprising defensive struggle. Ultimately, BYU was more effective in overcoming adversity and early-season mistakes.

"I'm very excited about the win for our program and the work ethic our young men showed and the determination to play and battle through," said Coach Bronco Mendenhall. "It was an amazing situation in terms of the opportunity to play Oklahoma in this setting. Our intent was to play worthy of the opportunity, and I believe that they did that and I'm proud of them for that."

"BYU just made plays when they needed to, and I give them all respect," said Sooners defensive lineman Gerald McCoy. "Of course it hurts. Who likes to lose?"

The complexion of the game shifted when, just before the end of the half, OU quarterback Sam Bradford, the 2008 Heisman Trophy winner, suffered an AC joint sprain in his shoulder and sat out the rest of the game. Bradford gave way to redshirt freshman Landry Jones.

Bradford was knocked out of the game by linebacker Coleby Clawson, a returned missionary who was married and had a young daughter at the time. That play on Bradford quite possibly made Clawson the most unpopular man in the state of Oklahoma. Clawson's clean hit on Bradford was replayed almost ad nauseam on ESPN and other sports networks that Labor Day weekend. Along with BYU's monumental upset, Bradford's shoulder was the most talked-about story of the young college football season in 2009.

Clawson, a senior from Wales, Utah (population: 300), watched the play a few times on the plane ride home. "Since then,

I haven't really turned on the TV to watch it," Clawson said. "But people have told me it's been on over and over again."

Clawson admitted he had some mixed feelings about the result of his hit on Bradford. "It's kind of the nature of the beast, I guess. I really do feel bad because he's a great player and a good person too. I feel bad he got hurt. As far as our game, I think it helped us win."

Though Clawson's hit on Bradford changed Oklahoma's season, he said Sooners fans were "classy" toward him and his family, for the most part. His wife, Breanna—who wore a T-shirt bearing Clawson's No. 41 and his name at the game—was among the Clawson clan at Cowboys Stadium. "OU's fans were really great. They treated my family and my wife good," Clawson said. "[Family members] were in the middle of all the BYU fans, so I think they felt safe. [OU fans] even came up and congratulated us."

Mendenhall called BYU's defense, which was much-maligned the previous season, "outstanding." It came up big time against Oklahoma, particularly in the fourth quarter. Early in the period, after a Hall interception, the Sooners had first-and-goal at the Cougars 2-yard line. On three straight plays, the BYU *D* turned the Sooners away, and after a delay-of-game penalty, OU had to settle for a 22-yard field goal that gave the Sooners a 10–7 advantage. "If I were to use words to describe the game," Mendenhall said, "it would be *grit* and *determination*, and that comes down to that goal-line stand."

After Jacobson's touchdown catch, which gave BYU its first lead of the game at 14–13, OU marched into BYU territory for the potential game-winning field goal. The Cougars forced the Sooners to attempt a 54-yarder that fell short with 1:23 left. "They played an excellent football game and really made the plays there at the end when they had to have them to win," OU coach Bob Stoops said about BYU.

Among the many unsung heroes in that game was walk-on running back Bryan Kariya, who rushed for 42 yards and caught four passes for 76 yards against the Sooners. "We made a lot of mistakes, but fortunately the defense kept us in it and we were able to put it down there at the end of the game and get a score," Kariya said. "It was a great win for us."

That victory at Jerry World was one of the biggest for BYU under Mendenhall.

29 Eat a Cougar Tail

A decade ago, the director of BYU's dining services, Dean Wright, entered the Wilkinson Center on campus and admired the stuffed cougars displayed, noticing their tails. That's when inspiration struck.

Wright and his staff were trying to come up with an item to sell at the concessions stands for BYU athletic events, something that would be unique to BYU. "It just dawned on me. What if we took a maple bar and extended it to represent a cougar tail?" Wright wondered. "It was right there. I took the concept home, and my wife and I worked on it. I took it to our bakery and asked them to duplicate it, and they did." And that's how the Cougar Tail—a 16-inch maple bar donut that sells for five dollars—was born.

In a relatively short period of time, the Cougar Tail became part of the BYU sports scene—a sweet-tasting confection that perfectly fits the school. "It's truly a signature item for BYU," Wright said. "I've never, in my entire career…and I started in 1974… seen anything take off with a school like Cougar Tails [did]."

In the fall of 2016, BYU concessions sold an average of 6,000 Cougar Tails during football games. "In total, we've sold nearly

40,000 of them," Wright said. "That's like nine miles long of Cougar Tails if you put them end to end."

Cougar Tails are the top-selling specialty concession nationwide among collegiate concessions, and ESPN called them "the most unique collegiate dining concession product."

Cougars Tails are the No. 2 most popular concession at BYU, only behind beverages. "When [someone buys] a Cougar Tail, they're more apt to buy our milk," Wright said. "People tell me nothing goes better with a Cougar Tail than a bottle of chocolate milk."

Almost 18 percent of BYU's dining services revenue comes from the sales of Cougar Tails, Wright said. Cougar Tails are made from scratch, and they're all made on campus. Crews start working through the night before a game to create the quota that will be sold during the game. "It takes about 20 hours," Wright said.

It took a while to get the word out about Cougar Tails. "At the very beginning it was like, 'What are you selling a donut for?' Then people tried them and discovered that they're much more than a donut," Wright said. "We made the decision to only sell them at athletic events. If we had them readily available, they wouldn't be as special."

Once Wright received an email from someone who wanted to buy Cougar Tails to eat from home while watching the upcoming bowl game. "My response was, 'Why don't you go to a basketball game, buy a Cougar Tail, and eat it at home?'" Wright said. "We really wanted them to be tied to athletics. The neat thing about it is, at first, children wanted [them].… Then once the adults started buying [them], [they] became a total hit."

Wright heard that not long after the Cougar Tail was introduced, the wife of one of the BYU players gave her husband a Cougar Tail before halftime. "The players were all jealous. They didn't know what it was," Wright said. "We operate the hospitality suite at the bowl games, and we always ask what they would like us to bring. The No. 1 thing is Cougar Tails. We'll have one of our employees drive a vanload of Cougar Tails to San Diego for the [Poinsettia] Bowl game. People just love them. They're very unique and symbolic of BYU sports."

There are other schools, such as Houston and Washington State, that share the Cougars nickname, but BYU has ensured that the Cougar Tail remains tied to the school. "We trademarked Cougar Tail from the very beginning. We own that trademark and the name," Wright said. "We have special bags made for the Cougar Tail. It's something we're very proud of. It's unique to be proud of a donut."

30 The Start of a Perfect Season

Unranked BYU's visit to No. 3 Pittsburgh on September 1, 1984, turned out to be historic on several fronts. That was the first live regular-season college football game televised by ESPN, and it was one of BYU's biggest road wins in school history.

Unheralded wide receiver Adam Haysbert—brother of actor Dennis Haysbert—caught a 50-yard pass with 1:40 remaining in a 20–14 upset of the Panthers in the 1984 season opener to kick-start what ended up being an undefeated season. "I remember that pass at the end of that game and Haysbert running through the end zone with his arms outstretched," remembered offensive lineman Trevor Matich. "That set off the season. From there, we didn't really talk about going undefeated, but there was an undercurrent that if we took care of business, at the end of the season, we could find ourselves at 13–0."

Pittsburgh boasted future NFL mainstays Bill Fralic, Chris Doleman, and Craig "Ironhead" Heyward. The Panthers returned

15 starters from a team that finished 8–3–1 in 1983, and they had their sights set on a national championship. Over the previous five years, the Panthers had boasted the nation's No. 1 defense. The Cougars, meanwhile, had the nation's top offense during that same period. But BYU had lost stars such as Steve Young and Gordon Hudson from the previous season.

"Once we got there [to Pitt], we knew the game wasn't going to be a pushover," Haysbert said. "We were confident we could win, but we knew we had to play our best game. When we got into town, I remember that the media [was] comparing us to a high school team. And before the game Pitt was taunting us and trying to intimidate us."

The game was a defensive struggle. It wasn't pretty offensively. It took junior quarterback Robbie Bosco, feeling the pressure of replacing Young, a while to feel comfortable in his first career start. "That first game, we were very raw. I was lacking confidence," Bosco said. "I didn't have any confidence. I always felt good in practice, but game time was a whole different thing. The way we won it and the way the defense stepped up, that brings back a lot of great memories. That was one of the great games."

At the half, BYU led 3–0. In the second half, Pitt surged to a 14–12 advantage thanks to a couple interceptions thrown by Bosco. With less than two minutes remaining in the game, the Cougars trailed by two points and had the ball, third-and-4 at midfield. The plan was to be conservative and move deeper into Pitt territory to give Lee Johnson the chance to kick a field goal, which, if successful, would give the Cougars a one-point advantage.

But first BYU needed to convert on third down. In the huddle, Bosco called for play 63, in which Haysbert would run a post pattern to clear out the defenders underneath the coverage while Glen Kozlowski would cut across the middle.

All afternoon long, it was apparent that Pitt didn't respect BYU's ability to go deep. So when Panthers free safety Bill Callahan left Haysbert, Bosco delivered a strike to his senior receiver, who hauled in the pass and dashed into the end zone, propelling the Cougars to a 20–14 lead.

Haysbert said later that throughout that game, he and other Cougars had noticed holes in the Panthers defense and were waiting for the perfect time to exploit them. "I knew that I could beat them deep," he said.

The touchdown was thrilling for BYU's defense, which had been waiting for the offense to make a big play. "Our defense was crushing Pittsburgh, which I think was a big surprise to them and everybody in the nation," remembered linebacker Leon White. "It was great to see Adam just break free for that touchdown. It was a crazy play and a great part of the history of that year." Two days later, the previously unranked Cougars jumped to No. 13 in the Associated Press poll.

The magnitude of this victory may have diminished in the eyes of some because, as it turned out, Pitt finished with a 3–7–1 record in 1984. But the fourth-quarter come-from-behind victory over Pitt jump-started the Cougars' improbable run to the national championship.

This game was an opportunity for the Cougars to showcase their program before an East Coast crowd, and it was a rare opportunity to play a game in the East. It was the closest the Cougars came all year to being seen by a national television audience. The 20–14 win in many ways validated the program. Many of those who eventually voted BYU No. 1 in early January 1985 remembered that the Cougars had traveled to the East Coast and knocked off a team that was, at the time, an East Coast powerhouse.

31 LaVell's Last Miracle

When BYU and Utah met on November 24, 2000, there were no conference championships or bowl bids on the line. Neither team had a winning record; the two teams had a combined record of 9–12.

LaVell Edwards, the man who had seen his team win plenty of amazing games in his career, said the 34–27 victory that night over the Utes "may be the best one ever." Why? Because this was Edwards' final game as BYU's coach, and because of the way it ended.

Going into the contest, BYU defensive lineman Hans Olsen analyzed the upcoming matchup. "Both teams could be 0–11 coming into that game and it would still be big," he said. "The fact we've both had dumpy seasons, that's going to make it more of a battle, to see which team had the dumpier season. Hopefully we can end up [victorious] and say they had the dumpier season." BYU needed to win the game against their dreaded archrivals to avoid sending out Edwards with just his second losing season in 29 seasons.

On the game's second play from scrimmage, quarterback Brandon Doman, making just his second career start, threw an interception that was returned for a touchdown by Andre Dyson. Then the Cougars scored 19 unanswered points, including four field goals by Owen Pochman, but they knew they should have scored touchdowns instead. "At halftime," Edwards said, "I felt our inability to score [touchdowns] in the first half was going to haunt us, and it did."

Still, BYU jumped ahead 26–10 late in the third quarter, and it appeared the Cougars had the game wrapped up like a farewell gift. But somebody forgot to tell Utah it was over. The Utes scored

17 unanswered points to take a 27–26 edge with 2:16 remaining. "They had me scared for a minute. I thought the game was over," said Cougars cornerback Mike Lafitte. "I said a little prayer." So did a lot of BYU faithful.

BYU started its final drive from its own 20-yard line. Doman threw an incompletion then was sacked for a 10-yard loss. "When I sacked Doman, I really thought we had sealed the victory," said Utah linebacker Kautai Olevao.

A seven-yard reception by Luke Staley on third down set up fourth-and-13. So it came down to this: BYU trailed by one point with about one minute remaining—in the game, the season, and Edwards' career—and the Cougars were huddled up in the shadow of their own end zone with the Utah crowd screaming in their earholes.

BYU knew it had one last chance to pull out a victory for Edwards in his final game. But it didn't look promising. Edwards stood on the sideline at Rice-Eccles Stadium wondering if this was how it was going to end, with another heart-wrenching loss to the Utes. "I was dying inside," Edwards said.

The play was called, but senior wide receiver Jonathan Pittman had other ideas. "Brandon wanted me to run an out pattern, and I said, 'Give me a fade,'" Pittman explained. "I'm surprised their DB didn't hear me. We ran that play three times in a row. We ran it all game. Finally, we completed it. I knew in my heart we were going to complete in on fourth down. I wasn't going to let my team down. Throw it up and hope for the best."

Doman rolled out and completed a 34-yard pass to Pittman near the sideline to give BYU new life. "Brandon made a heck of a throw," Edwards said. "When he completed the first one, I thought, *Hey, we're going to win this.* I didn't exactly think that down there when it was fourth-and-13."

Pittman beat Utah's cornerback by sealing him off, coming back to the ball, and making a 34-yard grab at the Utah 49. On the next play, Pittman caught another pass for 36 yards, going out of bounds at the Utes 13. Staley followed up with a nine-yard run to the Utah 4. Doman capped off the amazing series with a four-yard run, bulling his way into the end zone. Olevao later said, "A miracle like that was bound to happen, seeing that it was LaVell's last game."

After the breathtaking win, BYU players hoisted Edwards upon their shoulders and carried him to midfield. The victory all but erased the painful memories of past failures in Edwards' farewell season. "I can't think of a more fitting ending [than] that," Edwards said.

"To have Jonathan Pittman make a play like that, then to make another after that was incredible," Doman said. "And then for the coaches to call a quarterback sweep for me to score in LaVell's last game...you couldn't dream up something like this."

For Pittman, it was the right way to finish his career at BYU, as well as Edwards'. "There's no better way to go out than that," Pittman said. "It was almost like a miracle. Somebody was looking down on us. Somebody wanted to grant [Edwards] that wish."

After an arduous final season for Edwards amid a 6–6 campaign, it was a storybook ending to a storybook career.

32 Gordon Hudson

Gordon Hudson was one of the first of BYU's many star tight ends, and he was the first—and only—Cougars tight end enshrined in the College Football Hall of Fame, in 2009. "It's awfully special. It kind of adds an exclamation point to my career and my legacy," said Hudson, who was a unanimous All-America selection in 1982 and 1983. "What's really special is I'm the first non-quarterback or non-coach [from BYU] to be elected to the Hall of Fame. I don't know that it's completely sunk in. I guess one of these days I'll have a chance to sit back and reflect. I'm amongst an elite group now."

"Gordon was tremendous," said Coach LaVell Edwards. "No one played the tight end position like he did at that time." During his career, Hudson helped the Cougars win four WAC championships and earn four trips to the Holiday Bowl. He caught a total of 178 passes for 2,484 yards and 22 touchdowns. His stellar play came at a time when BYU was emerging as a national power. Many of the passes he caught were from fellow Hall of Famer, quarterback Steve Young.

"Gordon and I were teammates at BYU, so I know from first-hand experience just how good of a football player he was," said athletic director Tom Holmoe. "This is a great honor for both Gordon and BYU."

Hudson was the second Cougars tight end to receive All-America honors, after Clay Brown first accomplished the feat in 1980. Several others have followed.

"The tight end position has always been as important to that offensive scheme, almost, as the quarterback," Hudson said. "To be the first one to go to the Hall of Fame—and I'm sure there will be many more after me, like [former Cougar] Chad Lewis and [current Cougar] Dennis Pitta, who is a fantastic player—I guess the [National Football] Foundation is starting to recognize what great tight ends BYU continues to put out. There will be more to come after me, I'm sure."

Hudson's legacy includes setting three NCAA tight end records that still stand—most passes caught per game (5.4), most career yards per game (75.3), and most yards in a single game (259). That 259-yard receiving performance happened during a 56–28 rout of archrival Utah in 1981. "It's going to be hard to break," Hudson said of that mark. "I am surprised that 26 years later I still hold three of those records. It gives me a little validation for some of the things I did. But records are made to be broken, and I'm sure someday, someone will come along and nab them all. But until they do, it's something I can hang my hat on. The [single-game receiving] record I broke stood for 40-something years. It will be broken at some point."

Years later, BYU coaches still use Hudson's game film as a way to teach and train their tight ends, decades after the end of his Cougars career. "To be considered by the coaching staff down there to be the one who set the bar, who set the standard, is really special," Hudson said. "It's been a long time since I played, but I still follow [BYU], and I still root for these guys who are coming after me. To have them tell me they still use a lot of my game tape to do teaching, that's an awful high honor."

The other Cougars who have been elected to the College Football Hall of Fame are quarterbacks Gifford Nielsen (inducted in 1994), Marc Wilson (inducted in 1996), Jim McMahon (inducted in 1998), Steve Young (inducted in 2001), Ty Detmer (inducted in 2012), and LaVell Edwards (inducted in 2004).

33 Hike Y Mountain

It's the most recognizable symbol, and most famous letter, in Utah County. The giant white *Y* emblazoned on Y Mountain that hovers above campus stands as an iconic landmark representing Brigham Young University and the values the school espouses.

When people ask why a *Y* and not a *B* serves as the logo of BYU, well, it's because of Y Mountain. The mountain is 380 feet high and 130 feet wide, covering 32,847 square feet, and is one of the largest school emblems of its kind in the United States. The *Y* is larger than the letters spelling HOLLYWOOD in Southern California. It requires more than 200 individual lights to illuminate it at night; the letter can be seen all over the valley.

Hiking the Y is a must for any BYU fan, and it provides a magnificent view of campus and the entire Utah Valley. It's a 1.1-mile hike to the top of the Y from the trailhead. In terms of elevation gain, it's 1,074 feet to the top of the Y. While it is a steep hike, there are 12 switchbacks to ease the ascent.

And there's a fascinating story behind the creation and preservation of the 111-year-old *Y* emblem. In 1906 BYU president George H. Brimhall commissioned a professor and three of his students to design and survey the letters *B*, *Y*, and *U* on the mountain above the school. BYU students then stood eight feet apart, starting at the base of the mountain, to the site of the Y. The line of students shuttled lime, sand, and rocks up the mountain to create the *Y*. The process took so long that they gave up trying to create the *B* and *U*. So the *Y* stood alone, and has ever since.

But in the beginning, the *Y* wasn't a block *Y* but a sans serif version. According to BYU's website, "Constant repairs to the thin, lime-covered letter prompted students to add a layer of rock to the face of the Y in 1907. In 1908, 20,000 pounds of sand and cement were added to make a three-foot rim around the letter, and in 1910 and 1911, the blocks or serifs were added to create the Y as it appears today."

From 1911 to 1971, students observed and celebrated Y Day in the springtime by forming a bucket brigade and whitewashing the Y. Freshmen would haul water from a spring while sophomores carried the whitewash and mixed the substance in wooden troughs. Juniors and seniors would pour on the liquid, which required 500 pounds of salt, 110 bags of lime, and 3,000 gallons of water.

Then in 1972 helicopters were used to transport the whitewash to offset the wear and tear to the mountain. In 1978 that exercise was discontinued. Instead, the school applied gunite, rendering the annual whitewashings obsolete. Gunite is a charcoal-colored substance made from cement and sand. A fresh coat of paint—155 gallons' worth—has been applied every few years so the *Y* can maintain its white appearance.

When the *Y* received its first facelift in 20 years in 1998, the school had to obtain a conditional work permit from the US Forest Service to refurbish the emblem. BYU spent about $30,000 on the project.

In 2016 BYU announced it had finalized the purchase of 81 acres of the mountain from the US Forest Service for $180,000. Capitol Hill authorized the sale of Y Mountain, the Y Mountain Trail, the block *Y*, and the area around it in 2014. Also in 2014, the US Senate passed a bill—cosponsored by BYU alums Rep. Jason Chaffetz (a former BYU place-kicker), R-Provo, and Sen. Orrin Hatch, R-Utah—that stipulates BYU could purchase the land, approximately 80 acres, on Y Mountain from the US Forest Service. The bill passed by a vote of 89–11. The land would sell for about $500,000, according to government estimates. According to the bill, BYU would be required to guarantee public access to the mountain.

In 2016 BYU also announced plans to make major improvements to the trail and install permanent lighting to the Y. Roy Peterman served as BYU's director of grounds maintenance for 35 years and was considered, among other things, as the mountain's caretaker before retiring in 2013. "People look for identifying marks and symbols to give stability and meaning to their lives," he said. "The Y represents a sense of security and well-being."

In 2005, prior to his first season as BYU's head coach, Bronco Mendenhall started a tradition of having his players run to the top of Y Mountain. That first time, as he was trying to resurrect a program mired in three straight losing seasons, he told his team that their ascent was symbolic. "The view is much better from the top," Mendenhall said.

When people wonder why a *Y* serves as BYU's logo, all they have to do is look up at the mountain that looms above campus.

34 Missouri's Misery

BYU opened the 1983 season, and quarterback Steve Young's senior campaign, with a heartbreaking 40–36 loss at Baylor. After that, the Cougars won 10 consecutive games, captured another Western Athletic Conference title, jumped to No. 9 in the polls, and were invited to the Holiday Bowl for the sixth consecutive season. Their opponent? A 7–4 team from the Big 8 Conference: Missouri. The Tigers wanted to knock off a top-10 opponent they felt was inferior.

During the bowl festivities leading up to the game in San Diego, Missouri didn't show much respect for BYU. "All week long, they said that we don't get physical, and that makes me angry," said guard Craig Garrick. "These guys don't believe we deserve our ranking and they don't believe we have the No. 1 offense. The coaches have told us that we need to show them. Missouri's license plates have 'Show-Me State' on them. That's what we want to do— show them. I feel like we really have something to prove."

But the Cougars had five turnovers, three interceptions, and two fumbles, and the Tigers held the ball for 37 minutes, compared to 23 minutes for the Cougars. Meanwhile, Missouri running back Eric Drain ran 27 times for 115 yards to earn the game's offensive MVP honors.

The Tigers led 17–14 when the Cougars offense took over at their own 7-yard line with 3:37 remaining. On that final drive, Young completed a 53-yard pass to wide receiver Mike Eddo to the Missouri 36, and eventually BYU reached the 14-yard line with a little more than 30 seconds remaining. That's when offensive coordinator Norm Chow called the play: fake ride 28 screen left.

It was a trick play the Cougars tried at the end of practices—out of diversion, probably never dreaming it would be used late in a bowl game with the outcome in doubt. "I loved it," Young said of Chow's play call. "I thought it was a gutsy decision. It's one of those plays you just have to wait and see develop."

Young handed the ball off to running back Eddie Stinnett, who sprinted right. Suddenly Stinnett stopped, turned, and tossed an off-balance pass toward the opposite side of the field to Young, who had turned into a wide receiver.

Missouri defensive star Bobby Bell had read the play correctly and was bearing down on Young and the ball. Instead of waiting for Young to catch the ball and tackle him for a loss, Bell opted to try to bat away or intercept the pass. Bell jumped, but somehow the ball cleared his outstretched fingertips.

Young latched onto the back half of the ball then sprinted untouched toward the end zone. He was hit at the goal line and fell into the end zone with 23 seconds remaining. Young high-stepped around in the end zone with the ball aloft in his hand.

Fittingly the touchdown, which gave the Cougars a 21–17 victory, was the final play of Young's college career. "It's a Holiday Bowl. What else can you say about a finish like that?" said Coach LaVell Edwards. "Sometimes it seems like those things are meant to happen. The TD was a great call."

In the fourth quarter, Young completed 10 of 11 passes for 145 yards. And Young pulled off a rare college football hat trick. He scored three touchdowns in three different ways—he threw one, he ran for one, and he caught one.

The game's defensive MVP, Bobby Bell, wasn't exactly gracious in defeat. "BYU didn't give us the respect we deserve. We still probably won't get it from them.... BYU is right up there with Kansas [which went 4–6–1 that season]. BYU didn't beat us in the fourth quarter. We beat ourselves, and that's what we have to live with."

The Cougars finished the season with an 11–1 record, an 11-game winning streak, and a No. 7 ranking. It served as a prelude to BYU's national championship season the following year.

35 Jimmer Breaks Scoring Record

Just when it seemed like the world had seen it all from BYU guard Jimmer Fredette, he did the unthinkable in Las Vegas at the Thomas & Mack Center in March 2011. In the Mountain West Conference tournament semifinals, Fredette exploded for a career-high 52 points—shattering the career school scoring record (surpassing legend Danny Ainge) and the school single-game scoring record in the same game—to lead the No. 8 Cougars to an emotional 87–76 triumph over New Mexico. In a town known for entertainment, the Jimmer Show reigned supreme.

"He's a scorer, a great scorer at that," Lobo guard Kendall Williams said of Fredette. "It piled on. It was a great game. He's a great player."

"Obviously, Fredette had one of those career nights," said UNM coach Steve Alford. "Very, very special talent. He put on an incredible performance."

And what did Fredette think? "It was just a great night," he said. "I knew I was having a good game. I was just making shots tonight."

Making it look easy and fun, Jimmer Fredette celebrates a win in 2011.

The senior from Glens Falls, New York, knocked down 22 field goals, just eight fewer than the entire New Mexico team. He was 22-of-37 overall and 7-of-14 from three-point territory. Amazingly, Fredette attempted only one free throw, and that came with 4:24 left in the game.

The MWC Player of the Year, who had already been named National Player of the Year by several media outlets, scored his 49th point to eclipse Ainge's all-time scoring mark, and he tied the single-game school record of 49, which he already held. Fredette also drew a foul on the made shot. Then he calmly drained a free throw to reach the 50-point milestone, recording the highest-scoring performance in school history.

Fredette added one more bucket with 56 seconds left to give himself 52 points. Coach Dave Rose removed him from the game with 16.1 seconds on the clock, to the deafening roars of BYU fans in attendance.

"To get 52 and to do it…getting to the free-throw line just one time speaks volumes to how talented he is," Alford said. "I think we had five different guys guard him. We tried running some people at him. I think we've won the other two [games] because we haven't let the role players and a couple other players hurt us."

Rose emphasized that it was a tremendous win for the program. "Jimmer had one of those real special offensive nights that kind of kept a lot of energy with our team," he said. "But you watch it, it's amazing. You can have a team win, as big a team win as this is, with one player scoring 52 points."

36 John Beck

On his first collegiate play from scrimmage, in the 2003 season opener against Georgia Tech, John Beck was sacked for a 10-yard loss. On the second play, he fumbled the ball, which the Cougars recovered. And on the third play, on his first collegiate pass attempt, he threw an interception. What made it worse was that former Cougars star QB Steve Young watched it all at LaVell Edwards Stadium on the same night the school retired Young's jersey.

But Beck's inauspicious start eventually blossomed into a remarkable career. Right before Cougars fans' eyes during the 2006 season, John Beck—the senior who had taken his lumps as a callow, wide-eyed freshman just off a mission—grew up and wound up accomplishing feats that hadn't been seen on BYU's campus in years. Over a four-month period that fall, Beck transformed from a strong-armed quarterback with potential to a legendary Cougars quarterback who won over legions of BYU fans.

That transformation wasn't by accident. "John's such a hard worker," said tight end Daniel Coats. "You'll never see anybody on this team outwork him. He's constantly trying to make himself better, but within that, he's always trying to make his teammates better too."

Beck's defining moment to that point came when the Cougars, sporting a mediocre 2–2 record, traveled to nationally ranked TCU in late September. Playing on two sprained and heavily wrapped ankles, he guided BYU to a dominating 31–17 upset. It marked the Cougars' first road victory over a ranked team in nine seasons.

While Beck was impressive that night, it wasn't anything less than what his coach and teammates expected. "John has always been a tough guy and a competitor. It didn't shock me that he was going to play hurt—if John had to crawl or whatever," Coats said. "John is basically the captain of the offense. It's always impressed us when we hear stories about [Robbie] Bosco, when he played in [the 1984 Holiday Bowl]. John wouldn't have played if he thought he'd hurt the team. We trusted him, and he went out and had a great game."

That victory built momentum toward a stellar conclusion of the season as the Cougars won their final 10 games, including a last-second victory over Utah and a 38–8 blowout of Oregon in the Las Vegas Bowl. Beck became only the seventh quarterback to lead BYU to a bowl win. During the 2006 campaign, Beck posted amazing numbers and steamrolled Mountain West Conference opponents.

That's exactly what Beck wanted when he arrived in Provo—to help return the Cougars to glory. After he surpassed the career 10,000-yard passing mark, eclipsing Jim McMahon, during a 55–7 stomping of Wyoming, Beck reflected on that accomplishment. "When I came to BYU, my sights weren't set on beating these guys that were legends. My sights were set on just winning. Winning football games and winning a championship. These last couple of years have not been easy, not by any means. But to be able to be on the field and have a big win like that, and have my teammates, who have been through so much with me, celebrate—that's the feeling I came here for. Right now, I feel like I'm playing for the BYU that I chose to play for."

By the end of his career, Beck had reached the stratosphere of BYU's other quarterbacking legends. "For him to have the senior year he's had makes him probably as good as any quarterback we've had in the history of BYU," said offensive coordinator, and former BYU quarterback star, Brandon Doman. "To beat Utah in the last game, I think it sends him into the history books as one of the great ones."

Beck capped an outstanding regular season with a last-minute, game-winning 75-yard drive against Utah. With no time remaining on the clock, he completed an 11-yard touchdown pass to Jonny Harline, rallying the Cougars to a dramatic 33–31 triumph. "I can remember trying to buy time to my left, trying to get someone open by signaling with my hand, then running to my right and seeing Jonny swing back to the left. I remember jumping and throwing it," Beck recalled. "It's a play that I dreamed of being a part of since I was little. I grew up watching highlights of Jim McMahon in the Miracle Bowl, Steve Young against Missouri when they threw it back to him, and so many of Ty Detmer's amazing plays. To be able to be here at BYU, wearing that same *Y* on my helmet, to be able to be a part of a play like that, means a lot to me."

Beck was selected in the second round of the 2007 NFL Draft and played for the Miami Dolphins, Baltimore Ravens, Houston Texans, and Washington Redskins.

37 Watch a Game at the Marriott Center

When the Marriott Center opened in 1971, it was the largest on-campus arena in the country with a seating capacity of 22,700. In fact, it was larger than any NBA facility back then. These days, due to renovations, the Marriott Center seats slightly fewer than 19,000, making it the fifth-largest college basketball arena in the nation. And when the Marriott Center fills up with fans, it's one of the loudest facilities in the country.

After the Cougars suffered through their worst season ever—BYU went 1–25 and fans stayed away in droves during the 1996–97 campaign—new coach Steve Cleveland knew where to

Ring the Y Victory Bell

For an inanimate object, BYU's Y Victory Bell has experienced quite a history and has gone through several iterations. Like a (mountain) cat, it seems to have nine lives.

When the early Mormon pioneers traveled across the plains from the Midwest to present-day Utah in the 1840s, they had a bell that was used to announce meetings and deaths. That bell was donated to Brigham Young Academy in 1875 and was used to begin and dismiss classes. In 1884, however, that Y bell was destroyed in a fire and the school went without a bell for 28 years.

But when Brigham Young Academy became Brigham Young University in 1903, the student body size had increased significantly, creating a bigger need for a campus bell. In 1912 the school purchased a 36-inch-diameter cast iron bell from the American Bell Foundry in Michigan. However, the bell's sound didn't carry far and couldn't be heard outside the building that housed it. The Utah Stake presidency from the Provo Meeting House donated a nickel bell to BYU in 1919 and the old bell was gifted to the Boy Scouts of America. The new bell was perched in the education building belfry, and the Y Victory Bell was born, ringing loudly on campus to celebrate wins.

In 1949, after BYU defeated archrival Utah in basketball, several students climbed to the top of the belfry and beat on the bell until it sustained a crack. The bell was repaired with a bronze patch in 1954 and taken down from the education building. The Y Victory Bell was mounted on a trailer, and it traveled with BYU's team to road games. But at some point in 1958, the bell was stolen and turned up in a Springville, Utah, field. In response to the theft, the school constructed a bell tower on BYU's upper campus.

The bell tower was dedicated in 1959, but the bell crashed down while it was being rung during the dedication of the Marriott Center in 1973 and shattered. Using electric welding, the bell was repaired and returned to its spot in the tower. Amazingly, the bell maintained its tone despite the damage. The bell tower was moved to its current location at the southwest corner of the Marriott Center in 1978.

As BYU gained national prominence during the 1980s, frequent wins and frequently ringing of the bell changed the name from the Y Bell to the Victory Bell.

start to regain a competitive advantage at home. "Our theme is to recapture the magic in the Marriott Center," said Cleveland at the time, and he wrote letters to season-ticket holders and went door-to-door in the student dorms in an attempt to coax people back to basketball games. A couple years later, the Cougars started winning again, and the fans returned.

The Marriott Center, which was completed in 1971, replaced the George Albert Smith Fieldhouse, which had been the home of BYU basketball from 1951 to 1971. The popularity of BYU basketball outgrew the Smith Fieldhouse, which was needed for academic and intramural purposes.

When the Marriott Center debuted, BYU's administrators couldn't figure out what to call the new activities facility, so they held a contest. The first prize for the best name was $100. At the same time, hotel magnate J. Willard Marriott donated $1 million. Contest over.

Since then, considering the BYU basketball team's record at home going into the 2015–16 season was 448–119, it's safe to say very few visitors enjoy a good night at this Marriott. It's one of the country's most formidable home-court advantages.

The outside dimensions of the Marriott Center are the equivalent of two football fields placed side by side. The roof covers 130,000 square feet and will house 8 million cubic feet. The height of the building, from the playing floor to the top of the roof, is 10 stories.

Though the Marriott Center celebrated its 45th anniversary in 2016, you'd never know it thanks to some upgrades. During the summer of 2015, crews installed a new $4 million center-hanging scoreboard with four LED screens that measure 24 feet wide and 18 feet tall. The scoreboard also includes a pair of boards that are visible from the floor. As part of the renovation, the school added 8,000 padded blue seats that fill the lower bowl of the Marriott Center. With the changes, the Marriott Center's capacity dropped from 20,900 to 18,968. "The people will be a lot more comfortable," said men's coach Dave Rose. "Hopefully, we'll put out a product that will have people standing rather than sitting."

In addition to basketball games, the Marriott Center houses devotionals and other church meetings, as well as other events. Back in the 1970s and 1980s, it hosted the West Regionals of the NCAA Men's Basketball Tournament (1972, 1979, and 1982). On February 19, 1999, the Marriott Center set an NCAA record for highest attendance for a men's volleyball match: 14,156 fans watched BYU defeat the University of Hawaii, shattering the previous record of 10,225 set at home by Hawaii.

When the Marriott Center first opened, it hosted bands and singers in the 1970s and 1980s before school leaders banned those types of concerts. Billy Joel, Elton John, James Taylor, Boston, and the Cars all performed at the Marriott Center.

38 The Pitch

Boasting a 10–0 record, a No. 8 ranking, and a shot to clinch the Mountain West Conference championship, BYU hosted archrival Utah (7–2) on November 17, 2001, with Fiesta Bowl officials on hand in Provo. The Cougars were one of the top offensive teams in the country and the Utes were one of the top defensive teams in the nation. It was a slugfest, with a lot of big hits and big plays.

Late in the fourth quarter, BYU trailed 21–10, and things looked bleak for the Cougars, who had the ball on their own 8-yard line with 5:47 remaining. But because of the prolific nature of BYU's offense, which had already pulled out some tight games that season, there was hope on the sideline. Cougars linebacker Justin

Ena, for one, was brimming with optimism. "Put a smile on your face and have fun, because we're going to pull it out," Ena told his teammates. "I don't know how we're going to do it, but we're going to do it."

Sure enough, they did. The Cougars cut the deficit to four points on a seven-yard touchdown pass from quarterback Brandon Doman to Luke Staley, capping a 92-yard drive. Staley also added a two-point conversion to make it 21–18 with 3:22 remaining.

BYU's defense held to put the ball back in the hands of the offense. Eventually, Doman rolled right toward the sideline and, at the last moment, pitched the ball to Staley, who cruised down the sideline for a 30-yard touchdown run. That gave BYU a 24–21 lead with 1:16 remaining, touching off a deafening roar from the crowd.

"I kept saying, 'Pitch it, pitch it, pitch it!' I could see there was no defender there," said Coach Gary Crowton. "He pitched it right at the last second so they couldn't come off and squeeze the boundary."

With time still remaining, Utah drove into BYU territory before cornerback Jernaro Gilford intercepted Utes quarterback Lance Rice's pass to seal the win.

During that 2001 season, Doman pitched the ball to Staley many times. But that one for the late touchdown against Utah is etched in the memories of BYU fans. "There's a little magic toward the end of those games, if you're feeling it like that," Doman said. "There's a little destiny. At least that's the way I believe it." Before that season, who would have dreamed BYU would clinch an outright conference championship and polish off the dreaded rivals on…an option play?

That night, against a stingy Utah defense, Staley rushed 17 times for 169 yards and scored two touchdowns. That victory preserved BYU's undefeated season and kept them in the running for a BCS bowl game. And that play helped Staley earn the Doak Walker Award, emblematic of the nation's top running back.

Following Staley's performance, BYU officials began making plans to launch a 2002 Heisman Trophy campaign for the running back, who was set to return to Provo for his senior season. Part of the campaign was to feature highlight videos of Staley, including that 30-yard, game-winning touchdown run against Utah, to send to Heisman voters as part of a large publicity blitz. Before his arrival in Provo, nobody could have imagined a BYU running back as a Heisman candidate.

As fate would have it, however, in the Cougars' next game, at Mississippi State, Staley broke his ankle late in the fourth quarter, ending his season. Weeks later, Staley turned pro, short-circuiting the shortest Heisman campaign in BYU history.

But Staley's final carry at home, taking a pitch from Doman and streaking down the sideline, couldn't have been bigger.

39 1965: Triumph Amid Tragedy

In late November 1965 BYU beat New Mexico 42–8 to claim its first-ever Western Athletic Conference championship. It was a historic day, as it marked the Cougars' first league title in 42 years of football history.

But the day was marred by tragedy. On the morning of the game, 13 people, including eight BYU boosters and five crew members, boarded a chartered plane in Salt Lake City to travel to Albuquerque to watch the Cougars play for the championship. Those boosters realized the potential historical significance of the game. At the time, BYU was defined by losing. The Cougars had logged just 12 winning seasons before 1965.

The DC-3 charter flight ascended into the sky at approximately 7:00 AM amid wintry weather. The 28-seat aircraft was scheduled to stop in Provo to pick up about 20 more boosters and school president Ernest L. Wilkinson. But the plane never arrived, crashing before it reached the Point of the Mountain near northern Utah County. The wreckage was discovered about one and a third miles northwest of Camp Williams, some 23 miles from Provo. Cloud cover and poor visibility were cited as factors in the crash. It was determined that the aircraft was flying too low and clipped a hill—ripping off a wing—and then bounced across a ravine and slammed into a snowy mountain. The plane burst into flames and all 13 people on board were killed.

Among those who died were prominent Utah physicians, including Marion Earl Probert, a former BYU star. The eight BYU boosters on board were charter members of the Cougar Club, which was established in 1964.

News of the tragic accident was passed along to the team in Albuquerque during its pregame breakfast, rendering players and coaches in shock. Probert's wife, Beverley, sent a telegram to Coach Tommy Hudspeth to read to his team prior to kickoff. She expressed her husband's desire that BYU someday win a conference championship, and she asked the team to "do [their] best to see his wish fulfilled."

Perhaps fueled by the day's devastating accident, the Cougars played their best game of the season. BYU—led by quarterback Virgil Carter, wide receiver Phil Odle, and running backs John and Steve Ogden—crushed the Lobos. The Cougars had been projected by the media in a preseason poll to finish last in the six-team WAC.

Identical bronze plaques featuring that inspirational message from Beverley Probert to the team appear at the Smith Fieldhouse and LaVell Edwards Stadium. The plaques memorialize the BYU boosters who lost their lives that day and honor the widows of those who died, praising them for their courage.

In 1977 the school inducted Marion Probert into the BYU Athletic Hall of Fame. His No. 81 was retired as a tribute to him and those who died in the 1965 plane crash.

Despite the league title, there was no bowl invitation tied to winning the championship at that time. It would turn out to be the first of 23 WAC championships for BYU, but the next one wouldn't happen until 1974.

Then–BYU sports information director Dave Schulthess said the star-crossed date of November 27, 1965, was "a special date, which might be called a historical turning point. BYU came on to win the championship the hard way—by winning three of four conference games on the road."

Certainly, it was a day of triumph and tragedy in Cougars football history.

40 The Quarterback Factory

Sometime during BYU's national championship season, Coach LaVell Edwards knew he was experiencing a run of great quarterbacks that would be difficult to continue. "We've created a monster here," he said. "Every time another quarterback does well, it just grows bigger and bigger. Sometimes you wonder how long it can keep going."

The Cougars went almost seamlessly from Gifford Nielsen to Marc Wilson to Jim McMahon to Steve Young to Robbie Bosco during a nine-year stretch from 1977 to 1985. Each of those men went on to play in the National Football League, and McMahon and Young both led their teams to Super Bowl championships.

BYU's All-Time Leaders in Passing

Rank	Yards	Name	Years
1.	15,031	Ty Detmer	1988–91
2.	11,365	Max Hall	2007–09
3.	11,021	John Beck	2003–06
4.	9,536	Jim McMahon	1977–78, 1980–81
5.	8,400	Robbie Bosco	1983–85
6.	8,390	John Walsh	1991–94
7.	8,065	Kevin Feterik	1996–99
8.	7,733	Steve Young	1981–83
9.	7,637	Marc Wilson	1975–79
10.	7,464	Steve Sarkisian	1995–96

Seven BYU QBs have won the Sammy Baugh Trophy. No other school has won it more than four times.

And Edwards was right: it didn't last forever. Following that stint of record-setting, All-American, Heisman Trophy–candidate, NFL-bound quarterbacks, the school went through a bit of drought—until Ty Detmer arrived on campus and became the starter as a sophomore in 1989. When offensive coordinator Norm Chow watched Detmer work prior to the 1988 season, he told Edwards, "We're back in the quarterback business." Two years later, Detmer won the school's first Heisman Trophy.

After all those years of quarterbacking greatness, expectations were so high for BYU quarterbacks that it was difficult for any to live up to them. "I've heard it said that the quarterback position is the toughest position to play in all of sports," said John Beck, who played from 2003 to 2006. "Then when you add playing at one of the most recognizable schools for quarterbacks in the nation, there's a lot that goes into it. Because of that, you have a large responsibility as the BYU quarterback. A BYU quarterback is supposed to be nothing less than first-team all-conference. A BYU quarterback is supposed to be nothing less than being up for the awards for the top quarterbacks in the nation. That's what's expected at BYU. If you finish with not a great season record-wise, that doesn't cut it. A BYU quarterback is supposed to be someone who wins a lot of games and wins the big ones. In tight situations, a BYU quarterback is supposed to make the play."

Robbie Bosco recalled a sleepless night before his first start, against No. 3 Pitt, wondering if he could live up to his predecessors. All he did was win a national championship. But the following season, he was booed at home during a game because...well...he wasn't always perfect.

The mid-1970s to mid-1980s marked a golden era in BYU football history. Every year, a new quarterback would step forward and pick up where the last one had left off, and they wound up more decorated than the campus Christmas tree. Then, from 1992 to 1996 AD (After Detmer), John Walsh and Steve Sarkisian showed flashes of that familiar BYU QB brilliance. Still, inserting an heir apparent isn't as automatic as it used to be.

"It's the loneliest position in the world," said Blaine Fowler of being a BYU quarterback. He knows. He was Bosco's backup and now is a broadcaster. He remembers competing with Bosco for the starting job, losing it, and then hearing Bosco being booed lustily in 1985, a year after the national title. "You can never imagine the spotlight you're in," Fowler said. "It's unbelievable. High school kids can't understand the microscope you're under. Mentally, it has an effect on you. It takes so much more than being able to throw the ball. You have to deal with the mental side and be a leader."

"There's 10 times the pressure at quarterback than other positions at BYU because of the tradition," said Steve Clements, who transferred to BYU after a stint at Texas. He came in thinking he would be the next star, like fellow Texan Detmer. He started just one game. He said he didn't know what he was getting into when

BYU's Single-Game Passing Leaders

Rank	Yards	Name	Opponent	Date	Score
1.	619	John Walsh	at Utah State	October 30, 1993	56–58
2.	599	Ty Detmer	at San Diego State	November 16, 1991	52–52
3.	585	Robbie Bosco	at New Mexico	October 19, 1985	45–23
4.	576	Ty Detmer	Penn State	December 29, 1989	39–50
5.	571	Marc Wilson	Utah	November 5, 1977	38–8

he became a Cougar. "Not even close. Until you're thrown in with the dogs, you don't know. It's crazy."

Successfully surviving that heat doesn't necessarily guarantee your canonization as a BYU quarterback, either. Since the mid-1980s, BYU quarterbacks have been chasing ghosts—their predecessors. In the 2000s Brandon Doman, Beck, and Max Hall all established themselves as some of the all-time greats. But Jake Heaps, who was touted as the top high school QB prospect in 2010, transferred out of BYU after two rocky seasons.

There are a host of prevailing theories as to why BYU doesn't churn out quarterbacks like it used to. The Cougars are playing tougher competition than they were 20 to 30 years ago, and opposing defenses have figured out how to play the pass now that it's become a bigger weapon in college football offensive arsenals.

Coaches have pointed to other reasons too. Decades ago, quarterbacks waited their turn for two to three years before becoming the starter. Quarterbacks are less inclined to do that now. They want to play. "McMahon sat around for three years before starting," recalled Chow. And Young once said: "It takes at least two years to be really comfortable with the offense. You could play before that, but you'd be in a cloud."

Playing quarterback at BYU is an alluring thing. But living up to the hype can be overwhelming. During Edwards' 29 years at the helm, his quarterbacks completed more than 11,000 passes for more than 100,000 yards and 635 touchdowns. In 13 of his first 17 seasons, BYU finished either No. 1 or No. 2 nationally in passing.

41 Kresimir Cosic

On March 4, 2006, thousands of BYU students who weren't even born when Kresimir Cosic displayed his freewheeling brand of basketball for the Cougars in the early 1970s wore white T-shirts emblazoned with No. 11. During halftime of BYU's 76–68 victory over New Mexico, when the school officially retired Cosic's No. 11 jersey—which will forever hang from the Marriott Center rafters—those same students chanted, "Co-sic! Co-sic! Co-sic!" And at one point some of them held up a Croatian flag in honor of Cosic's homeland.

Members of the Cosic family—wife Ljerka, daughters Ana and Iva, and son Kresimir—attended the jersey retirement ceremony in Provo and were visibly moved by the outpouring of affection for the former Cougars All-American, who died in 1995 of non-Hodgkin's lymphoma.

"It is very impressive that Kreso is not forgotten here. Kreso never forgot Provo. I don't think he ever really left it," said Ana, who had recently graduated from BYU. The family made the 20-hour flight from Croatia to attend Saturday's event.

Tears welled up in Ljerka's eyes as she took in the sights and sounds of the fanfare directed toward her husband. "I am touched to see that they honor him here so far away from his country and seeing that he is not forgotten," she said.

Cosic arrived at BYU as a communist and an atheist, and he ended up becoming a devout member of the Church of Jesus Christ of Latter-day Saints. As a junior, Cosic was an All-America selection in 1972, becoming the first non-American player to receive that honor after averaging 22.3 points and 12.8 rebounds per game. He was twice drafted by NBA teams but rejected those offers and instead returned home to Croatia. Cosic played in four Summer Olympic Games—in 1968, 1972, 1976, and 1980, when he led his team to the gold medal in Moscow. After he finished playing, he led the former Yugoslav team to a silver medal in the 1988 Olympics in Seoul.

Later, Cosic served as a Croatian diplomat in the United States at the embassy in Washington, DC, and in 1996 Cosic became only the third international player and the first BYU player elected to the Basketball Hall of Fame.

Among those who spoke during the halftime ceremony of his jersey retirement were Cosic's former teammate Steve Kelly, his former coach Glenn Potter; and LDS Church president Thomas S. Monson, a member of the First Presidency of the Church of Jesus Christ of Latter-day Saints.

The man who introduced Cosic to basketball, longtime Yugoslavian coach Ranko Zeravica, spoke through an interpreter to the media prior to the game. "He was an outstanding person. A born leader," Zeravica said. "He gave 100 percent in everything he did. He had a brilliant basketball IQ. He looked like a coach on the court. I'm glad his jersey is being retired. It's the biggest honor an athlete can receive in his career."

Cosic stood 6'11", but he was quick and agile. He was also charismatic and possessed an uncanny ability to entertain on the court. "He basically thought he was a guard in a 6'11" body," Steve Kelly recalled. "He would dribble and pass. If you weren't looking, you'd get hit in the head with a pass. He was an all-around player."

President Monson recalled a meeting he had with Cosic when Cosic was playing at BYU: "I asked him how he got along with Coach Stan Watts. He said, 'Wonderful in every respect except one. He told me not to dribble, but I could dribble better than the guards. And I dribbled and I shot.'"

"Over 30 years has passed since the last game Kreso played in the Marriott Center. It was 1973. Many of you probably remember his game. You probably also remember his conquering smile," Ana said. "It is a great honor for us to be here. Being his family, this makes us proud and happy. Thank you on behalf of Kreso and my family for this great honor, and thank you, Kreso, for getting us all together."

42 Gifford Nielsen

Having grown up in the shadow of BYU's campus and starred in three sports at Provo High School, Gifford Nielsen dreamed of playing for the Cougars. And he did play two sports at BYU, basketball and football. But he was destined to be a quarterback, and he was one of the best the Cougars ever produced—despite his career being cut short by injury.

Nielsen struggled early on being a BYU quarterback, but the hiring of Doug Scovil as offensive coordinator in 1976 changed that. As a junior that season, Nielsen led the nation in passing and touchdown passes and was No. 2 in the country in total offense. He earned first-team All-America honors and finished sixth in Heisman Trophy voting—the highest for a BYU player at that time.

Going into his senior year in 1977, Nielsen, nicknamed the Mormon Rifle, was a preseason Heisman Trophy candidate. Three games into the season, with three straight lopsided victories, Nielsen was taking the nation by storm. The Cougars captured attention for being a perennially downtrodden program that was nationally ranked and led by a quarterback putting up prodigious passing numbers. At that point, he was regarded as one of the Heisman Trophy front-runners.

But in the fourth game of the season, at Oregon State, Nielsen suffered a season-ending knee injury late in the contest, though he stayed in for 11 more plays despite his medial collateral ligament having become detached from the bone in his left knee. His college career, and his Heisman Trophy hopes, were over.

Nielsen's successful knee surgery enabled him to be drafted by the Houston Oilers in the third round of the NFL Draft. Nielsen played six years as the Oilers' quarterback.

From there, Nielsen became a sportscaster for KHOU-TV in Houston and later the station's sports director. Nielsen joined KHOU in May 1984 and was involved in the coverage of some of the biggest sports stories in Houston since then, including the Houston Rockets' two NBA championships and the Houston Astros' World Series appearance.

In 1994 Nielsen was inducted into the College Football Hall of Fame. In 2003 he received the NCAA Silver Anniversary Award, which recognizes student-athletes on their 25th anniversary of graduating from college.

Retired Football Numbers and Jerseys

BYU has retired the numbers of two football players in its history—Eldon Fortie (40) and Marion Probert (81). The numbers 40 and 81 won't be worn again in honor of Probert, who was tragically killed in 1965, and Fortie, the Cougars' first All-American. Meanwhile, four players have had their jerseys retired: Steve Young (8), Jim McMahon (9), and Gifford Nielsen and Ty Detmer (both 14).

Honorees must be, among other criteria, a first-team All-American; recipient of a major national award; a university graduate; make significant accomplishments after BYU graduation; and be a faithful member of the LDS Church or other religious affiliation.

Gifford Nielsen, shown here in 1978 with the Houston Oilers, was a big part of BYU's winning ways.

During his years in Houston, Nielsen made major contributions to the community, helping raise money for charities and organizations. He and his wife, Wendy, have six married children and nine grandchildren.

A few years after his retirement from KHOU in 2009, Nielsen was called as a general authority of the Church of Jesus Christ of Latter-day Saints and a member of the First Quorum of the Seventy.

In 2010 Nielsen spearheaded a BYU quarterbacks reunion, as the school honored the Cougars' great QBs. "There's a special feeling when we get together and when our paths cross. There's a feeling of respect for what we were able to do at BYU and how we were able to play a part in putting the program on the map," Nielsen said. "Every stage was absolutely vital in the progress of the program, even back to the time of Virgil [Carter, who starred at BYU, finishing in 1966, then went on to a career in the NFL], then just building upon this succession of All-America quarterbacks. For us to win a national championship and for Ty to win the Heisman Trophy, I honestly believe we all had to do what we did and really get the program to the point where there was respectability throughout the country. We all had a small part to play in the success of where that program is today."

43 Sit with the ROC

Coach Kalani Sitake hadn't even coached his first football game at BYU and he had already made himself at home in the ROC. If you're not familiar with that acronym, it stands for Roar of Cougars—the name of BYU's student section, created in 2013. The ROC began as the brainchild of BYU's athletic marketing department, which created the ROC name as a way to rebrand and unify the student section. Purchase of a ROC pass gets a student into any game; in 2016 the cost of a ROC pass was $125.

The ROC is known for being loud and distracting to opposing teams. Sitake has dubbed it "the rowdy, rowdy ROC." During a game in the 2016 National Invitation Tournament at the Marriott Center, Sitake joined the ROC wearing a royal blue Cougars baseball shirt, and he danced, cheered, and chanted with the student body.

Cougars basketball coach Dave Rose loved the atmosphere. "It was awesome. The crowd was so good from start to finish," Rose said of the crowd of 12,000-plus. "It was a large crowd, and they were loud and they came to support the guys. I'm glad we were able to send them home happy."

Rose didn't notice Sitake's presence in the student section during the game. But he appreciated his support. "We've had a conversation, and he told me he loves basketball," Rose said. "He told me he was a great basketball player as a younger guy. His body kind of grew out of basketball. He told me he'd be here for all the games he could. Those students must have had a good time."

Guard Kyle Collinsworth spotted Sitake in the crowd. "He hit me when he gave me a high five," he said. "I was like, 'This guy is kind of strong.' Then I saw who it was."

Those who want to sit in the ROC often wait in long lines (called the "ROC line") or camp out at night in order to secure a favorable spot for the first-come, first-served seating at big BYU sporting events.

Former coach Bronco Mendenhall was known for buying pizza for those starving students camping out. "Our team was doing a walk-through at 10:00 PM, and there's…I don't know, 100-ish people there, and there's tents," he said. "It kind of felt like an amazing college football experience. I'd just as soon have them sleep out there and stay and have a ROC concert going as well and make it an event. So I just wanted, in a small way, to show my appreciation and thanks. You never know, it might be a tradition."

During its brief time at BYU, the ROC has increased the decibels at games, for sure. It has also been able to pay tribute to its favorite players. When quarterback Taysom Hill suffered a season-ending injury at Nebraska, the following week, each member of the ROC held up signs bearing No. 4 (Hill's number). And when running back Jamaal Williams broke the school's all-time rushing record, students held up signs acknowledging his feat.

44 Messin' with Texas

Perhaps no opposing player in college football history had the University of Texas' number like Taysom Hill did. In back-to-back seasons, the BYU quarterback wreaked havoc on the Longhorns. For Texas' defense, he gave a whole new meaning to the term "burnt orange."

The nationally ranked Longhorns came to Provo in September 2013, and just prior to kickoff, a nasty storm featuring a torrential downpour, black clouds, and fierce winds raged through LaVell Edwards Stadium.

But that was nothing compared to what Hurricane Taysom unleashed that night on the No. 15 'Horns. Hill rushed for 259 yards, a BYU quarterback record, in a commanding 40–21 win. As a team, the Cougars set a school record with 550 rushing yards. It was also the most ever surrendered by a Texas team. BYU ended up with 679 yards of total offense. "We expected to run on them," Hill said after the game. "We didn't expect to break the school record."

The next day, then–Longhorns coach Mack Brown fired defensive coordinator Manny Diaz. By the end of the season, Brown resigned after a remarkable 16-year career in Austin that had featured a national championship in 2006. Hill's performance helped hasten that end. "In 2013," wrote *Austin American-Statesman* columnist Kirk Bohls, "the Longhorns defense made quarterback Taysom Hill look like a cross between Tim Tebow and Jim Brown."

As part of Texas' reboot, Charlie Strong was hired to replace Brown. The following season, BYU visited Texas and, of course, the Longhorns hadn't forgotten being humiliated at the hands of Hill and the Cougars. "As a pride factor, that ought to be something you have circled on your calendar—if you're a man," senior cornerback Quandre Diggs said. "We got beat down that day. Y'all want me to keep it real? We got beat down. Those guys played a better game, and they beat our tail." Texas vowed it wouldn't happen again.

While BYU didn't roll up the eye-popping stats it did in Provo, Hill and the Cougars trounced, tormented, and terrorized Texas in Austin before a crowd of 93,463. For Strong, it set a dismal tone for his first season at the helm as part of a tenure that lasted just three years.

In the first half, Hill ran for a 65-yard touchdown that was negated by a holding call on a wide receiver, some 20 yards behind the ball. BYU's first drive of the second half, which jump-started a 28-point third-quarter outburst, produced what many believe was Hill's signature play as a Cougar. Hill took the snap, saw a hole and burst up the middle, ran toward the sideline, and hurdled Texas defensive back Dylan Haines inside the 10-yard line before gliding into the end zone in a phenomenal display of speed and athleticism. "They'd been going for my knees and ankles all game," said Hill, "and that time I took a leap of faith."

Over the next week, that play was replayed thousands of times on ESPN, YouTube, and everywhere else. "I was right next to the safeties," said receiver Jordan Leslie, "and I turned and saw it and my mouth dropped open." It was a Heisman moment for Hill, though just weeks later, his season would be cut short due to a broken leg.

At the end of the game, Hill had thrown for 181 yards and rushed for 99 yards and three touchdowns in the 41–7 victory that catapulted the Cougars into the national rankings. Yes, BYU hooked 'em all over again.

Nobody in Texas will forget Hill's heroics. "It's something you just don't coach," said Coach Bronco Mendenhall. "Sometimes you just have to let him go."

Even without Hill in the lineup, don't count on the Longhorns scheduling BYU ever again.

45 Sunday Play and "the BYU Rule"

For decades, BYU has fought to compete at the highest levels of college athletics while upholding its longstanding commitment to keeping the Sabbath Day holy by not competing on Sundays. BYU's unbending refusal to compromise on Sunday play has stirred up controversy in the past and has prevented its athletes from competing in certain cases.

BYU, owned and operated by the Church of Jesus Christ of Latter-day Saints, will not back down from its stance that it will not play on Sundays, even if that means forfeiting a chance at a championship. It's nonnegotiable. "People might look at BYU and say, 'Why do they send kids on missions, why do they have an Honor Code, why do they not play on Sunday?'" athletic director Tom Holmoe said. "But that's who we are, that's what we thrive on, that's why people come here. The closest thing I can say is that the mission of our athletic department is aligned with the mission of our school, and that makes it easy to keep what matters in focus."

Not only do the Cougars not play on Sunday, they don't practice on Sunday either. Coaching staffs at BYU try to avoid working on Sundays and make other arrangements to do their jobs, such as arriving earlier than usual on Monday mornings.

While the Sunday play policy generally doesn't affect BYU's football team, the NCAA basketball tournament committee places the Cougars men's basketball team in a Thursday–Saturday bracket instead of a Friday–Sunday bracket. A similar accommodation is made for other BYU teams.

BYU is the only major athletic department in the nation that doesn't compete on Sundays, which has left it standing alone at times. According to current NCAA rules, if a university competing in an NCAA championship has a written policy against competition on a particular day for religious reasons, the championship schedule must be adjusted to accommodate that institution. But that hasn't always been the case. In 1958 and 1961, the Cougars baseball team failed to advance to the College World Series, though they had qualified, because games were scheduled on Sunday. This, though "team members voted unanimously to uphold the university in its stand against Sunday competition," according to a *Deseret News* article in 1958.

In 1963 the NCAA included a provision known as the BYU Rule to accommodate the Cougars' position on Sunday play. Still, that didn't solve all potential conflicts. The BYU football team made it clear it would turn down an opportunity to play in the 1977 Fiesta Bowl—then held on Christmas Day—if it were to win the Western Athletic Conference championship, because that year Christmas fell on a Sunday. The Cougars ended up winning the WAC title that year to earn a bid to the Fiesta Bowl, but instead traveled thousands of miles across the Pacific Ocean to play a pair of exhibition games in Japan.

Then in 1998, the NCAA voted to eliminate the 35-year-old BYU Rule because accommodating BYU would "unduly disrupt the conduct of the championship." That ruling was aimed primarily at the women's soccer and women's basketball tournaments, which had scheduled their championships on Sundays. As a result, BYU and Campbell University, a small, Baptist school from North

Carolina that has a similar policy, battled fiercely behind the scenes to reinstate the rule.

Not long after the BYU Rule was done away with, then–BYU president Merrill J. Bateman rallied support among other NCAA institutions. Within two months, 99 schools petitioned the NCAA to hold an override vote by the entire 300-plus NCAA Division I membership. That list of schools that supported BYU included at least one from every major conference, and institutions from coast to coast.

Fortunately for BYU, 18 months after the BYU Rule was eliminated, it was reinstated by the NCAA board of directors. During meetings in Indianapolis in 1999, the NCAA rescinded waivers previously granted by committees from women's soccer and women's basketball that voted not to invite schools such as BYU that refused to participate on Sundays into their tournaments. Though the championships were still scheduled for Sundays, if the Cougars had advanced to the title games, the contests would have been staged on other days.

When BYU's football program decided to go independent in 2010, the Cougars needed a home for the rest of their teams. BYU joined the West Coast Conference, and its membership of faith-based institutions, for almost all of its other programs, without having to worry about competing on Sundays. Before the Cougars joined the WCC, the league played its annual basketball tournament on Sundays. That stopped with the addition of BYU. Now all the teams participating in the tournament take a day off on Sunday for religious observance and then resume games on Monday.

It remains to be seen how much the Sunday play issue will affect BYU athletics in the future, but one thing is certain—the school won't compromise its standards. As history has shown, BYU is determined to keep the Sabbath Day holy, regardless of the consequences.

46 1996 WAC Championship

There's no catchy name or traveling trophy involved, but there's no doubting the intensity of the BYU-Wyoming rivalry. Never had this game meant more than it did in the inaugural Western Athletic Conference Championship Game at Sam Boyd Stadium in Las Vegas. It was a game for the ages.

It was nationally televised by ABC, and billed as the biggest game in WAC history. There was plenty at stake aside from the WAC championship. The Cougars boasted a No. 6 ranking and a 12–1 record. The Cowboys were 10–1 and ranked No. 20. BYU was looking to bust the Bowl Alliance to a possible Fiesta Bowl berth and an $8.5 million payday.

Wyoming was clinging to a five-point lead, 25–20, with 2:57 remaining in regulation. The Cowboys had the ball on their own 2-yard line, when Coach Joe Tiller opted to take a safety on fourth down—rather than risk a possible blocked punt or kicking to dangerous punt returner James Dye. After Wyoming's punter went out the back of the end zone for a safety, the Cowboys' ensuing free kick gave the BYU offense the ball. That safety was one of the most controversial decisions in Wyoming football history.

"We took the safety with the thought in mind that if we punt from the 20, we'll at least have them pretty deep on their side of the 50, but that didn't happen," Tiller explained. The Cowboys' punt gave BYU the ball at its own 45-yard line.

The Cougars drove the ball deep into Wyoming territory, moving inside Wyoming's 10-yard line with less than one minute remaining. On that final drive, with 12 seconds left, quarterback Steve Sarkisian scrambled and threw a pass to Mark Atuaia, who made a diving catch inbounds at the 3-yard line.

The clock was still running and it looked as though time would expire before BYU could get off another play. Wyoming players began celebrating. However, Cougars wide receiver Kaipo McGuire alertly had started calling timeout with four seconds remaining and managed to get the attention of the official, who blew his whistle with one second on the clock—setting the stage for place-kicker Ethan Pochman's heroics. Pochman, a walk-on and former high school soccer player who had never kicked a football in a game situation prior to that season, booted a 20-yard field goal to send the game into overtime. "The game was over," Tiller lamented afterward, "and they put a second back on the clock for some reason."

In overtime, Wyoming was forced to settle for a 47-yard field goal, which missed wide left. On BYU's overtime possession, it picked up nine yards then sent in Pochman again for the game-winning field goal. Pochman drilled a 32-yarder to lift BYU to a heart-stopping 28–25 victory and the WAC title.

"In the pandemonium that followed (kids flooding the field and some decidedly unwholesome attempts to bring down a goalpost), it was briefly forgotten that Pochman's kick might have been an $8 million boot," wrote *Sports Illustrated*'s Richard Hoffer.

Yes, that kick might have been worth $8 million had the Cougars earned a berth to the Fiesta Bowl. Instead BYU clinched the Cotton Bowl berth and a $2 million payday, while Wyoming stayed home for the holidays without a bowl game. Back in 1996 there were only 18 bowl games, and there wasn't room for a Wyoming team with a 10–2 record. For the Cowboys, it was a bitter defeat that lingers to this day.

For the Cougars, they had won the first WAC Championship Game and they were headed to the Cotton Bowl—the team's first, and only, New Year's Day bowl appearance. "It's every kicker's dream to kick a last-second field goal to win a game," Pochman said at the time, "and tonight I got to kick two."

Ratings for that WAC Championship Game exceeded those of both the Big 12 and Southeastern Conference title games that day, shown as part of a triple-header on ABC.

47 Attend a Fireside

For more than a decade, the BYU football program held religious firesides on the night before games. They were held in church meetinghouses in places as far-flung as Seattle to Hartford, and many places in between.

It was a tradition started by former coach Bronco Mendenhall as a way to share the gospel. And huge crowds showed up, filling seats that stretched all the way to the back of the Cultural Hall. They were so popular that some meetinghouses showed the firesides on closed-circuit TV to other meetinghouses in the area to accommodate the crowds.

During Mendenhall's inaugural campaign, the Cougars opened with a 1–3 record and were set to travel to New Mexico, where he had served as defensive coordinator for several years. The week of that game, Mendenhall informed his coaching staff that the team should organize a fireside that Friday night in Albuquerque.

His assistant coaches were caught off guard and confused. Fewer than 20 people showed up for that first fireside. But a tradition was born. The Cougars rallied to defeat New Mexico the next day, and from that point on, BYU's football program continued winning and the firesides continued too. "Some folks come from two or three states away just for the fireside," Mendenhall once said. "They don't have tickets to the game; they just want this connection, which is really special."

Almost as amazing as the big crowds that would turn out for the firesides was the large contingent of players who would always attend. Consider that fireside attendance was voluntary, not mandatory. Both LDS and non-LDS players, dressed in jackets and ties, would go and participate. Players would prepare talks on being a disciple of Jesus Christ, and they would sing uplifting hymns and songs, such as "We'll Bring the World His Truth."

It was at a fireside in Seattle in 2008, on the eve of the second game against Washington, when Mendenhall first publicly explained his priorities as the head coach of BYU's football program. He said the outcome of the game against the Huskies wasn't the most important part of the weekend for him. "It might be fourth or fifth," Mendenhall said, adding that being a part of the fireside and the opportunity to spend time with his wife, his children, and his parents ranked higher on his list than a football game. "I won't back down from that," he said.

Fans in attendance didn't know quite what to make of that comment. When you win, people will go along with such comments, and indeed the Cougars won the next day. But as time went on, if BYU lost, Mendenhall drew criticism for holding firesides the night before games.

But Mendenhall understood that the firesides made a lot of sense for the BYU football program. "I think it is possible to integrate the spirit with football. It's not only possible, but it's necessary and desirable at BYU," he once said. "If not, what are we doing having a team? No one wants to win more than me, because of what it can do for those who are looking for more than just football. Maybe you came here tonight for a pep rally. But this is first and foremost about developing ourselves spiritually."

On the eve of the 2015 season opener at Nebraska last September, a large throng gathered at a stake center near Lincoln. The building was filled to capacity for the team's first-ever visit to the Cornhusker State.

During the question-and-answer portion of the fireside, when a microphone was passed to those in the congregation, one fan asked quarterback Taysom Hill how he was able to overcome a season-ending leg injury the previous season. Hill was about play in his first game in almost one year. Little did anyone know, Hill would suffer yet another season-ending injury, this time to his foot, less than 24 hours later, in the first half against Nebraska. As it turned out, BYU defeated the Cornhuskers 33–28 in miraculous fashion.

When Mendenhall left for Virginia at the end of last season, many people wondered if his successor would continue to put on firesides. The answer was yes, but not in the same way. First-year BYU head football coach Kalani Sitake decided to discontinue the night-before-a-game firesides. However, Sitake held firesides during the off-season at places the Cougars would play during the 2016 season. That way, his team could focus on football during the season. "It's one of those things where the players see the positive things, especially being returned missionaries, of what firesides do for the program and what they do for others as well," Sitake said.

Sitake praised Mendenhall for implementing the firesides and said he'll continue it in his own way. "We feel like this is one thing where we have the best of both worlds—we get to do the firesides at a different time and be able to play the game and not do it the night before," Sitake said. "It will be a good change."

48 Shaking Down the Thunder at Notre Dame

In the locker room at Notre Dame Stadium prior to kickoff, BYU president Rex Lee delivered a pregame speech to the Cougars, and a bold prediction. "In the five years I've been at BYU," he said, "we've always had an upset in an even-numbered year. In 1990 it was Miami. In 1992 it was Penn State. Now in 1994 it will be Notre Dame. Today is the day, and this is the team."

Turned out, President Lee was prescient. The Catholics couldn't withstand the Mormon battalion on that October day in South Bend. BYU's victory march out of historic Notre Dame Stadium after a stunning upset had a distinctive feel to it. The Cougars played smash-mouth football and seized an unforgettable win against the Fighting Irish.

Just how good was this win for BYU—which entered the game as 15-point underdogs? Besides giving Notre Dame coach Lou Holtz and 59,075 Irish fans a serious case of the south bends, the Cougars' win rocked the foundation of Notre Dame football, home of Touchdown Jesus, the Four Horsemen, Knute Rockne, Joe Montana, and Rudy. It prompted questions about Holtz's job security; knocked Notre Dame (ranked No. 17 going into the game) out of the polls for the first time in eight years, snapping a string of 85 consecutive regular-season games with a national ranking; and saw the Cougars hold the Irish to their lowest point total at home in eight years.

"It's like a nightmare," said Notre Dame defensive coordinator Bob Davie. "It's devastating. There is no way to hide that or downplay that. This is a devastating loss." Keep in mind that in the two previous seasons, Notre Dame had demolished BYU by scores of 42–16 and 45–20.

This time the Cougars defense shut down Notre Dame in the red zone. Late in the third quarter, the Irish failed to score from the BYU 3-yard line. The Cougars offense, despite four turnovers, won the battle of the line of scrimmage, opening up holes for running back Jamal Willis, who reached the end zone twice. Touchdown Jamal scored on a nifty catch-and-run in the second quarter and another on a Superman plunge from the 1-yard line in the fourth quarter. "What a clutch player he is for them," Holtz said. "Willis is big, strong, and has a heart. He's also got a lot of dimensions to him, which gives BYU more options. Looking around the country, it would be hard to find a better back or a more versatile runner."

After the game, a smiling Edwards engaged in a spontaneous group hug with assistant coaches Barry Lamb and DeWayne Walker. It was a belated gift for Edwards, who had celebrated his 64th birthday four days earlier. Said Todd Christensen, the former Cougars running back who worked as the color commentator for NBC that day: "I have known this man for 20 years, and I have never seen him show that level of emotion."

Indeed, it was one of BYU's biggest road victories ever. And how satisfying was it for senior receiver Tim Nowatzke, who hails from Michigan City, just 40 miles west of South Bend? "After growing up right there, always wanting to go to Notre Dame," he said, "there's nothing really sweeter than this right now."

Two years earlier, in 1992, Nowatzke's return to his hometown was bittersweet. His grandfather had died just three days prior to the game, and Nowatzke attended the funeral the day before the game. On game day, Nowatzke scored BYU's only touchdown.

In 1994 more than 100 boisterous friends and relatives of the Nowatzkes were in attendance. Later that evening, all of them, as well as all the other BYU fans who were in South Bend, fully expected the moon above the Golden Dome that night to come up BYU blue. "We talked about that all week [about Notre Dame's tradition and aura]," Nowatzke said. "Like we told the media, we're not playing the Four Horsemen, we're not playing Joe Montana. We're not playing those guys. We're playing the Notre Dame of this year. They've been beat. You've got to overcome that intimidation. We have history. We've played well. I don't ever have to play them again, and this is something I can brag about for the rest of my life. Hey, this is what I'm going to remember forever."

49 Robbie Bosco

Of all the great quarterbacks BYU has produced, only one led the Cougars to the pinnacle of college football and an undefeated season. Under Robbie Bosco, BYU posted a 13–0 record—the only perfect season in school history—and won the 1984 national championship.

On the eve of the Cougars' season opener at No. 3–ranked Pittsburgh, Bosco, who would be making his first collegiate start the next day, could not sleep. What flooded his head was self-doubt. Many figured 1984 would be a rebuilding year for BYU after losing Steve Young and several other stars to graduation. "I questioned myself," Bosco recalled. "BYU had won countless championships. The quarterbacks before me had been successful. I wondered, 'What if we don't win any games?'"

Turned out Bosco worried in vain. Not only did the Cougars upset the Panthers, they won *all* their games that season, en route to a perfect season and a national title. But it didn't come until after all of the skepticism had raged. "Before the season, that's what was being written about—people were wondering if we could do it," Bosco said. "You just want to get out there and prove you can do it."

The pressure was on again at the end of that season, when No. 1–ranked BYU matched up with Michigan in the Holiday Bowl in San Diego. The Wolverines did everything they could to smash BYU's hopes of a national title. In the first quarter, Bosco dropped back and completed a pass to Kozlowski. At the end of the play,

Join the Cougar Club

In 1964 Ron Hyde and Ray Beckham started the Cougar Club, and BYU athletics haven't been the same since. "Prior to 1964," Hyde said, "BYU football had been an exercise in character building." BYU's athletic department receives no funding from the LDS Church. The athletic department is responsible for raising all funds to run the program and meet costs for all BYU's 21 team sports. With the donations and support of almost 5,000 members nationwide, the Cougar Club has helped BYU establish one of the nation's top athletic programs.

That's why the Cougar Club has been instrumental in BYU's success—by raising funds for the athletic department. Fans can donate to the Athletic Scholarship Program; Coaches Circle (revenue for this endowment helps supplement benefit packages and allows BYU to pay and retain its coaches); and Touchdown Club (which provides fans a way to support walk-on scholarships by pledging a donation for every touchdown scored).

Cougar Club membership offers a variety of levels, and Cougar Club members enjoy numerous benefits, including priority seating at games, parking passes, and tickets to exclusive events.

Dale McCann served as executive director of the Cougar Club for 24 years, up until he died of cancer in 1998. "The Cougar Club got off to a pretty good start, but when Dale took over, it leaped forward light years," said LaVell Edwards. "He was just a guy who had a great vision and work ethic. He made a big difference. He was just tremendous in terms of the programs he started and the amount of money raised. He helped us immeasurably." Mike Middleton succeeded McCann in 1998.

For more information about how to join the Cougar Club, call 801-422-2583 or 1-800-426-4298, or email CougarClub@byu.edu.

Michigan's Mike Hammerstein unloaded on Bosco, injuring his left leg. An official whistled Hammerstein for a late-hit penalty, and Bosco was removed from the game as trainers and doctors attended to his left knee and ankle.

At that moment, many BYU fans believed the Cougars' shot at a national title was gone with Bosco. Bosco was replaced by capable backup Blaine Fowler until Bosco returned in the second quarter, hobbling on his heavily wrapped knee. "When [the injury] first happened, I wasn't sure I'd return," Bosco remembered. "But the doctors said it wasn't that bad, and I was able to walk on it a little. If I was able to walk, I knew I would play. When you are playing in a big game, you don't feel much pain as long as you are playing. It hurt on the sidelines."

Injury or no injury, he wanted to be out on the gridiron. Inside the locker room at Jack Murphy Stadium, Bosco could hear the muffled sounds of the crowd—and it was killing him. "After I was checked, I asked the trainers, 'If I get hit on it again, is it a career-ending injury? Can I play on this?'" Bosco recalled. "They said I could. I said, 'Wrap it up and let's go!' They wrapped it up and I went out there. Warming up, I wasn't sure if I could do it or not."

Bosco returned early in the second quarter. Because of his lack of mobility, the Cougars turned to the shotgun formation, something they hadn't attempted all year. "The injury took away a little of our offense," Bosco said. "We wanted to roll out more and use some reverses. All I could do was fade straight back." Somehow the Cougars made it work. A gimpy Bosco made plays when he needed to, completing 30 of 42 passes for 343 yards and two touchdowns. He also threw three interceptions.

"Never have I seen a more courageous performance by a kid," Coach LaVell Edwards said of Bosco after the game. "He was in pain. But as long as he could stand up, he wanted to play."

While BYU rolled up 483 total yards compared to 202 for Michigan, the Cougars' many turnovers kept the game close. In fact, the Wolverines enjoyed a 17–10 advantage early in the fourth quarter.

Bosco led two touchdown drives in the final 11 minutes, starting with a leaping grab in the back of the end zone by Glen Kozlowski, who soared over a Michigan defender to tie the game at 17. On the Cougars' final drive, Bosco threw a touchdown pass to Kelly Smith. A couple weeks later, BYU was voted No. 1 in the polls and won the national championship.

Bosco's senior season in 1985 was affected by injury, but he still led the Cougars to a 24–3 record in two seasons as a starter. Bosco finished third in the Heisman Trophy voting in 1984 and 1985 and was drafted in the third round of the NFL Draft by the Green Bay Packers, where he played for two years before a shoulder injury ended his career for good.

Bosco returned to BYU in 1989 and served as BYU's quarterbacks coach for several years. He currently works as an administrator in the school's athletic department.

50 1951 and 1966 NIT Championships

BYU won two National Invitation Tournament championships 15 years apart, in 1951 and 1966, when the NIT champion was considered by some as the national champion. "It was a national championship," legendary coach Stan Watts used to say. "Football championships are mythical. We won ours on the court."

And in 1951 and 1966, the Cougars were the toast of New York City. Both BYU's NIT titles were won at Madison Square

Garden (the self-proclaimed Most Famous Arena in the World) in the Big Apple. "Madison Square Garden had a lot of magic to it," remembered Dave Schulthess, BYU's former sports information director, who was with the team for its 1966 championship. "For most of us it was a first shot at New York City. We were drinking it all in."

Today, a pair of signs commemorating BYU's two NIT championships hangs in the Marriott Center rafters. Back in the 1950s and 1960s, the National Invitation Tournament had a different connotation than it does now. Then it had only 14 teams, and it was more prominent than the NCAA tournament, which featured conference champions and prohibited multiple teams from the same conference. The NIT was the place to be.

Why? New York City offered teams major media exposure, and a chance to play in front of NBA scouts. "The NIT 50 years ago is a lot different than it is today," said Richard "Dick" Nemelka, who was a starting guard on BYU's 1966 team. "The NIT was almost as big a tournament as the NCAA. It was very prestigious to go to the NIT and to win it. It was a pretty big deal."

"That was basketball in those days," said Pete Witbeck, a former BYU assistant coach. "Back then, the NIT champ was the big champ. We could have gone to either the NCAA or NIT. We chose the NIT because it was more prestigious. Playing basketball at Madison Square Garden is like playing football at Notre Dame."

In 1951 BYU posted a 24–7 record before accepting an invitation to the NIT. It was Watts' second season at the helm, and he had Mel Hutchins, who was named an All-American and went on to become the NBA Rookie of the Year in 1952–53.

With Hutchins and six-foot forward Roland Minson, who ended up as the NIT MVP, the Cougars defeated Saint Louis, Seton Hall, and Dayton to claim the championship. One newspaper account read that the Cougars had "stolen away the hearts of the Garden fans with their fight, sportsmanship, and clean play." The 1951 team was inducted into BYU's Hall of Fame in 1976.

In 1966 BYU had a 17–5 record when it headed to the NIT. The Cougars beat Temple handily in the first game. In the second game, BYU played Army and its 25-year-old coach, Bobby Knight, who would go on to lead Indiana to national championships and become the second-all-time-winningest coach (now third) in college basketball history.

In the waning moments of the game, Army had a two-point lead when Nemelka drove to the hoop and drew a foul. "I made two foul shots to tie the game," Nemelka said. "Army brought the ball down the court and Jim Jimas stole it and scored, and we won."

The championship game was against New York University, a school that has since given up athletics. "They had two or three All-Americans," Witbeck said. "It was a classic game—fast-break basketball. It was a wonderful win. They had a parade for us in Provo. It was like winning a national championship, which it was. We had our day in the sun in New York City. Fans back there are very knowledgeable. You had better play well or they'd come after you. Watts was revered in New York City. When we came home everyone told us they were pinned to their radios and praying for us while they were listening."

At the championship game, the Boston Celtics' legendary coach Red Auerbach and Celtics star Bob Cousy were there scouting. In the game against NYU, BYU prevailed before a Garden crowd of 18,479. Nemelka scored 15 points and center Craig Raymond scored 21 and grabbed 18 rebounds.

The Cougars averaged 94.4 points per game for the 1966 season, and they shot 59 percent in the championship game against NYU. After the game, Auerbach said, "BYU simply overpowered them. They outplayed them all over the court."

The Cougars finished the year with a 20–5 record. During the summer before the season, BYU played 20 exhibition games in South America. The Cougars averaged 99 points per game in 1966—without the assistance of a shot clock or the three-point shot (the three-point line wasn't introduced until 20 years later, in 1986). The 1966 team was inducted into the BYU Hall of Fame in 1980.

51 Wrecking Texas A&M

On the eve of the 1996 Pigskin Classic in Provo, as BYU and Texas A&M were preparing to square off in the first college football game of the season, Cougars players filed into a meeting room for their usual pregame pep talk and film session. When the lights went out, music blared, and the huddled masses watched an 11-minute highlight show choreographed to contemporary (circa mid-1990s) rock tunes. The film—put together by Duane Busby, LaVell Edwards' administrative assistant, and Chad Bunn, BYU's video coordinator—showed dramatic scenes from great BYU victories over the years.

But the most poignant, inspiring moment came toward the end when the image of Philadelphia Eagles quarterback Ty Detmer filled the screen. Detmer, in his practice uniform, addressed the 1996 Cougars: "I want to wish you the best of luck against A&M," Detmer drawled. "You're not going to get respect, like we didn't against Miami in 1990. You gotta believe in yourselves. Play hard and let it roll. As you know, I'm not a big fan of Texas A&M." Detmer was referring to the 1990 Holiday Bowl when the Cougars lost 65–14 to the Aggies and Detmer had both shoulders separated just weeks after he had won the Heisman Trophy.

None of the players or coaches had any idea Detmer would be speaking to them, and they were spellbound. They were stunned.

"It was a great show," tight end Chad Lewis said. "It really focused us on the game. It was the reason why we won. Ty's comments pumped me up."

That matchup between BYU and No. 13 Texas A&M that day—it was August 24, the earliest start of a season in school history—was also a great show. The upstart Cougars from the lowly Western Athletic Conference were 10-point underdogs to the Big 12 powerhouse with a defense nicknamed the Wrecking Crew. The game featured plenty of spectacular plays and dramatic comebacks. There was just a feeling in the air that it would be BYU's day, even after Texas A&M drilled a 52-yard field goal with 1:27 remaining to give the Aggies a 37–34 lead.

But the Cougars had another patented comeback left in them. On first-and-10 from the Aggies 46, with 1:11 left on the clock, the plan was for the receivers to clear out some space for Lewis, who would run an underneath route. And while Lewis was wide open as the play unfolded, quarterback Steve Sarkisian threw the deep ball.

The inability, or unwillingness, to throw deep was something Sarkisian had been criticized for the previous year. But the Aggies corner cheated up, wide receiver K. O. Kealaluhi sprinted free, and Sark tossed a perfect over-the-shoulder pass into his arms. "Steve threw the ball over my head, and I thought, *What are you doing?*" Lewis said. "But that was the best pass he threw at BYU."

After catching the ball, Kealaluhi raced into the end zone with a sliding finish. He lay flat on his back with his hands over his face mask, acting as stunned as the 55,229 in attendance. Pandemonium reigned as the Cougars won 41–37.

"I was supposed to run my corner back so Chad could get open underneath," Kealaluhi said. "For some reason the corner came up and pressed me, so I just ran as fast as I could. Sark threw a perfect, perfect pass. It seemed like it took forever to get in my hands. I couldn't believe I caught it. I just kept thinking, *Man, don't drop this ball. Don't drop this ball on national television.*"

BYU's victory that day resonated throughout the nation. The Cougars, previously unranked, jumped to No. 19 in the Associated Press poll days later. BYU and LaVell Edwards became, once again, media darlings.

Did the victory make up for not going to a bowl game in 1995—snapping a streak of 17 consecutive seasons of going bowling? "It was like a bowl game," Lewis said about beating Texas A&M. "But it was also not like playing in a bowl game because the second a bowl game is over, the season's over and you feel a lot of emotions. We felt a lot of emotions after beating Texas A&M, but our season wasn't over."

Indeed, the victory set the tone for the Cougars' amazing 14–1 season that culminated with a Cotton Bowl triumph and a No. 5 national ranking, their second-highest finish in history.

That upset of Texas A&M not only avenged BYU's embarrassing loss to the Aggies in the Holiday Bowl six years earlier but was yet another memorable performance to add to BYU's highlight reel.

52 Dennis Pitta

Despite a solid high school career as a wide receiver at Moorpark High School in Moorpark, California, Dennis Pitta received no Division I scholarship offers. Because he grew up a BYU fan, he chose to walk on with the Cougars. Soon, coaches decided to turn the 6'4" freshman into a tight end, though he weighed just 210 pounds, and put him on scholarship.

Late in the 2004 season, Pitta, who was merely an obscure name on the roster—at one point that season, then-coach Gary Crowton mistakenly called him "Dustin"—had a breakout game

Pitta's speed and agility made him a standout in the college game and defined his play in the NFL.

151

at Air Force. First, he caught an 11-yard screen pass for a touchdown, the first of his career, midway through the third quarter to give BYU a 17–10 lead. Two minutes later he blocked a punt that resulted in another TD—the first time the Cougars had scored off a blocked punt since 1992. Then he registered the game's final score with three minutes remaining in the contest. His one-yard touchdown catch slammed the door on the Falcons and sealed a 41–24 win.

"It was difficult to make the adjustment to tight end," Pitta said at the time. "It's a lot more physical playing tight end, having

Special Deliveries, by George

Not long after BYU tight end Andrew George arrived in Albuquerque with his team on the afternoon before the Cougars' game against New Mexico on November 14, 2009, he found out that his pregnant wife, Tawny, was going into labor back in Provo. Her water had broken while the team was in flight.

Arrangements were made for George to catch a flight back to Utah to be with his wife. He landed at about 8:30 PM, and he made it to the hospital in Provo in time to see Tawny give birth to an 8-pound, 14-ounce baby boy the couple named Jack Andrew George.

After only a couple hours of sleep, the proud father caught a 6:00 AM flight back to Albuquerque on Saturday morning and arrived at University Stadium at around 10:00 AM, just a couple hours before kickoff. Late in the second quarter, George caught a 27-yard touchdown pass from Hall, giving BYU a 17–7 lead in what turned out to be a 24–19 win.

But that wasn't George's only special delivery during the final month of his senior season. Having spent most of his career overshadowed by his teammate, All-America tight end Dennis Pitta, George's big moment came on second-and-10 from the 25-yard line in overtime against archrival Utah. Quarterback Max Hall threw a strike between two Utah defenders to George, who secured the ball and immediately turned and raced untouched into the end zone—sparking a delirious celebration on the field. Going into the 2017 season, it marked BYU's most recent win over Utah.

to be a part of the offensive line and having to block. It's a part of the game I had to develop."

After the season, Pitta left for a two-year LDS mission in the Dominican Republic. Pitta had been planning to leave the previous summer, but the coaches convinced him that if he waited and left in December, after the season, he'd return prior to spring ball. Plus they figured he could contribute as a freshman, which he did.

When he returned prior to the 2007 season, he added weight and muscle—and looked more like a tight end. Though his frame carried 247 pounds as a senior, he still made athletic catches like a wide receiver.

Over the next three seasons, he became the most prolific tight end in school history. Pitta stands No. 1 in receiving yards by a tight end (2,901) at BYU and No. 4 in all-time receiving yards, No. 2 in career receptions (221), and No. 1 in receptions by a tight end, No. 9 in single-season receiving yardage (1,083 in 2008), and No. 9 in receiving touchdowns (21). Pitta was a two-time All-America tight end, the 10th Cougar to be so honored at that position.

Pitta became BYU's all-time leader in tight end receiving yards—surpassing Gordon Hudson—during the 2009 season at Qualcomm (formerly Jack Murphy) Stadium, the same venue where Cougars tight end Clay Brown made one of the most famous catches in school history to win the 1980 Miracle Bowl against SMU.

One of Pitta's most memorable catches came early in the fourth quarter of a wild 45–42 win at Colorado State. Quarterback Max Hall threw a pass as he was being hit, and Pitta snatched the ball while falling backward in the end zone and was sandwiched by two Rams defenders. Pitta's helmet popped off, but the ball did not pop out, for a 23-yard touchdown.

"BYU has a great tradition of great tight ends. I'm kind of the next in line," Pitta said at the time. "We're fortunate enough to be in a position to be able to contribute to our team and follow in the footsteps of the guys who have come before us—the Gordon Hudsons and Chad Lewises and guys who have played the position so well here at BYU. Chad's a guy I've looked up to. I'm happy to follow in his footsteps."

While he was at BYU, Pitta married Mataya Gissel, the sister of Hall's wife, Mckinzi Gissel. So during part of his career as a

Tight End Tradition

The argument can be made that after quarterback, tight end is the most tradition-rich, and talent-rich, position in BYU football lore. Most of the great quarterbacks in Provo have had great tight ends to throw to. "This is a very tight end–oriented offense," longtime offensive coordinator Norm Chow said. With its pass-happy, wide-open offensive attack, BYU helped put the tight end position on a pedestal in college football.

The Cougars have produced a string of All-America performers at that position, much like they've produced a string of All-America quarterbacks. Ten times a BYU tight end, and his pass-catching skills, have earned All-America status, starting with Clay Brown, who caught the most famous pass in BYU history—the game-winning Hail Mary at the end of the 1980 Miracle Bowl. Gordon Hudson was so prolific as a receiver that he was inducted into the College Football Hall of Fame in 2009. Former Cougars tight ends Doug Jolley (2002 with the Oakland Raiders), Chad Lewis (2004 with the Philadelphia Eagles), Itula Mili (2005 with the Seattle Seahawks), and Gabriel Reid (2006 with the Chicago Bears) all helped lead their teams to the Super Bowl.

Todd Christensen, meanwhile, didn't play tight end at BYU. He played fullback. But he ended up earning five trips to the Pro Bowl with the Oakland / Los Angeles Raiders as a tight end. Still, as a running back at BYU, he led the team in receiving for three straight years.

Starting in 1976 with Brian Billick—who would go on to lead the Baltimore Ravens to a Super Bowl championship as a head coach—12 BYU tight ends have earned first-team all-conference honors. Among them are David Mills, Trevor Molini, Chris Smith, Byron Rex, Lewis, Mili, Jolley, Jonny Harline, and Pitta.

Cougar, many of the record number of passes he caught came courtesy of his brother-in-law.

Pitta was drafted in the fourth round of the NFL Draft by the Baltimore Ravens, where he ended up becoming one of the league's productive tight ends before hip injuries forced him to sit out the entire 2013 season and almost all of the 2014 and 2015 seasons before returning in 2016. In the 2016 season finale, Pitta set two Ravens records, surpassing Todd Heap's record for most catches by a tight end in a single season (86) and most catches in a single game (11).

53 Visit Legacy Hall

Inexplicably, two of the greatest and most memorable moments in BYU sports history transpired just a few months apart. Clay Brown caught a 41-yard Hail Mary touchdown pass from Jim McMahon to cap the wild 1980 Holiday Bowl in December, and the following March, Danny Ainge led the Cougars to the Elite Eight by driving the length of the court and scoring a layup to beat Notre Dame.

There's a place where true blue fans can relive those moments and many more. Ever wonder what happened to the football Brown caught and the basketball Ainge dribbled in those historic games? You'll find them inside Legacy Hall, a new 7,400-square-foot, goose bump–inducing BYU sports treasury, a one-stop location for devout Cougars fans to bask in the athletic program's rich tradition. And if that weren't enough, admission is free. "If you're a BYU sports junkie, it's great," said associate athletic director Duff Tittle, with a broad smile.

Within the three-level atrium in the new Student Athlete Building, hundreds of pieces of memorabilia are on display, including trophies, game balls, jerseys, shoes, and tributes to great athletes, teams, and coaches. It also showcases perhaps the most famous piece of sports hardware at BYU: the 1990 Heisman Trophy, won by quarterback Ty Detmer. "For the first time, our fans won't have to ask, 'Where are you guys hiding the Heisman?'" Tittle said. "You walk in the building, and it's right there."

The hallowed walls of Legacy Hall, which opened in 2004 with 34 display cases and 21 wall displays, unleash a tidal wave of memories for Cougars fans. Simply put, this is BYU's version of Cooperstown, Canton, and Springfield rolled into one.

The assignment of collecting the memorabilia to fill the vast space was charged to Tittle, who grew up a rabid BYU fan in Orem, Utah. For several months Tittle played the role of museum curator, hunting for rare, tough-to-find Cougars relics from every sport BYU plays. Although the task has required plenty of hard work and networking, there have been some serendipitous moments. Such as the time Tittle got a phone call from a BYU fan who received an original Ainge home basketball uniform as a birthday gift years before. Someone else sent Tittle a piece of the goal post that was torn down following BYU's first-ever football victory over archrival Utah—in 1942.

More than 100 former athletes, from various eras and representing 21 sports, have generously donated items to Legacy Hall. Eldon Fortie, BYU's first All-America selection in football, contributed the helmet he wore in 1961. Former BYU golf star Mike Weir sent the bag that held his clubs when he won the Masters in 2003. Quarterback Steve Young loaned his 1995 NFL MVP trophy and a game ball from his MVP performance in the 1995 Super Bowl with the San Francisco 49ers. "We've had some big-time people step up to the plate," Tittle said.

Still, Tittle's goal goes beyond gee-whiz souvenirs. "I don't want you to just come in and look at the Heisman Trophy and say, 'Wow, that's cool,'" he said. "I want you to be able to see Ty Detmer's jersey and his helmet. Then I want you to learn what Ty's all about. He came here as an 18-year-old kid out of Texas and left as a man who embraced the gospel, met his wife, and it just so happened he won the Heisman Trophy along the way."

To help instill that message, Legacy Hall features interactive kiosks with video touchscreens to allow visitors to watch or listen to highlights of some of the greatest moments in BYU sports history. Included are in-depth player biographies as well as video presentations documenting each of BYU's 12 national championship teams— men's basketball (1951 and 1966), men's track (1970), men's golf (1981), football (1984), women's cross-country (1997, 1999, 2001, and 2002), and men's volleyball (1999, 2001, and 2004).

Tittle hopes Legacy Hall entertains and educates all campus visitors. "Maybe they're a sports fan, maybe they're not," he said. "Maybe they're an alumnus, maybe they're not. But everyone that visits Legacy Hall will learn what BYU is all about. It's more than just championships and trophies."

54 Rob Morris

When he was an All-America middle linebacker at staid, buttoned-down BYU in the mid-1990s, Rob Morris carved out a reputation for being outspoken, flamboyant, and a little crazy. Aside from being regarded as one of the best defensive players in school history, Morris craved the spotlight, regaling reporters with his antics, such as taunting eight-foot alligators while on vacation in Florida.

The BYU media relations department nicknamed him Freight Train to promote him for the Butkus Award. Once, after scoring a touchdown on a 51-yard interception return, he celebrated by making a snow angel in the end zone grass. He also publicly criticized the school's Honor Code Office for the way it handled disciplinary issues involving non-LDS athletes.

But after an eight-year National Football League career with the Indianapolis Colts—he was a first-round pick—that included a Super Bowl championship, Morris mellowed. Life can do that to a guy. "A lot of that was building a reputation in college that matched football. Not that I was being fake, or that it wasn't me," said the Colts' first-round pick in 2000. "To some extent, I was like that. Now I'm more harnessed. I guess I'm more humble, more meek. That's growing up."

While the Colts were marching toward the Super Bowl during the 2006 season in what could be considered the pinnacle of Morris' football career, he and his wife were dealing with a profound personal loss. In Week 9, when the Colts played at New England, it was reported in the Indianapolis newspapers that Morris was out because of a hamstring injury. In reality, he missed that game so he and his wife, Tracie, could travel to Highland to bury their triplets, who died 20 weeks into Tracie's pregnancy.

"Nobody really knew about it except for people in my [LDS] ward back there," he said, talking about the experience publicly for the first time. "I really didn't want my personal business out there [in the media]. We flew back to Highland and had a little ceremony here at the city cemetery. The Super Bowl was a blessing because we came back, and people wanted to talk about the Super Bowl."

Morris credited LaVell Edwards for putting him on a course toward the NFL. When Morris was a high school star in Nampa, Idaho, he was being recruited by schools such as Stanford and BYU to play two positions—linebacker and fullback. "I knew in the back of my mind that eventually I would be a linebacker," Morris said.

"When I was a freshman at BYU, and having a hard time with the switch from fullback to linebacker, LaVell told me, 'I think you can be a great running back, but I think you can play on Sundays as a linebacker. You have the potential to go a long way.' And LaVell [didn't] throw out idle things like that, so I took that to heart. LaVell [had] a nose for where a guy should be."

Morris could have turned pro after his junior year in 1998 but elected to return for his senior season. While he didn't regret the decision, he was disappointed to miss a handful of games due to injury during his senior season.

He was projected as a first-round draft pick, which wasn't something Morris necessarily aspired to while growing up. "I'm pretty much a country boy from Idaho. My dream was to play at Boise State or Idaho State, and now people are telling me I can be a first-round draft pick," Morris said as a senior in 1999. "I'm thinking that's ridiculous. I'll take it, though. I'm not complaining. I dreamed about playing in the NFL, but it was never real to me. I played the game because I loved it, not because I thought I was going to be a first-round draft pick."

55 Eldon Fortie

The first real star BYU football produced was Eldon Fortie. He was the Cougars' first All-America football player and he was the first to finish in the top 10 in Heisman Trophy balloting (No. 10) in 1962. Fortie was the first BYU player to have his jersey (No. 40) retired.

Nicknamed the Phantom because of his elusive running style, he rushed for a school-record 272 yards against George Washington in 1962, a record that stood for 54 years until 2016, when it was broken by Jamaal Williams. Fortie ran for 1,039 rushing yards in 1962, making him the first BYU player to rush for 1,000 yards in a season.

At 5'9" and 169 pounds, Fortie played quarterback, though he wasn't a quarterback in the traditional sense. In 1962 BYU coach Hal Mitchell installed a single-wing offense. "In this offense, you have a tailback who handles the ball 90 percent of the time," Fortie's former teammate Bill Wright said. "Eldon took the direct snap from the center about five yards deep and either ran it or passed it. I was the fullback and only blocked for Eldon, until he got injured and they switched me to tailback for the remainder of the year. The single wing has disappeared with the dinosaurs, thank goodness, but tailback isn't a true quarterback—he is a halfback with passing options."

Alas, despite Fortie's running prowess, the Cougars finished with a 4–6 record that season. Still, that was viewed as progress considering BYU had come off a two-win season.

Fortie participated in four postseason games after his senior year ended—the 1963 North-South Game in Miami, the All-American Game in Tucson, the Hula Bowl in Hawaii, and the Coaches All-American Bowl.

Fortie was named to the All-Conference Academic Team in 1961 and he played for the Edmonton Eskimos of the Canadian League for one season. In 1963 he received the Dale Rex Memorial Award for his contribution to amateur athletics in Utah.

Since 1962 no BYU player has worn the No. 40, in honor of Fortie. In 2004 Fortie was honored at halftime of a game. Fortie reminisced about his BYU football career and had a message for the current team. "There's a lot of guys who went before me, that shed their blood—blue blood. They achieved, much like we are achieving now," Fortie said. "Just remember, these guys left their legacies. It's your turn to leave your legacies."

56 1974: A Season on the Brink

Six weeks into the 1974 season, nobody would have guessed BYU would end up going to a bowl game. Besides the fact that the Cougars had never been to a bowl game before, they started the season with a miserable 0–3–1 record. Furthermore, they didn't earn their first win until October 12. To begin the season, both Hawaii and Utah State defeated BYU without scoring a touchdown (the Cougars lost 15–13 and 9–6, respectively, giving up a flurry of field goals). Iowa State then pummeled BYU 34–7.

BYU tight end Brian Billick recalled how tenuous things were for Coach LaVell Edwards, who was in the middle of his third season at the helm, and how the program's losing ways could have short-circuited Edwards' Hall of Fame career. In Week 4 the Cougars visited Colorado State in the Western Athletic Conference opener, and Edwards addressed the team. "We did not start well that year. To this day, I believe in my heart what LaVell said to that team the night before; you could read between the lines," Billick said. "If we didn't get it turned around now, that was probably going to be it for LaVell."

Edwards called those weeks "the low point of [his] coaching career." But it was also the turning point of his coaching career. BYU battled to a 33–33 tie with the Rams and went on to defeat Wyoming the following week, 38–7. BYU then went on to win their next six games.

"As you look back at it, it was really a pivotal time. It was great to become a part of the emergence of BYU football," Billick recalled. "Coming in with LaVell, and they hadn't had a lot of success, but you could tell they were on the verge of it. LaVell was obviously a great coach. That first team that worked itself through into the first bowl game overcame so many obstacles. That was a pivotal time to be a part of that…it was a great time to be on the ground floor of everything BYU accomplished at that time. I'm very proud of that time."

The Cougars won the WAC title and were invited to the Fiesta Bowl, which automatically took the league champion. After playing football for 52 years, BYU finally earned a trip to a bowl game. "It was one of the major early accomplishments we had," Edwards said. "We had won a championship when I was an assistant [in 1965], but we had never gone to a bowl game. It was an exciting period of time. As a boy growing up, I remember listening to bowl games on the radio. So for us to go to a bowl was very special." As it turned out, there would be many more WAC titles and bowl games to come over the next 20 years.

BYU fans gobbled up their allotment of 8,333 tickets for the game. The Cougars fell 16–6 to Oklahoma State, and quarterback Gary Sheide suffered a dislocated shoulder in the first quarter after leading his team to an early 6–0 lead. He was sidelined for the rest of the game.

Still, reaching a bowl for the first time was a huge accomplishment, and 1974 was the year BYU's bowl tradition began. "That was the group of kids that totally changed the direction of my life and the direction of our football program," Edwards said of the 1974 team. "I hadn't really accomplished anything yet."

57 Paddling the Ducks

Going into the 2006 Las Vegas Bowl, the pressure was squarely on BYU. The No. 19–ranked Cougars boasted a Mountain West Conference championship and a nine-game winning streak. Plus, they hadn't won a bowl game in a decade. To lose to Oregon, a team that had finished in a fifth-place tie in the Pac-10 and a team mired in a three-game losing streak, would have meant another blue Christmas in Provo.

As it turned out, though, it was the Ducks who quacked under the pressure—of BYU's dominating defense and prolific offense. The Cougars made Oregon look like just another MWC opponent with a convincing 38–8 victory before a Sam Boyd Stadium–record crowd of 44,615.

With that, BYU's bowl-win drought ended emphatically. The Cougars won their first postseason game since defeating Kansas State in the Cotton Bowl after the 1996 season. With the win, BYU put the finishing touches on a memorable 11–2 campaign. "I couldn't think of a more fitting ending, one that this team deserved," Coach Bronco Mendenhall said.

And it all came at the expense of the Cougars' former head coach Gary Crowton, who was Oregon's offensive coordinator. "Our dream," said senior quarterback John Beck, "has been fulfilled. This is the way we wanted to end the season, winning the conference, winning a bowl game, and sending the seniors out on a winning note. This senior class went through so much, and this program has seen such a tremendous turnaround since Coach Mendenhall arrived."

As they had all season, the Cougars seniors led the way against the Ducks, from Las Vegas Bowl MVP tight end Jonny Harline's highlight-reel, career-best performance (nine catches, 181 yards) to running back Curtis Brown's two touchdowns to Justin Robinson's two interceptions (which tied a Vegas Bowl record).

And Beck broke his own Las Vegas Bowl record, passing for 375 yards and a pair of touchdowns. BYU rolled up 548 yards of total offense and limited Oregon to 260. The Cougars were looking to validate their outstanding season, and they accomplished that in impressive fashion before a national television audience. "We wanted to show we could come out and compete with anyone," Harline said.

After going scoreless through the first quarter for the first time all season, BYU's Jared McLaughlin booted a 24-yard field goal to cap a 92-yard drive early in the second quarter. The Cougars struck again on their next possession on a six-yard touchdown run by Brown, and they added another TD on a 41-yard pass from Beck to Harline.

At halftime, BYU led by the relatively comfortable score of 17–0. After driving into Oregon territory on the Cougars' first drive of the second half, Beck threw his second interception of the night. But the Cougars responded by stopping the Ducks on a Robinson pick that set up another Brown touchdown run late in the third quarter.

Oregon's score came on a long TD pass with 10:27 remaining. "We didn't play very well. I think we got outcoached, outplayed, and outhustled," Ducks coach Mike Bellotti said. "We didn't win the battle at the line of scrimmage. I give credit to BYU. They played with great discipline and they are a very, very good team."

While much was made of Oregon having the eighth-best offense in the nation, BYU's defense rose up once again. "People seem to forget, this is a defense that allowed just 15 points a game all season," Mendenhall said.

Following the game, fans rushed the field. Bowl officials awarded BYU the Las Vegas Bowl trophy as fans, players, and coaches savored the moment. "It felt like a home game for us," Beck said. "We went undefeated this year at LaVell Edwards Stadium, and it felt like Edwards Stadium to us tonight."

The day before the game, Bellotti was asked if BYU could compete at the highest levels of the Pac-10. Bellotti flatly said no. "As a team, I can't say that they would play with the highest-level Pac-10 teams," he said. "But you better ask me that after the game."

Naturally, after the game, the question came up again. "We didn't play like a mid-level Pac-10 team, but no, my opinion of them hasn't changed," Bellotti said.

Said Cougars running back Curtis Brown: "They can say whatever they want. The scoreboard says 38–8."

58 Dave Rose

During his career as a player and a coach, Dave Rose established a reputation for being a fiery competitor and a winner. In college at the University of Houston, he played with two future Hall of Famers, Clyde Drexler and Hakeem Olajuwon, on a team known as Phi Slama Jama, a team many consider one of the greatest of all time. Rose was a cocaptain of that team.

When he joined BYU's coaching staff as an assistant in 1997, Rose was part of a staff trying to resurrect a program that had won one game the previous season, and when he became the head coach in 2005, he led the Cougars to an NIT berth after a 9–21 campaign.

But Rose had never faced a battle like the one that confronted him during the summer of 2009, when he was diagnosed with a pancreatic neuroendocrine tumor—a rare form of cancer and the only type of pancreatic cancer that can be successfully treated. The news stunned the sports world.

Rose underwent emergency surgery in a Las Vegas hospital to stop internal bleeding, and his spleen and pancreas were removed. "There was so much blood—he was lying in pools of blood," his wife, Cheryl, told ESPN about that fateful day at the hospital. "That's when I'm thinking, *He's dying*. I kept saying that he can't leave us, that he has to fight. I kept screaming to everyone, 'You have to save him. He means everything to me: a husband, a grandfather, a friend—people need this man. You have to help him.'"

Long before the shocking diagnosis, Rose was well aware of the devastating effects of insidious diseases. Dave and Cheryl became involved with what was known as the Children with Cancer Foundation in the late 1990s. Every year, the Cougars basketball program assists children with cancer, and their families, by putting on a party attended by players and coaches that includes gifts, a dinner, and a visit from Santa Claus and Cosmo the Cougar. The annual event took on deeper meaning for Rose and his family after he was diagnosed with pancreatic cancer.

Rose survived his bout with cancer, and his cancer scans have come back normal since then. Ever since, the Rose family has felt an even stronger connection with, and a more profound empathy for, families that are fighting cancer.

Months after his surgery, Rose was back on the sideline to coach the Cougars again. "I believe that I am a lucky guy," Rose said. "I believe that I've been hit with a challenge but that it's a challenge that is manageable, a challenge that I can handle and continue to do what I love to do.... It's been as difficult as anything I've ever been through, but I feel like I got a second chance, and I'm ready to go."

On the court, Rose led BYU to a school-record six consecutive NCAA Tournament berths, highlighted by the Cougars' first Sweet 16 appearance in 30 years in 2011.

Head coach Dave Rose shouts instructions to his players in the first round of the 2015 NCAA Tournament.

Rose is one of more than 2,000 Division I, II, and III college basketball coaches that belong to the National Association of Basketball Coaches. Coaches vs. Cancer is a national collaboration between the NABC and the American Cancer Society. The group has raised $50 million since it was founded to fund cancer research.

"Dave's profile on the college scene has really increased over the last number of years," said BYU athletic director Tom Holmoe. "I've always loved him from the day we hired him. But I think more and more people are getting to know him and know that he's a class act. He says the right things and runs a great program. The players are great representatives of the program. I think Jimmer [Fredette] did a lot to bring that BYU name back to the forefront again. Dave had his cancer, and people realize that [Coaches vs.

BYU's All-Time Basketball Coaches

Name	Years Coached	Record (Pct.)
W. A. Colton	1902–03	4–5 (.444)
—	1903–05	12–6 (.667)
C. T. Teetzel	1905–08	22–6 (.786)
Fred Bennion	1908–10	16–6 (.727)
Henry Rose	1910–11	8–0 (1.000)
E. L. Roberts	1911–20; 25–27	87–49 (.640)
Alvin Twitchell	1920–25	50–20 (.714)
G. Ott Romney	1927–35	139–71 (.662)
Edwin R. Kimball	1935–36; 1938–41	59–38 (.608)
Fred "Buck" Dixon	1936–38	25–23 (.521)
Floyd Millet	1941–49	104–77 (.575)
Stan Watts	1949–72	371–254 (.594)
Glenn Potter	1972–75	42–36 (.538)
Frank Arnold	1975–83	137–94 (.593)
LaDell Andersen	1983–89	114–71 (.616)
Roger Reid	1989–96	152–77 (.664)
Tony Ingle	1996–97	0–19 (.000)
Steve Cleveland	1997–05	138–108 (.561)
Dave Rose	2005–present	305–111 (.733)

Cancer] does a really good job. They're a close, tight-knit group…
and Dave's lived what he's doing."

When he hired Rose more than a decade ago, Holmoe couldn't
have imagined the Cougars achieving an impressive string of
25-win seasons and NCAA Tournament berths. Rose guided BYU
to the biggest comeback in NCAA Tournament history in 2012 as
the No. 14 seed Cougars rallied from a 25-point deficit to beat Iona
78–72 in a First Four contest.

In 2017 Rose won his 300th game as BYU's head coach, tying
coaching legends Bobby Knight and John Thompson for the 25th-
fastest to 300 wins (407 games). Rose is the second-winningest
coach in Cougars history, trailing only Stan Watts, who won 371
games in 23 seasons from 1949 to 1972.

In the regular-season finale in 2016–17, BYU upset No. 1,
undefeated Gonzaga on the road—the Cougars' first-ever win over
a top-ranked team. It was BYU's third consecutive victory over the
Zags at the Kennel.

As important as basketball is to Dave Rose, his perspective is
much broader than the game. Rose is as competitive as ever, but
he's simply grateful to be coaching.

59 Steve Sarkisian

With a big junior year in which he led BYU to a 10–3 record in
1994, quarterback John Walsh elected to forgo his senior campaign
to enter the NFL Draft. But Walsh played a big role in finding his
replacement—his friend Steve Sarkisian.

Sarkisian had already replaced Walsh as the starting quarterback at West Torrance High School in California. So when Walsh

let Sarkisian know he'd be leaving BYU, Sarkisian signed with the Cougars from El Camino Junior College.

"We don't play many [JC transfer quarterbacks] here," said BYU assistant coach Lance Reynolds. "It's an unusual thing for us to take a junior college quarterback and have him play right away. It was very unusual for us. He did a great job for us, no question."

Before enrolling at BYU in the winter of 1995, Sarkisian was confident about what he could accomplish in his two seasons of eligibility in Provo. "I expect to win," he said. "I expect to go in and lead BYU to two WAC championships. And in two years possibly lead BYU to the Cotton Bowl. I don't think BYU has ever been to the Cotton Bowl."

"He had a determination to be great. He wasn't afraid of anything. He was confident in his abilities," said tight end Chad Lewis. "He was a leader. He was a non-Mormon at BYU who fit in seamlessly. That's not always easy to do. I loved my time with Steve."

Before throwing a pass in a Cougars uniform, Sarkisian, whose father is Armenian and grew up in Iran, embraced the pressure of being the next BYU quarterback. "There will always be the comparisons. The fans expect me to come in there and be another great BYU quarterback," he said. "They don't want anything less, and I think the media will keep those comparisons in the headlines. But I think that pressure is healthy. I think if you are pressured and you don't want to become better, then you go into this shell. If you are a competitor and if you are a guy that wants to win and wants to be the best, you want those pressures. You want those things that are going to make you a better quarterback and help you succeed."

As a junior, in Sarkisian's BYU debut, the Cougars lost to Air Force 38–12. Then he lost his home debut to UCLA 23–9. But as the season progressed, he got more comfortable.

In the final game of the season, at Fresno State, he set an NCAA completion percentage record that stood for 18 years, completing 31 of 34 passes for 399 yards and three touchdowns. But the Cougars failed to go to a bowl game for the first time in 17 seasons. That lit a fire under BYU, and Sarkisian was determined to lead the Cougars to a big season in 1996.

BYU opened with an upset of Texas A&M on national television at home—Sark threw for 536 yards, the most ever by a player against the Aggies—and, except for a September loss at Washington, the Cougars rolled. In the end, Sarkisian fulfilled his promise of leading BYU to the Cotton Bowl. Playing in its first and only New Year's Day game, the Cougars defeated Kansas State 19–15.

BYU finished with a 14–1 record and a No. 5 national ranking. There was a certain symmetry to that campaign. Sarkisian threw a game-winning fourth-quarter touchdown pass to wide receiver K. O. Kealaluhi in the opener against Texas A&M, and then he completed a 28-yard touchdown pass to Kealaluhi in the fourth quarter of the Cotton Bowl. Bookend knockout touchdown passes.

Sark posted a 21–5 record as a starter and holds the record for the highest completion percentage (.669) in school history.

In 2000, after a short stint in the Canadian Football League, Sarkisian began his coaching career at El Camino JC, then became an assistant under then–USC coach Pete Carroll. He worked for seven seasons with the Trojans, interrupted by a one-year stint, in 2004, with the NFL's Oakland Raiders.

In December 2008 Sarkisian was hired as Washington's head coach and he returned to Provo for the first time in 14 years when the Huskies visited the Cougars. "I think all in all, it was a great experience for me at the Y," Sarkisian recalled. "The fans were tremendous to me. The community was very good to me and my family."

Sarkisian was the head coach at USC for one and a half seasons before being fired. He was hired by Alabama in 2016 and called the plays in the Crimson Tide's national championship game loss to Clemson. Weeks later, he accepted the job as offensive coordinator for the Atlanta Falcons.

60 BYU and Conference Expansion

In at least one circle, BYU received unofficial overtures to join the Pac-10 in the 1980s. Former Cougars athletic director Glen Tuckett said if Pac-10 athletic directors would have had their way, BYU would have been invited decades ago. But it's the presidents who call the shots, and they've always been resistant to the idea of BYU being in that league. "On the AD level, they told us they'd love to have us," Tuckett said. "On the presidential level, it was a different story. But we were always an attractive entity. The Pac-10 would have traded Washington State, Oregon State, and Oregon in on us at anytime."

In the late 1990s, athletic director Rondo Fehlberg said almost every Pac-10 athletic director was beating down the door to schedule the Cougars. BYU draws well on the West Coast. But it's the university presidents who decide who to invite to their party, and BYU, as a private religious institution, was never high up on that list of potential invitees.

The common theme heard about why the Cougars are not in the Pac-10 is that BYU is a teaching institution rather than a research institution, and that questions about academic freedom on campus make the presidents uncomfortable. Yet insiders believe this is merely a smokescreen. They point out that if "research" is

Outland Trophy Winners

Two BYU linemen earned the prestigious Outland Trophy a few years apart. And both were junior college transfers. Jason Buck, a native of St. Anthony, Idaho, arrived at Ricks College to try out as a quarterback but left school to work. When he came back, he put on weight and was moved to defensive line. Buck ended up setting the record at Ricks for sacks in a season with 17 as a freshman, and he was a first-team All-American as a sophomore, with 25 sacks.

Buck was recruited by Texas, Alabama, Ohio State, Arizona, Maryland, Kansas, Texas Tech, Illinois, and Georgia Tech. He transferred to BYU and made an immediate impact, leading the Cougars with 11.5 sacks and 26.5 quarterback hurries. Hawaii coach Dick Tomey called Buck "the most dominating player I've seen."

As a senior, the 6'6" 270-pounder recorded 13 tackles for losses, 17 quarterback hurries, and 13 sacks. BYU created a publicity campaign called One Buck, featuring Buck's face on a dollar bill. At the end of the season, Buck received the Outland Trophy, emblematic of the nation's top interior lineman. "For me it was just a thrill to be on the field every Saturday at BYU," Buck said. "To win the Outland Trophy was a dream come true."

That following spring, Buck was picked in the first round of the 1987 NFL Draft by the Cincinnati Bengals, No. 17 overall. He tallied six sacks in the 1988 and 1989 seasons and later played for the Washington Redskins and earned a Super Bowl ring when the Redskins defeated the Buffalo Bills in Super Bowl XXVI.

Three years after Buck left BYU, Mohammed "Mo" Elewonibi transferred in from Snow Junior College. The 6'5" 290-pounder from British Columbia grew up in Nigeria and didn't play football until after high school.

Nicknamed Mount Mohammed, Elewonibi graded out four times with perfect pass protection as a senior and earned the 1989 Outland Trophy.

Elewonibi played professionally in the NFL and CFL. He was Buck's teammate on the Washington Redskins team that won Super Bowl XXVI.

part of the criteria, there are schools already within the Pac-10 that don't qualify as research institutions either.

Sources contend the presidents blackballed BYU simply because of their biases against the school, for such reasons as the school's refusal to compete on Sundays. "It's religious prejudice masquerading as academic snobbery," said one source who did not want to be identified back in the late 1990s. "They're trying to find an excuse to avoid the real issue, that they don't want a school that is tied to the LDS Church." The source added that the idea of BYU going to the Pac-10 was "a dead issue," saying, "The door is slammed shut." When the Pac-10 expanded to the Pac-12 in 2010, the league selected Utah and Colorado.

The Big 12 has long been viewed as the best fit for BYU, should it join a Power 5 conference someday. In 1994 BYU was strongly considered to be invited to the newly created Big 12. There were reports that Texas governor Ann Richards pulled some strings to get her alma mater, Baylor, into the Big 12 ahead of the Cougars.

BYU became an independent in football in 2011, and that fall the Big 12 had discussions with the Cougars about becoming a member of the conference. Instead, the league invited TCU and West Virginia to help offset the departure of Nebraska, Missouri, Texas A&M, and Colorado to other conferences.

In the summer of 2016, the Big 12 decided to explore the possibility of expansion and return to a 12-team league. But in October, the Big 12 announced it would not be adding more schools after all. That left BYU, once again, on the outside the Power 5 looking in.

It's odd, because the Cougars are No. 5 nationally in total wins (366) since 1976, trailing only Nebraska, Florida State, Ohio State, and Oklahoma. Since 1974 BYU has recorded 20 top-25 finishes, played in 35 bowl games (including 12 in a row), won 23 conference titles, and produced 57 All-Americans.

And BYU is one of only six schools in the nation with a Heisman Trophy, Outland Trophy, Doak Walker Award, and Davey O'Brien Award (the others are Boston College, Iowa, Ohio State, Penn State, and Texas). In fact, BYU has garnered 17 major football awards in its history.

BYU looks like a Power 5 program, and is regarded by some conferences as a Power 5 program in terms of nonconference scheduling, but it is not part of a Power 5 conference. The Cougars are likely to remain an independent for the foreseeable future, but as current athletic director Tom Holmoe has affirmed, they are poised to make the jump should the opportunity arise.

61 Kyle Van Noy

There was no easy path to BYU stardom and to the NFL for defensive playmaker extraordinaire Kyle Van Noy. A highly regarded recruit from Reno, Nevada, Van Noy had committed to the Cougars when, on the eve of signing day, he sent a letter to Coach Bronco Mendenhall informing him he had received a DUI citation just days earlier. Van Noy admitted his mistake and apologized.

Van Noy remained committed to BYU, but Mendenhall insisted he not enroll until nearly one year later, in January 2010. Before becoming a Cougar, he needed to earn an ecclesiastical endorsement and free himself from legal issues. That's exactly what Van Noy did, though things didn't come easily even after he arrived in Provo.

Throughout his football career prior to arriving at BYU, ever since Pop Warner ball, Van Noy wore the No. 3. If there's one thing Mendenhall despised, it was a sense of entitlement. So instead of No. 3, Van Noy donned No. 45 as a freshman. Then, as a sophomore, he returned to his familiar No. 3. "I guess I worked hard for this No. 3," Van Noy said. "That's a good thing we have here. You work hard for the number you have. I had to earn it. It's kind of an accomplishment for me, because Coach Mendenhall said, 'If you work hard and do the right things on and off the field, then it works out for you.' It means more than just a number to me. It means how I got here and what I've gone through. It's more than the No. 3 to me."

And what an impact he made. Van Noy played at BYU during a stretch when Cougars offenses struggled. Sometimes Van Noy single-handedly influenced the outcomes of games. For example, at the start of his sophomore season, BYU played in its first game as an independent at Ole Miss. Van Noy helped the Cougars celebrate with defensive fireworks. Trailing 13–0 midway through the fourth quarter, BYU rallied for two touchdowns, including the game-winning TD by Van Noy with 5:09 remaining, to earn a dramatic 14–13 season-opening victory at Vaught-Hemingway Stadium. "I just got lucky. That's all it was," Van Noy said of his touchdown. "I tried to make something happen."

Van Noy, who played wide receiver in high school, was always looking for a chance to score points. While the Cougars offense had hung nothing but a donut on the scoreboard for most of the game, Van Noy found the end zone with relative ease. The Rebels faced third-and-27 from their own 21-yard line when Van Noy lined up wide, sped past the Ole Miss right tackle, and swatted the ball away from quarterback Zack Stoudt. Van Noy scooped up the ball at the 3-yard line and scored.

BYU offensive tackle Matt Reynolds, who was watching that play unfold from the sideline, knew what was going to happen even before the ball was snapped. "It's funny. I saw Kyle Van Noy line up.... I thought, *That tackle has no idea what's coming*," said Reynolds, who had spent the previous month lining up against

Van Noy in practice. "I've seen that stance in camp. I know what's coming. Sure enough, he came flying off that edge."

At the end of his junior season, in the Poinsettia Bowl against San Diego State, Van Noy dominated in the fourth quarter. While BYU struggled moving the ball and scoring points, Van Noy, who spearheaded another strong Cougars defensive effort, pretty much took matters into his own hands and took control of the defensive slugfest. Van Noy scored two touchdowns in the Cougars' come-from-behind 23–6 Poinsettia Bowl victory over San Diego State before a crowd of 35,422 at Qualcomm Stadium.

Early in the fourth quarter, BYU trailed 6–3 before Van Noy burst around the corner and drilled SDSU quarterback Adam Dingwell in the end zone, forcing a fumble. Van Noy pounced on the ball for a touchdown, giving the Cougars their first lead in the Poinsettia Bowl, 10–6. It was the beginning of a 20-point fourth-quarter onslaught.

"It happened to land in my lap. I'm grateful that it did," Van Noy said. "We were talking about how someone needed to cause a turnover. All 11 guys were working as a unit. I just happened to get lucky and make the play."

Van Noy scored another TD with 6:09 left, returning an interception 17 yards into the end zone. Van Noy scored two touchdowns that night; the BYU offense scored one touchdown, and the Aztecs had zero. And by the way, he also recorded a blocked punt in the third quarter.

That was one of the hallmarks of Van Noy's career—his uncanny ability to score points. He holds the BYU record for most defensive touchdowns—five—which includes a pick-six on the first play of BYU's game against Utah State in 2013. And he was a stat stuffer. He holds the school record for career tackles-for-loss (61.5), career quarterback hurries (32), forced fumbles (11), and is No. 5 in career sacks (26).

That's why Van Noy was drafted by the Detroit Lions in the second round as the 40th overall pick in 2014. He was traded to the New England Patriots in 2016, and it proved to be a good move for both Van Noy and the Patriots. Van Noy was a better fit for the New England defense than he had been in Detroit. And at the end of the third quarter of Super Bowl LI in Houston, Van Noy teamed up with Trey Flowers for a nine-yard sack of Atlanta's Matt Ryan on a third-and-11 play. At the time, the Patriots trailed 28–9.

That sack played a role in the largest comeback in Super Bowl history as the Patriots rallied from a 25-point deficit to beat the Falcons 34–28 in overtime.

62 Austin Collie

During the summer of 2007, Collie had been home from his mission in Argentina for just a few months. He was sitting inside BYU's Legacy Hall, talking to a reporter about the upcoming season. While some people had lofty expectations for Collie, others thought he'd never be the same player after serving a mission and being out of football for two years. He was fully aware of what people were saying.

Then Collie opened a window to his soul. "For all those people who think I'm going to come out and perform even better than I did, I want to prove them right," he said. "For all those people who think I can't hack it anymore and it's going to take me a while to get back into it, I want to prove them wrong. I think about that when I'm catching a ball and I think about that when I'm dead tired and don't want to keep going. It's definitely one of those things that drives me."

As it turned out, Collie became BYU's all-time leader in receiving yards with 3,255—in just three seasons. He's also No. 3 in career all-purpose yards (4,649), holds the single-season record for all-purpose yards (2,112 in 2008), and holds the school record for single-game all-purpose yardage (366). He's also No. 1 in receptions in a season (106).

One of his most memorable plays came against Utah in 2007, when he caught a fourth-and-18 pass that set up the game-winning touchdown. "I wouldn't say it was lucky," Collie said of the play. "Obviously, if you do what's right on and off the field, I think the Lord steps in and plays a part in it. Magic happens."

Collie was a highly rated recruit and prep All-America selection out of El Dorado Hills, California. Under different circumstances, Collie probably would have played for Stanford. Collie grew up a 90-minute drive from Palo Alto and he spent plenty of time there while playing at Oak Ridge High School. "I used to go there every weekend," he said. "As soon as I was done with a football game, the next day I'd go over there and visit with all of the coaches."

It wasn't until about a month before signing day in 2004 that he settled on the Cougars. "I think that coming here, and being the same faith as everybody, makes you feel more comfortable rather than going somewhere where your faith really isn't that known," Collie said. "Up until that month before signing day, it was tough. It involved a lot of praying and thinking about it."

In his first game as a Cougar, Collie made a big splash on national television, scoring what turned out to be the game-winning 42-yard touchdown in the Cougars' 20–17 victory over Notre Dame.

Of course, Austin wasn't the first Collie to play at BYU. His older brother, Zac, played with Austin, and their father, Scott, was a Cougars receiver from 1979 to 1982. Scott Collie taught his boys everything he knew about catching the football. He learned from his BYU coaches, Norm Chow and Doug Scovil, the following mantra: "You will make the great catch all of the time and the impossible catch some of the time."

Scott drilled that philosophy into Zac and Austin. "They didn't ask me about being a receiver. I told them," he said. "And they both come from an excellent high school program. I always stressed to them that you have to catch everything. In the era I played in, BYU receivers didn't drop balls. You have to have mental toughness." Austin Collie was one of BYU's most dangerous weapons during his time in Provo.

In January 2009 Collie announced he was skipping his senior season and making himself eligible for the NFL Draft. "After the year that I had and the success that I had, I feel like I'm ready to take on the next challenge," Collie said. "I don't know what will happen, but I feel pretty confident in my decision and what's in store for me in the future.... I do realize it is the NFL and anything can happen. It's a choice I feel comfortable making. I'm just looking to make an NFL team. It's been my dream. Always has. I feel that it's the right time."

In December 2009 the *Sacramento Bee* named Collie the Sacramento Area's Player of the Decade (2000–2009). Collie was drafted in the fourth round of the draft and enjoyed a few very productive seasons with quarterback Peyton Manning and the Indianapolis Colts before concussions led to the end of his career. Collie caught 179 passes for 1,908 yards and 16 touchdowns during his NFL career.

63 Tyler Haws

Marty Haws fondly remembers those early mornings. The door to his bedroom would swing open, and from the comfort of his bed he'd hear his young son, Tyler, whispering through the darkness. "Dad." It was Marty's wake-up call, and it happened like clockwork. Some days, Marty would think to himself in semi-amazement, *Man, here he is again.*

Together they would head to their local church gym in Alpine, Utah, for a predawn basketball workout. Tyler was in elementary school when these daily father-and-son outings began, and they happened because Tyler wanted to hone his hoops skills.

Marty, who starred for BYU from 1986 to 1990, was both happy and willing to help, whether that was to rebound for his son or teach him a new move. After his BYU career, Marty played professionally in Belgium, where Tyler was born. "My deal with Tyler was, 'I'll go with you every day, but I won't wake you up,'" he recalled. "I told him, 'I have to go to work at eight, so we need to go at six.' It was very rare that he ever missed a day. I never had to coax him."

Tyler would hoist up hundreds of shots—up to 800 some days—and Marty would keep track of them on a chalkboard as a tangible way to monitor his progress. "I knew if I wasn't working, somebody else was," Tyler said of those workout sessions. "I wanted to go into my season knowing I did everything I could to be a better player."

His hard work paid off. In 2015 Haws became BYU's all-time leading scorer with 2,720 points, eclipsing Jimmer Fredette. But Haws didn't become a relentless scorer without having a relentless work ethic.

Yet Tyler's collegiate success wasn't part of some grand design. At first, the Haws' hope was that he would be able to play high school basketball. Tyler was cut from a team in the third grade, which fueled his desire to improve. Then came what Marty calls "a perfect storm of things that helped Tyler reach his potential"— growing to 6'5" (Marty is 6'2") and playing for one of the best high school coaches, Quincy Lewis, who led one of the best programs in the country at Lone Peak High.

Over the years, Tyler has developed a repertoire of shots and a midrange game that is a rarity in a world that glorifies long three-pointers and rim-rattling dunks. In fact, the countless hours spent in that particular church gym as a kid played a major role

BYU's All-Time Leading Basketball Scorers

Rank	Name	Years	Points
1.	Tyler Haws	2009–10, 2012–15	2,720
2.	Jimmer Fredette	2007–11	2,599
3.	Danny Ainge	1977–81	2,467
4.	Michael Smith	1983–84, 1986–89	2,319
5.	Devin Durrant	1978–80, 1982–84	2,285
6.	Russell Larson	1991–95	1,885
7.	Fred Roberts	1978–82	1,841
8.	Jeff Chatman	1984–88	1,824
9.	Mekeli Wesley	1997–01	1,740
10.	Mark Bigelow	1998–99, 2001–04	1,715
11.	Kyle Collinsworth	2010–11, 2013–16	1,707
12.	Brandon Davies	2009–2013	1,680
13.	Ken Roberts	1990–91, 1993–96	1,652
14.	Lee Cummard	2005–09	1,569
15.	Jonathan Tavernari	2006–10	1,519
16.	Kresimir Cosic	1970–73	1,513
17.	Joe Nelson	1946–50	1,494
18.	Jay Cheesman	1973–77	1,408
19.	Roland Minson	1948–51	1,407
20.	Andy Toolson	1984–85, 1987–90	1,388

Triple Double King

In the West Coast Conference Championship Game against Gonzaga in 2014, BYU guard Kyle Collinsworth suffered a devastating season-ending knee injury. The timing and severity of the injury made some wonder if he would be able to return, let alone play at a high level, the following season.

Collinsworth heard the doubters. Overcoming that major setback has been a motivating factor for him. "Right when I went down, the talk was redshirting and not even playing that [next] year. Talk was about taking 10 months and maybe making it back for conference play," Collinsworth said. "It never was, at the beginning, about me coming back and playing in the first game. Just hearing people in the community saying I would never be the same again and I [wouldn't] be athletic anymore. I wasn't supposed to really come back, and if I did, I wasn't supposed to be as good." Collinsworth returned that next season as a junior and set the NCAA single-season record, and tied the NCAA career record, with six triple doubles.

As a senior, Collinsworth became BYU's all-time leader in assists (703) and rebounds (1,047), and he ranks No. 2 in steals (229) and finished No. 11 in scoring (1,707). The 6'6", 215-pound point guard and team captain also ended up with an NCAA career record 12 triple doubles. He surpassed LSU's Shaquille O'Neal and Drexel's Michael Anderson to become college basketball's triple double king. All of Collinsworth's triple doubles came in his final two seasons, after the devastating injury.

in shaping his game. "We've chuckled over the years because our church has a 'midrange' gym," Marty said. "That's what we call it. So many churches have small courts. The corners don't go out to three-point range. I don't know how much that has played into it, but that's where we practiced a lot."

At one point, BYU coach Dave Rose hinted that some people might be taking for granted Haws' consistent scoring ability. "The reason we take him for granted is because of Jimmer Fredette, and what we saw a few years ago," said former Cougars basketball great Jeff Chatman, who was Marty Haws' teammate at BYU in the

1980s. "Jimmer was really flashy. He shot a lot of NBA threes. He carried the team to a Sweet 16. Following Jimmer, it's a tough act to follow. But when all things are said and done, they're going to see that Tyler is one of the greatest players ever to play [at BYU]."

Ainge was BYU's top all-time leading scorer until Fredette came along. "Ainge's record lasted for so long, and Jimmer came 30 years later," Chatman said. "You think that the next time you'd see it would be a long time from now. That's pretty incredible that we could have two players like that in one generation." When games were close in the waning moments, there was nobody BYU would rather have at the line than Haws, who was an 88 percent free throw shooter.

As a freshman, Haws averaged 11.3 points per game before leaving for a two-year mission to the Philippines. Amazingly, just months after returning home, Haws was even better as a sophomore. He averaged 21.7 points in 2012–13. Haws' transition back to college basketball has served as the blueprint for other returned missionaries.

Besides his willingness to work, what impressed observers about Haws was the way he fought through screens, double teams, and physical defenses to get open for his shot.

"What he does on the court is fun for me to watch," said BYU athletic director Tom Holmoe. "Most of the time, I just watch him trying to [shake] rub people off and seeing people grab him and claw him and bump him and give him a hip check and all of those things. And he just keeps going like the Energizer Bunny. It's a physical war for that kid to play a full game."

As good as Haws is on the court, "off the court, he's even better," Holmoe said. "He's an incredible leader. He's soft-spoken, but when he speaks, the team listens. He's admired by the rest of the athletic department because of the way he handles himself on and off the court."

64 Mangum-Mathews Miracle at Memorial

No doubt, BYU's last-second victory against Nebraska in the 2015 season opener, in front a sea of red at Memorial Stadium, will go down as one of the most memorable in school history. It also produced a final play that will live forever in Cougars football lore—a miraculous Hail Mary that was reminiscent of the Jim McMahon–to–Clay Brown touchdown pass 35 years earlier. It was also a bittersweet win.

With starting quarterback Taysom Hill out of the game due to a season-ending foot injury, the Cougars trailed by one point, 28–27, and faced fourth-and-3 with one second left on the clock in a legendary stadium against a storied program. Taking the snap was freshman quarterback Tanner Mangum, just three months after finishing his mission in Chile and making his college football debut. Mangum calmly launched a desperation pass into the wind that fell into the arms of Mitch Mathews, who had Cornhuskers defenders behind him just inside the goal line. Final: BYU 33, Nebraska 28.

"I've grown up as a huge BYU fan. Always watching every game," said Mangum, who replaced Hill briefly in the first half and took over for good in the fourth quarter. "I guess to be in this moment, it is still a little surreal. More than anything, I'm just happy about the win. As crazy as the story might seem, I'm just happy we came out on top. I'm so glad we could rally together in a tough environment against a tough team. I'm glad we could come together and win."

The game-winning play was more or less unrehearsed. "Practiced it one time, never with Tanner," Mathews said. "You just hope that you can go jump ball and get that thing. Tanner didn't practice it, but he ended up being in the perfect place at the right time, and I had to come down with it for my guys. You see them on the sidelines and you see them look at you, and you know what you've got to do."

The six-play game-winning drive featured plenty of anxious moments as the Cougars drove from their own 24-yard line to the Nebraska 42. Time could have run out on BYU, but somehow the Cougars were able to set up the play. That day, BYU snapped Nebraska's 29-game season-opener winning streak in their first meeting against the Cornhuskers.

"I'm just proud of the resiliency of our team in an opening game on a big stage in a historic stadium and finding a way to pull it out," said Coach Bronco Mendenhall. "Pure elation is how it felt in the locker room. There hasn't been a bigger win for me personally, and maybe it's just the way it came about.... I'm humbled and just lucky to be a part of it."

For Mangum, what a way to start a career. His first TD pass as a Cougar couldn't have been more dramatic. "I rolled out and threw it," Mangum said. "It wasn't my best ball. It came out a little wobbly. But I'm just glad it got there. Mitch made an incredible catch."

The last time Mangum had suited up for a game was in January 2012 for the Under Armour All-America Game, nearly four years earlier. Just before returning home from his mission, Mangum was preaching the gospel in the town of Tocopilla, Chile. "A little bit different than Memorial Stadium in Lincoln, Nebraska," said Mangum, who completed 7 of 11 passes for 111 yards and a touchdown. And no, he wasn't a typical freshman. He turned 22 three days after the game.

On the last play, Mathews lined up on the left side of the line of scrimmage and rolled all the way over to the opposite side of the field in the end zone. "I think that guy came in from across the field," said Coach Mike Riley, who made his Nebraska debut that day. "And obviously we need to have someone in front of him rather than behind him at that point. We must have been out of position at that point. He came all the way from our sideline."

After catching the pass from Mangum, Mathews remembered fellow wide receiver Nick Kurtz "laying on [him] just looking at the ref, and [he] just started screaming," he said. "I felt more and more weight come on me, and I knew it was game over." Wide receiver Terenn Houk was so elated after the play, he hugged one of the referees.

As excited as the Cougars were to win the game, there were plenty of tears in the locker room when they learned Hill would be lost for the season. Still, that improbable touchdown pass from Mangum to Mathews became an instant classic in the annals of BYU football.

65 Luke Staley

Watching Luke Staley take a handoff, bounce outside, and sprint into the open field was like watching poetry in motion. He effortlessly glided downfield, running through and past would-be tacklers. There has never been another running back like him in BYU history. He's the only Cougars running back to be a consensus All-American and the only one to win the Doak Walker Award.

Blessed with massive calves and a chiseled upper body, Staley was a sight to behold on the football field, looking like he had been sculpted by Michelangelo. Legendary coach LaVell Edwards once said about Staley, "he's the most perfectly built guy you're ever going to see."

Staley turned in the greatest season of all time for a BYU running back as a junior in 2001. He rushed for 1,582 yards (a school record) on 196 carries, averaging an astounding 8.1 yards per attempt, and ran for 24 touchdowns. He also caught 32 passes for 334 yards and four TDs. At the end of the season, Staley earned the Doak Walker Award, emblematic of the nation's top running back. Not bad for a school known for its quarterbacks and passing game. "At the beginning of the year, I set some goals," Staley said. "One of my goals was to win the Doak Walker Award. I wasn't sure if I would, but I thought it was possible."

Most telling about that 2001 season was that with Staley in the lineup, BYU was 11–0. The Cougars were 0–2 without him. He missed the final two games that season (one game due to an academic issue), and with Staley sidelined, the BYU offense wasn't the same.

Staley missed those final two games because he broke his left leg in the final seconds of the Cougars' victory over Mississippi State on December 1 to preserve their top-10 ranking and undefeated season. He underwent surgery to repair damaged ligaments in his ankle and accepted the Doak Walker Award while moving around on crutches.

Throughout his career at BYU, Staley was plagued by a variety of injuries, and he was not able to remain healthy for an entire year. He showed glimpses of his potential as a freshman and sophomore, but both those seasons were shortened due to knee and shoulder injuries.

Staley scored three touchdowns in his first game as a Cougar in 1999, leading BYU to a 34–13 win over Colorado State in the inaugural Mountain West Conference football game. There was plenty more where that came from—in only 29 career games, he set the BYU record for career touchdowns, with 48.

Heading into his junior year, he had rushed for 911 yards and scored 20 touchdowns. After his sensational junior year, Staley opted to turn pro. He was drafted in the seventh round by the

In A Pickle (Juice)

Two days before BYU was to face defending national champion Florida State in the 2000 Pigskin Classic in Jacksonville, Florida, Cougars defensive tackle Chris Hoke choked down a small cup of pickle juice. He wasn't the only one. BYU was hoping that swallowing doses of the sour stuff would maximize their performance when they took on the Seminoles. How? We'll get to that...

In the previous game BYU had played in the Deep South, in the 1998 season opener, the Cougars had cramped up in the steamy 90-degree heat. BYU lost 38–31. Fullback Kalani Sitake, one of the Cougars who was affected that night, said Jacksonville wasn't quite the sauna Tuscaloosa was. "It's cooler here," Sitake said. "Over there it was hot. We were sweating in the buses on the way to the stadium."

The memory of the Alabama game was still fresh in the mind of BYU head trainer George Curtis, who had taken every precaution imaginable to guard against the effects of the South's heat and humidity. "We're trying everything," Curtis said. Including pickle juice.

He asked BYU personnel who served training table meals to the team in Provo to save all the pickle juice they could during the last couple weeks so Curtis and his staff could take it to Jacksonville for players to drink. Which brings us back to the question: Why pickle juice?

"It has to do with the vinegar and saline content it has," Curtis explained. "It is supposed to reduce cramping. I heard about it at a national convention, and teams like the Philadelphia Eagles are using it. It's been theorized that it works."

That may have ben so, but it didn't make the pickle juice taste good. "George says it will give us a little more energy, a little more jump in our legs," Hoke said. "It really helps. I felt good. Except for when it went down and burned my throat."

In addition, BYU had purchased eight Cool Zone machines—large fans that sprayed cool air and mist—that were on its sideline to offset the 80-degree heat.

Yet despite all his best efforts, Curtis knew cramping was inevitable. "Early in the season, you're going to have cramping," Curtis said. "There's so much adrenaline and emotion there. That makes it prevalent. It's not just a heat issue. Some of it may have to do with emotions. Heat, humidity, and emotion are all factors. We're shooting in the dark in this. I guarantee you that someone will cramp up no matter what we do. If there was a bona fide answer, wouldn't everybody be doing it?"

Detroit Lions but he tore the ACL in his right knee in training camp. A year later, Staley tried out for the Lions but was let go.

Former BYU running backs coach Lance Reynolds recalls his recruiting trip to visit Staley in Tualatin, Oregon.

"He comes walking down the hall and he's this big, physical, six foot two, 220-pound, great-looking guy that runs a 10.6 [in the 100 meters]" Reynolds said. "I turned to the coach before the coach even got there and said, 'Hey, we want to offer this guy [a scholarship]. He's a guy we want."

Staley grew up wanting to be a Cougar, and the fact that his older brother, Dustin, was playing safety at BYU was another reason for him to play in Provo. And he quickly became a fan favorite. During his BYU career, when Staley would break off a big run or score a touchdown, he'd prompt the following cheer: "Luuuuuuuuuuuuuke!"

Just before the end of his career, he was asked what he would miss most about BYU. "Running out of the tunnel before every game. The first time I ran out I felt like Rudy," he said. "You get the chills, you get the butterflies, you're running with the band, and the fans are cheering. That's something that is special. And to be running with your brother is something else that's special and something that'll be remembered."

Staley left an indelible mark on the BYU football program. "He had a quiet confidence but an air of unbelievably focused competitive instincts," Reynolds said. "Certainly, he's the most explosive big-play running back we've ever had both running the ball and catching the ball. Unbelievable size, speed, balance."

66 Hang Out with Cosmo the Cougar

BYU's mascot, the cougar, was selected by former coach Eugene L. Roberts in 1923, after he had said BYU athletes played like cougars. In 1924 BYU purchased two cougar cubs for 50 cents each that prowled the sideline at sporting events through the 1940s. By the 1960s, the cougars were only brought out on special occasions.

The original cougar cubs were kept on the south side of campus until 1929. That's when they escaped from their cage, killed two dogs, and stalked livestock on farms in the area. While both were recaptured later that day, one of them died a few weeks later and the other was donated to the Salt Lake Zoo. After that, nearby zoos and local bounty hunters allowed BYU to use their cougars, but BYU was out of the live-cougar-owning business.

Pep chairman Dwayne Stevenson noticed the lack of a mascot at BYU and created Cosmo the Cougar, which made its official public appearance in front of BYU fans on October 15, 1953. Stevenson spent $73 for the costume, and he convinced his roommate, Daniel Gallego, to wear it, becoming the first Cosmo. The name Cosmo references BYU's diverse student body that hails from all over the world.

Over the years, the identity of each year's Cosmo is kept secret until the final home basketball game of the year. Some school presidents, such as Ernest L. Wilkinson and Dallin H. Oaks, surprised the student body by wearing the Cosmo suit at basketball games.

Cosmo received a dramatic facelift in 1997, when BYU announced that Cosmo had fallen 100 feet while hunting a red-tailed hawk, which is Utah's mascot, in Rock Canyon. According to the school, several students called Utah Valley Search and Rescue and Cosmo underwent "cosmotic" emergency surgery.

Who wouldn't want to spend time with this breakdancing cat?

Cosmo emerged with a smaller and more athletic-looking head. The size was reduced to allow Cosmo more range of motion. The new Cosmo was then able to perform more difficult stunts, enabling him to do flips, walk on stilts, and ride motorcycles.

For many decades, Cosmo the Cougar has established a reputation for crowd-pleasing antics and ways to pump up the crowd through gestures. One of the most popular stunts came when Cosmo was part of a triple-decker dunk. Cosmo stood on the shoulders of a student who stood on the shoulders of other students, and then he leaned forward toward the hoop and dunked with authority—prompting a thunderous roar from the Marriott Center crowd. An ESPN commentator once said Cosmo was "probably the most athletic mascot in college basketball."

Cosmo has become an iconic member of the BYU community and he has had an influence on younger fans through the Cosmo's Kids Club, Team Cosmo, and Cosmo's Corner. He even has his own set of wheels—the Cosmobile, a custom van that travels around the community and is invited to be in the procession of local parades.

The Cosmobile features a 1,600-watt 12-speaker stereo system, a dance stage on top, a basketball hoop, a variety of specialty lights, several sirens, fog lights, and a cordless public address system.

Cosmo's fame has also propelled him into the media. He has been featured in national television commercials, and BYU dedicated a series of short films to Cosmo and his legacy—*Cosmo Begins* and *Cosmo: Reloaded.* Those films have been shown on the big screen at LaVell Edwards Stadium between the third and fourth quarters.

Twice Cosmo was invited to participate in the Capital One Mascot Bowl. Cosmo didn't win Mascot of the Year, but he received a lot of exposure through the Mascot Bowl's nationally televised commercials.

When ESPN's *College GameDay* came to Provo in 2009 for a game against TCU, Lee Corso, in his signature move, put on the mascot head of the Horned Frogs. Legendary coach LaVell Edwards, who joined the *GameDay* crew for predictions, donned Cosmo's head to counter Corso's pick. Alas, TCU won.

67 Honor Before Championships

It's one of those "what-ifs" in BYU basketball history. What if center Brandon Davies had played the entire 2011 season? Days after BYU's epic victory at San Diego State, and one day after the No. 3 Cougars achieved their highest ranking in 23 years, school officials released a stunning announcement: Davies had been suspended for the rest of the season due to an honor code violation.

While the news put a serious damper on the off-the-charts excitement surrounding the Cougars basketball program, the shock waves extended well beyond Provo. Because the Cougars had knocked off the Aztecs on the road, numerous national media and prognosticators projected 27–2 BYU as a No. 1 seed in the upcoming NCAA Tournament, and a legitimate contender to reach the Final Four. The Cougars boasted the eventual consensus Player of the Year, Jimmer Fredette; the all-time leader in steals, Jackson Emery; and a host of other talented role players. But BYU couldn't fully overcome the loss of Davies.

In the next game, at home against New Mexico, the Lobos routed the disillusioned Cougars 84–62. At the end of the game, Fredette sat at the end of the bench, his head down, staring at the floor. Fredette's posture symbolized what the program had been through in the previous 24 hours.

In the span of a few days, the Cougars went from the highest highs to the lowest lows. BYU lost in the Mountain West Conference Tournament Championship Game to San Diego State and entered the NCAA Tournament as a No. 3 seed. BYU defeated Wofford and Gonzaga to reach the Sweet 16, then it dropped a close game to Florida. With Davies in the lineup, who knows what might have happened? Maybe BYU would have advanced to the Final Four for the first time in the school's history.

For weeks after Davies' suspension, the BYU basketball program received a vast, unprecedented amount of media attention. The school's stringent honor code, and Davies, were the subjects of intense media scrutiny. "Our student-athletes have received incredible adulation. With the media, you're going to see great things for publicity. And you're going to see times now where it affects Brandon adversely," athletic director Tom Holmoe explained. "I don't think there's a way that we can take a student-athlete and say, 'You're an athlete; we have to protect you from the media.' We don't want to throw them to the wolves. That's not our intention at all. But we understand that with high-profile players, and high-profile people, they're going to be in the media. We won't relax the honor code for a situation that has to do with a basketball player."

Holmoe acknowledged that most people around the country wouldn't understand the honor code and BYU's actions. "This is something for us. We live this. This is who we are," Holmoe said. "We understand that people across the country might think this is foreign to them. They're shocked and surprised. But for us, we deal with this quite often. This situation, because of the timing, brings a lot of attention. But we've handled it exactly [the] same way [as] if there was no media [attention]."

News of the suspension shined a bright light on the honor code and the standards at BYU. But many admired BYU for holding its student-athletes accountable for the honor code they had agreed to abide by.

While Davies left school, he was readmitted to BYU the next fall and played his final two seasons. No player faced the intense scrutiny and publicity that Davies did for his honor code violation.

And everyone wondered about Davies' future. "With having a top-5 team and all the hype around that group and the situation that happened, it put Brandon in a special spot as far as the limelight is concerned," Rose said. "He had so many different options of how he could have handled it."

All-time, Davies ended up No. 12 at BYU in scoring (1,680 points), No. 6 in rebounds (840), and No. 5 in blocked shots (123). He also led the Cougars to the NCAA Tournament in his final two seasons.

Holmoe was happy with the way Davies rebounded from his setback. "I'm just so proud of the kid. I've seen him grow in so many ways off the court," Holmoe said. "I like the kid a ton. I just like him. Whenever I see him, we'll chat for a while. He asks me how things are going for me. He'll ask me about football, and he talks about football. He's just a good guy."

68 Marc Wilson

When Gifford Nielsen, a leading Heisman Trophy candidate, suffered a season-ending knee injury at Oregon State in 1977, many BYU fans believed they had seen their last great quarterback on campus for years.

Neilsen's backup was a lanky 6'6" unheralded sophomore named Marc Wilson, who was understandably nervous about being the team's new starting quarterback. Wilson's mood improved slightly when he met with quarterbacks coach Doug Scovil, who asked him what he liked to do best. Wilson said he liked to roll out and run.

So Scovil altered BYU's playbook to fit Wilson's strengths. In Wilson's first start, at Colorado State, he threw for seven touchdown passes and ran for an eighth TD in a 63–17 win, becoming a star overnight.

The following week at Wyoming, Wilson threw six interceptions as BYU held on to beat the Cowboys 10–7. In the first two weeks of his Cougars career, he had experienced both highs and lows. And there would be more of both for Wilson.

Before the 1978 season, Scovil left BYU for the Chicago Bears. His replacement, Wally English, was not a fan of Wilson's low-key style and favored the more demonstrative approach of Jim McMahon. Under English's new offensive attack, the two quarterbacks platooned for much of the year, and the Cougars slogged to a 9–4 record.

The season took such a toll on Wilson that he nearly quit playing football. But he changed his mind when Coach LaVell Edwards told him Scovil was returning to the Cougars and McMahon would be redshirting.

When BYU traveled to face nationally ranked Texas A&M in the 1979 season opener, few believed the Cougars were ready for prime time. The Cougars hailed from the lightly regarded Western Athletic Conference. BYU was a 16-point underdog.

Just weeks prior to the season, Wilson had suffered a ruptured appendix during a camping trip and nearly died. He made a miraculous recovery, although the night before the game, he still had a temperature of 102. Wilson wore a special flak jacket to protect his body from the physical A&M defense.

"One of my friends on the team, Neils Tidwell, was going on his mission, so we went on a farewell fishing trip with his dad and brother in the Sawtooth Mountains [in Idaho]," Wilson recalled. "We took horses to get back up in there. When we got there I felt sort of funny, and the next day I felt faint, like I was going to black out every time I got up. So I lay in the tent all day, and that night we decided I'd better get back home. In the morning we rode our horses out of there and I took a train back to Provo. I felt better so I didn't go into the doctor. I even went golfing. One morning I got really sick again and they found out I had appendicitis. I

BYU's All-Americans

The following players earned All-America status by being named to the first team, second team, third team or All-Freshman or All-Sophomore teams by major news outlets or award organizations.

Name	Position	Year
Jessie Wilson	HB	1934
Vaughn Lloyd	OL	1939
Lonnie Dennis	OL	1959
Eldon Fortie	QB	1961, 1962
Phil Odle	WR	1967
Gordon Gravelle	OL	1969
Peter Van Valkenburg	RB	1972
Jay Miller	WR	1973
Wayne Baker	DL	1974
Orrin Olsen	OL	1975
Brad Oates	OL	1975
Gifford Nielsen	QB	1976
Jason Coloma	DB	1978
Rod Wood	LB	1978
Tom Bell	OL	1979
*Marc Wilson	QB	1978, 1979
Clay Brown	TE	1980
*Nick Eyre	OL	1980
*Jim McMahon	QB	1980, 1981
*Gordon Hudson	TE	1982, 1983
Bart Oates	OL	1982
*Steve Young	QB	1983
Robbie Bosco	QB	1984, 1985
Kyle Morrell	DB	1984
Leon White	LB	1984
David Mills	TE	1984
Trevor Matich	OL	1984
Mark Bellini	WR	1985
Trevor Molini	TE	1985
*Jason Buck	DL	1986
Shawn Knight	DL	1986
Pat Thompson	P	1988
*Mo Elewonibi	OL	1989
Rob Davis	LB	1989
*Chris Smith	TE	1989, 1990

Name	Position	Year
*Ty Detmer	QB	1990, 1991
Randy Brock	DL	1991, 1992, 1993
Eric Drage	WR	1992, 1993
Derwin Gray	DB	1992
Byron Rex	TE	1992
Shad Hansen	LB	1992
Alan Boardman	P	1993
John Walsh	QB	1993
Todd Herget	LB	1993
Mike Empey	OL	1993
Jamal Willis	RB	1993
Evan Pilgrim	OL	1992, 1994
John Raass	DL	1995
Stan Raass	LB	1995
Itula Mili	TE	1996
Steve Sarkisian	QB	1996
John Tait	OL	1996
Jaron Dabney	RB	1997
Dustin Johnson	TE	1997
Rob Morris	LB	1998, 1999
*Luke Staley	RB	2001
Ryan Denney	DL	2001
Daniel Coats	TE	2003
Matt Payne	K/P	2004
Austin Collie	WR	2004, 2008
Dallas Reynolds	OL	2005, 2008
Jonny Harline	TE	2006
John Beck	QB	2006
Jake Kuresa	OL	2006
Jan Jorgensen	DL	2006
Harvey Unga	RB	2007
Ray Feinga	OL	2007
*Dennis Pitta	TE	2008, 2009
Matt Reynolds	OL	2008, 2009
Braden Hansen	OL	2009
Riley Stephenson	RB	2012
Kyle Van Noy	LB	2012, 2013
Tejan Koroma	OL	2014
Thomas Shoaf	OL	2016

*Consensus All-America selection

started practicing with the team a week before the [Texas A&M] game. I was 15 or 20 pounds underweight. They had been watching for a fever as a sign of infection, and when we left to go down to Houston I had one. It hit me Friday night, of all nights. I went to the hospital while the team went to work out. Fortunately, in the morning it was gone and I was fine. Everybody on the team stepped up to compensate for my condition, and we ended up beating them." Wilson was weak and weighed only 179 pounds, but he found the strength to will the Cougars to victory.

Strangely, the Aggies had outgained the Cougars 404–217 in total offense. BYU rallied, overcoming a 14–3 third-quarter deficit. With a little less than three minutes remaining, Tim Halverson partially blocked a Texas A&M punt that gave the Cougars first-and-goal at the Aggies 19.

With 52 seconds left in the game, Wilson threw a two-yard touchdown pass to Clay Brown, and a subsequent two-point conversion on a Wilson pass to Mike Lacey sealed the 18–17 victory. "That was a big one for us," Edwards said. "It was the highest-ranked team we had beaten to that point. It got the thing going for us. It was really big from that standpoint."

BYU ended up earning its first-ever 11-win season, finishing the regular season with an 11–0 record before losing by one point in the Holiday Bowl to Indiana. Wilson ended up winning the Sammy Baugh Award, was a consensus All-America selection, and finished third in the Heisman Trophy balloting. He led the nation in total offense and set nine NCAA records before being drafted in the first round of the 1980 NFL Draft, No. 15 overall. He had an 10-year NFL career and threw for 14,391 yards. Wilson was inducted into the College Football Hall of Fame in 1996.

69 The Protest Years

During the period from the late 1960s to the early 1970s, BYU's football and basketball teams competed with a constant threat of protest and violence. It was a turbulent time in American history, with demonstrations and protests abounding around the country, sparked by the civil rights movement and the Vietnam War.

The Church of Jesus Christ of Latter-day Saints, which sponsors BYU, prohibited African Americans from holding the priesthood at the time, and BYU athletics became a target for those who disagreed. They accused the LDS Church and BYU of practicing discrimination and racism.

There were several incidents during that period that illustrated the perilous situation BYU players and coaches found themselves in when they traveled. In 1968 San Jose State University sociology professor Dr. Harry Edwards promised violent demonstrations would persist against BYU until the LDS Church ended its prohibition against African Americans holding the priesthood.

BYU's trip to San Jose that year included a police escort to Spartan Stadium for a walk-through the day before the game. Later, at 3:00 AM, the hotel received a bomb threat, which proved to be a hoax. African American players refused to play against BYU and promoted a boycott of the game. There was a heavy police presence at the game and not many fans in the stands. As it turned out, there was no incident that day, and San Jose State, playing without 21 of their African American players, defeated the Cougars 25–21.

In 1969 BYU and Wyoming met at War Memorial Stadium in Laramie for a football game that turned out to be much more than a game. And the ramifications of the Black 14 incident resonated for decades.

During the week of the 1969 BYU-Wyoming game, the Black Student Alliance at UW announced it was planning to stage a demonstration outside the stadium. The 14 African American players on the team, who became known as the Black 14, insisted on being part of that protest by wearing black armbands as a symbolic gesture, but Coach Lloyd Eaton rejected that plan and kicked them off the team for violating team rules prohibiting players' involvement in protests. Reporters from the *New York Times* to *Sports Illustrated* descended upon Laramie to chronicle the episode.

Marc Lyons, who was BYU's starting quarterback in 1969, remembered staying at the Holiday Inn in Laramie the night before the game and hearing people throw bottles at the hotel. On game day, the Cougars encountered protestors as they arrived at War Memorial Stadium. "It was definitely a strange atmosphere," said Lyons, a longtime color analyst for KSL Radio. "It was hard to understand. A lot of our players weren't LDS. It was odd that this was happening at a football game. We were the news. It was the first time we encountered protesters. People were holding signs as we got to the stadium to play. We walked through those people, and they were badgering us a little bit."

At that time, Wyoming was a dominant team in the Western Athletic Conference while the Cougars were perennial also-rans. Yet going into that contest, BYU was confident about their chances for victory because they knew the Cowboys had lost seven starters. "We were kind of excited. We thought, 'Man, we're going to beat those guys,' " Lyons recalled.

Instead the incident, at least on that day, galvanized the rest of Wyoming's team. "Once the game started, man, they got all over us," Lyons said. "I was surprised about that. They beat us pretty good." The Cowboys, who were unbeaten and ranked in the top 10, crushed the Cougars 40–7.

From there, however, the two programs started courses in opposite directions, and Wyoming football was never the same as

African American athletes stayed away from the school. From 1966 to 1968, the Cowboys had won 27 games, but over the next seven seasons, they won only 24 times and suffered six consecutive losing campaigns. Eaton was fired after a 1–9 season in 1970.

BYU, on the other hand, went on to become the WAC's dominant team from the late 1970s through the 1990s. Through the years, many Wyoming fans saw BYU as being responsible for the Cowboys' demise.

The year after the Black 14 incident, BYU coach Tommy Hudspeth added the program's first African American player, Ronnie Knight, a junior college transfer defensive back from Oklahoma.

The impact of the protests was felt on the basketball courts as well. For example, in February 1970, when BYU visited Colorado State for a basketball game, student protestors poured onto the floor at halftime and a Molotov cocktail was hurled from the stands and onto the floor, disrupting the start of the second half. Those were dark times for BYU.

In 1978 LDS Church president Spencer W. Kimball announced a landmark policy change, stating that every faithful, worthy man in the LDS Church, regardless of race, would be able to receive the priesthood.

70 Fourth-and-18

BYU had dug itself into a major hole against Utah on November 24, 2007, in Provo. The Cougars were staring down the barrel of a fourth-and-18 situation at their own 12-yard line, with a little more than one minute remaining in the game. BYU was down 10–9.

"On fourth-and-18," Coach Bronco Mendenhall said afterward, "your chances aren't very good."

Quarterback Max Hall was playing with a third-degree separation of his throwing shoulder. Trainer Kevin Morris taped and wrapped Hall's shoulder, and it was a minor miracle Hall played at all. "I had no ligament holding my collarbone down," Hall said. "They just strapped some tape on top of it to hold it down so my collarbone wasn't sticking up through my skin."

He had injured the shoulder the previous week in a 35–10 drubbing of Wyoming, and he visited the trainers' room 20 times for treatment before the Utah game. BYU coaches downplayed the seriousness of the injury publicly, calling it "a shoulder sprain," but at practice on the Monday of game week, Hall spent the afternoon handing off the ball. Hall didn't attempt a pass during practices by order of the coaching staff. The injury could have forced him to miss the final two games of the season and perhaps return for the bowl game. But there was no way Hall was going to miss the Utah game—his first one. Understandably, Hall didn't have one of his better performances that afternoon. At one point in the first half, he was 2 of 9 passing, including seven straight incompletions.

The game came down to this fourth-and-18 play, with Hall facing the biggest challenge in the biggest game of his young career. He had fumbled on first down, losing eight yards, and then threw two straight incompletions, including one that was nearly intercepted.

The reality was that the Cougars hadn't scored a touchdown all day. Utah, which had won six of the previous seven meetings in Provo, had registered its first TD of the day just moments earlier to take a 10–9 lead.

The primary receiver on fourth-and-18 was to be either one of the tight ends. But if they weren't open, Hall was going to look for wide receiver Austin Collie, who was to run a stop-and-go pattern. As the play unfolded, Hall's tight ends weren't open. The pocket began to collapse around him, and he instinctively scrambled to his right. That, the Cougars said, was what made the play successful, because a couple Utes defensive backs cheated up, anticipating Hall running for a first down. But when they started to converge on Hall, Collie found himself all alone behind the secondary.

Hall let fly a long pass using all the strength his badly damaged shoulder would allow. Collie caught the pass and, after gaining a few yards, was forced out of bounds at the Utes 39 for a 49-yard gain. BYU fans cheered in both relief and disbelief.

"I saw Austin make a good move and he was wide open," Hall said. "Austin made a great move on the guy. It did surprise me to see how open he was. I just threw it as far as I could, and Austin came down and made a great play."

"I was a little surprised they didn't play a prevent package so when I came out of that double move, I was kind of surprised that [Utah's defense] bit on it," said Collie, who earlier in the game had a 67-yard touchdown nullified due to an offensive pass interference call. "I was amazed they didn't play deeper."

Even after that improbable completion, BYU's offense still had work to do. Three plays later, Harvey Unga barreled into the end zone from 11 yards out with 38 seconds to lift the Cougars to a 17–10 victory.

After the game, Mendenhall acknowledged that Hall's shoulder injury was "pretty substantial." He added, "For him to go out and play the way he did was remarkable, considering the severity of the injury."

"I'm a big believer that if you work on your execution and if you work hard and do the right things on and off the field, then [what we call] 'magic' happens," Hall said. "Certain things happen that allow you to win games. I think it was definitely a magic play. This is a magical place to play football. I knew something magical was going to happen." And for the Cougars, it did.

71 Listen to Tom Holmoe at Education Week

Every August thousands of people descend on BYU's campus for Education Week, the largest continuing-education program of its kind in the country. It offers more than 1,000 classes on a variety of topics, such as religion, marriage and family, history, communication, and genealogy. During Education Week, parking lots fill with recreational vehicles from all over the country so families can attend classes at BYU.

For Cougars fans, one class not to be missed in August is presented by athletic director Tom Holmoe. About 200 people show up and fill up the classroom to get the inside scoop on BYU athletics. In August 2016, the crowd was so large that an overflow room was set up in another part of the building, with a TV feed, for those who couldn't get inside the classroom.

During his annual 45-minute presentation and question-and-answer session, Holmoe is candid, insightful, and humorous. The class is a chance for Holmoe to share his unique perspective about BYU athletes and BYU-related issues. But he's careful not to reveal too much.

On that occasion, BYU fans were hopeful that the Cougars would be getting an invitation to join the Big 12 Conference. Holmoe shared early on what his job had been like lately. "I'm grateful for the [opening] prayer," Holmoe said. "I've been praying a lot these days about athletics. Seriously." (All classes, even Holmoe's, begin with a prayer.)

The audience laughed, then Holmoe addressed the elephant in the room. "I'll kick this off with the obvious," Holmoe said. "I know there are a lot of questions regarding our conference and membership. But I won't be able to say anything about any of those."

During his comments, Holmoe stressed how much he appreciates the fan base. "Cougars Nation is the fans, not just BYU alums, not just LDS [Church members]. What I've found from traveling all over the country is that we have people who support BYU sports athletics that aren't members of the church and [are] not BYU alums. I love that. Beards and beer. We welcome everyone."

In recent years, with archrival Utah joining the Pac-12, the series in both football and basketball has been interrupted. But Holmoe let fans know how he feels about the rivalry and how to respect it. "Be good sports," he said. "Support the rivalry. Don't say anything crazy or negative about our opponents. Respect them. On the field, it's one of the best games or matches you'll ever see. Nobody will get more anxious, nervous, excited, and have a chance to fall apart or excel than in that game. In the history of our tradition, some of the very best performances in the history of BYU have happened against Utah. Why in the world would we ever throw that away?"

72 Cody Hoffman

In wide receiver Cody Hoffman, BYU coaches discovered a diamond in the rough from Crescent City, California. He was the final player to be offered a scholarship in the Cougars' 2009 recruiting class.

More than four years later, Hoffman became BYU's top all-time wide receiver in receiving yards (3,612), receptions (260), and receiving touchdowns (33). He's also No. 1 in career all-purpose yards, with 5,015.

Though he was a star at Del Norte High, Hoffman received only two scholarship offers. One was from Sacramento State of the Big Sky Conference. The other was from BYU. Hoffman said he did talk to coaches at Oregon State, but he wasn't offered.

Why such little interest? Why did he fly so low under the radar? "I think it's where I was from," Hoffman said. "It's out in the boonies. Nobody really knew about [Crescent City]. There haven't been any big names to come out of there." Crescent City (population: 7,542) is located in the northwestern corner of the California coast, about 20 miles south of the Oregon border.

Coach Bronco Mendenhall credited a former college roommate at Oregon State for letting the BYU staff know about Hoffman. "It's not a place people normally go to recruit because it's a hard place to get in and out of," Mendenhall said. "So without having a personal connection, we might not have found him."

"Bronco went blindly on the kid," BYU athletic director Tom Holmoe said. "The kid had no [scholarship] offers. Bronco took him."

Redshirting as a freshman in 2009 gave Hoffman a chance to learn the offense and play on the scout team. It also allowed him to get used to life at BYU. Before being recruited by BYU, Hoffman knew of the school but didn't know much about it. But he soon found a home in the BYU record book.

During his time in Provo, Hoffman was known for acrobatic catches, such as the ones he had against Oregon State and Georgia Tech. Former Cougars tight end Chad Lewis has referred to Hoffman as the "best in-traffic receiver ever" at BYU.

And Hoffman made game-winning plays, such as against Tulsa in the Armed Forces Bowl in 2011. Quarterback Riley Nelson led the Cougars on a 12-play, 48-yard drive in the closing four minutes. With 11 seconds remaining, Nelson stood at the line of scrimmage

BYU WR and game MVP Cody Hoffman (2) celebrates after scoring a touchdown on a 30-yard pass from BYU QB Riley Nelson in the 2011 Armed Forces Bowl.

on second-and-2 at the Tulsa 2-yard line. BYU's coaches had called a spike play to stop the clock. Instead, Nelson decided to call an audible and execute a Red Alert, or a fake spike. Nelson's fake spike caught Tulsa's defense off guard, and he found Hoffman open in the end zone for the game-winning touchdown in a 24–21 Cougars victory. "Cody's stance was not a receiver's stance at all. He was standing there waiting for it to get hiked," Nelson said. "When Cody took off, the first thing the corner did was spring back to not get beat on a fade. I had Cody's eyes. He stopped. I was able to put the ball back-shoulder. Great play by him." Hoffman earned Armed Forces Bowl Most Outstanding Player honors after catching eight passes for 122 yards and three touchdowns.

Earlier that season against Central Florida, Hoffman's 93-yard kickoff return for a touchdown—marking the first time that's

The Helmetless Block

In the first half of the 2011 Armed Forces Bowl between BYU and Tulsa, Cougars left tackle Matt Reynolds delivered an unusual, memorable block that had long-lasting repercussions.

On first down, as Nelson scrambled left toward the sideline, Reynolds lost his helmet as he tussled with a Golden Hurricanes defender. "I probably got a little too aggressive," Reynolds said. "I think I hit his knee with my helmet and my helmet popped off. When I stood back up, I saw them running for Riley. I just tried to stop them."

Stop them he did, by peeling back and delivering a crushing block near the sideline that allowed Nelson to keep the play alive. Nelson completed a pass to Cody Hoffman in the middle of the field, at about the 3-yard line. After catching the ball, Hoffman battled through a couple Tulsa defenders, then stretched the ball over the goal line for the score. It was BYU's first touchdown in the game.

The postscript of this story: Reynolds' helmetless block prompted the NCAA to create a new piece of legislation, a rule that states that a player can no longer participate in a play if he loses his helmet.

happened since Mike Rigell accomplished the feat in 1998 against Hawaii—tied the game and propelled the Cougars to victory. In 2012 Hoffman caught a career-high 12 passes for 182 yards and a school-record five touchdowns against New Mexico State. Not bad for the last player to receive a scholarship in the Cougars' recruiting class of 2009.

Homes Away from Home: Las Vegas and San Diego

BYU and Las Vegas make quite the odd couple. The LDS-owned school is perennially voted the No. 1 stone-cold-sober university in the nation. It has a stringent honor code that students—and players—subscribe to. Las Vegas is nicknamed Sin City and is known for its glitz, glamour, and gambling. It features the Strip, showgirls, and racy billboards that can make a grown man blush.

BYU's reputation, and that of Las Vegas, clash like the Mormon Tabernacle Choir and Elvis impersonators. But when it comes to the Las Vegas Bowl, the two disparate entities complemented each other very well for years. Thanks to the annual December football game held at Sam Boyd Stadium, it's a place where "Come, Come Ye Saints" and "Viva Las Vegas" converge.

When BYU, under first-year coach Mendenhall, accepted an invitation to face Cal in December 2005—marking the Cougars' first bowl berth since 2001 and snapping three consecutive losing seasons—everyone connected with the program was thrilled about going to the Las Vegas Bowl.

And the feeling was mutual. At that time, the Las Vegas Bowl needed to sell more than 29,000 tickets to the 2005 game in order to maintain its bowl charter with the NCAA. That year, BYU delivered the Las Vegas Bowl's first-ever sellout.

Before that game against Cal, both Holmoe and Mendenhall figured it would not be the last time BYU would play in the Las Vegas Bowl. And they were right. Starting in 2006, the Las Vegas Bowl became home to the Mountain West Conference champion. "We want to go every year," Holmoe said prior to the 2005 Las Vegas Bowl. "Under Coach Edwards, we got a stranglehold on the bowl game and the conference championship. That success bred more success. Winning stimulated more winning. We got to be a powerhouse because of that and that's what we're going for right now."

In retrospect, it's somewhat surprising to realize that prior to 2005, BYU had never played in the Las Vegas Bowl. But from 2005 to 2009, the Cougars played in five consecutive Las Vegas Bowls

Go to a Bowl Game

BYU didn't go to its first bowl game until 1974—the Fiesta Bowl. When the Cougars played in their third bowl, the inaugural Holiday Bowl in 1978, it started a streak of 17 consecutive seasons of bowling. In 2005, after four straight years without going to a bowl, the Cougars started a new streak that, as of 2016, has reached 12 in row.

For many BYU fans, attending a bowl game has become an annual tradition during the holidays. The Cougars have had a colorful bowl history and have played in bowls all over the country. They've played in 15 different bowl games (Fiesta, Tangerine, Holiday, Citrus, Freedom, All-American, Aloha, Copper, Motor City, Liberty, Las Vegas, New Mexico, Armed Forces, Poinsettia, and Fight Hunger) in 10 different states (Arizona, Florida, California, Alabama, Hawaii, Texas, Tennessee, Michigan, Nevada, and New Mexico).

From 1974 to 2016, BYU earned 35 bowl bids. In that time, only six FBS programs have played in more bowl games.

Going into the 2017 season, the Cougars' record in bowl games was 14–20–1.

(and later returned in 2015 when they faced archrival Utah), and it was simply what athletic director Tom Holmoe and then-coach Bronco Mendenhall had predicted for the program back in '05.

Holmoe said the situation reminded him of when he was a BYU player in 1978, the year of the inaugural Holiday Bowl. "People were going, 'It's the Holiday Bowl. What kind of game is that?'" Holmoe explained. "But our team, and our fans, helped establish the Holiday Bowl. I really believe we can actually help start a great tradition down there. It's up to us, football-wise, to get in and make it special.... The WAC started the Fiesta Bowl and the Holiday Bowl. Those are two great bowls right now. We'll establish a great strength down there in Las Vegas. This is the time for our fans to get used to coming back."

Cougars boosters responded overwhelmingly (and it helps that Las Vegas is not far from Provo and has a strong LDS population), selling out Sam Boyd Stadium every year BYU appeared in the Las Vegas Bowl. Though it's not the holiday destination that seems to fit BYU, it's a place, oddly enough, where the Cougars feel right at home.

San Diego is another city where the Cougars feel at home; outside of Utah, BYU has played more games in San Diego—29 at the end of 2016—than in any other city. And for Cougars fans, some of the most unforgettable plays occurred at what was once known as Jack Murphy Stadium in San Diego, now Qualcomm Stadium.

More specifically, it's where BYU clinched the 1984 national championship. And some of the most famous touchdowns in BYU football history all took place in the same west end zone:

- The Miracle Bowl pass from Jim McMahon to Clay Brown in 1980
- The halfback pass to Steve Young for the game-winning touchdown against Missouri (Young's final college play) in 1983

- Glen Kozlowski's leaping catch in the back of the end zone in the fourth quarter against Michigan in the 1984 Holiday Bowl
- Robbie Bosco's game-winning touchdown pass to Kelly Smith in the 1984 Holiday Bowl to clinch the national championship
- Jamal Willis' five-yard touchdown run late in the game against San Diego State to tie the game 52–52. (The Cougars had been down 42–17 early in the fourth quarter before rallying to earn the Cougars' the highest-scoring tie in college football history)
- Chad Lewis' one-handed touchdown catch on a fade pattern against Ohio State
- Kyle Van Noy's two defensive touchdowns in the fourth quarter to beat San Diego State in the 2012 Poinsettia Bowl

"This park," Holmoe said, "has extra special meaning for all Cougars."

74 Chad Lewis

Just after Utah had beaten BYU in Provo for the first time since 1971, Utes fans and players were relishing the moment. But Chad Lewis, looking like a Clint Eastwood character, took Utah's victory celebration personally. While the Utes had made their own day, Lewis—a freshman tight end from Orem who had joined the team as a walk-on—wouldn't stand for it.

The Utes had split the uprights on a 55-yard field goal with 25 seconds left to give Utah a 34–31 win. When the game ended, several Utah players pointed toward the north end zone and defiantly charged toward the goal post. Then things got ugly. As pandemonium broke loose on the turf, a few Utes fans joined the players in a raucous celebration by trying to pull down the goal post.

Cougars fans and players watched as the scene unfolded on the field. Lewis, who was recruited by Utah but opted to walk on at BYU, sprinted toward the north end zone and defended the school's honor—not to mention $2,500 worth of school property—by chasing the crimson-clad enemies off the post and restoring territorial rights. The uprights teetered and were bent to the right, but they remained standing. "I buckled up my helmet and dove in there," Lewis explained. "That's just pride. That's *my* field. I figured it was my duty, so I did it."

Lewis' older brother, Mike, who had played at Utah in 1986 and from 1990 to 1992, assisted Chad in the fracas and was called a traitor by the Utes players and fans for defending BYU. "They are my friends," the elder Lewis said, "but that's crazy."

Other BYU players soon jumped into the fray, and after some punches had been thrown and insults had been exchanged, both teams returned to their respective locker rooms. The end result was a cockeyed goal post and bitter feelings.

But Chad Lewis earned plenty of respect that day. "Chad Lewis," said BYU linebacker Todd Herget, "is a guy who has a lot of pride. He's the epitome of what BYU football is all about."

When he arrived on campus after an LDS mission to Taiwan, Lewis was a skinny kid looking for a chance to play. As a freshman, he made an impact both on and off the field. He and teammate Itula Mili continued the tradition of big tight end production at BYU. Lewis finished his career with 1,376 receiving yards, No. 7 all-time among Cougars tight ends. He was also a key leader on BYU's 1996 team that posted a 14–1 record, won the Cotton Bowl, and finished No. 5 in the rankings.

The Lewis family never had much luck when it came to the BYU-Utah rivalry. When Mike played for the Utes, they lost all four games to the Cougars. And going into his senior year in 1996,

BYU's Academic All-Americans

Name	Year
Virgil Carter	1965, 1966
Casey Boyette	1966
Paul Ehrmann	1966
Dan Taylor	1972, 1973
Steve Stratton	1973
Steve Miller	1976
Steve Smith	1976
Scott Phillips	1980
Dan Plater	1981
Steve Young	1983
Marv Allen	1984
Ty Mattingly	1986
Chuck Cutler	1987, 1988
Tim Clark	1988
Fred Whittingham	1989
Andy Boyce	1990
Brad Clark	1992
Bruce Jenne	1992
Eric Drage	1992, 1993
Cory Cook	1994
Alan Boardman	1994, 1996
Chad Lewis	1996
Ben Cahoon	1997
Jared Lee	2000
Ryan Denney	2001
Nathan Meikle	2005
David Oswald	2008
Kellen Fowler	2008
Scott Johnson	2009
Matt Bauman	2009
Bryan Kariya	2010

Chad had lost the first three games to the Utes. Score it: Rivalry 7, Lewises 0.

So entering his final battle against Utah, Lewis wanted to end that streak—no matter how. He did, thanks to his friends in the backfield, Ronney Jenkins and Brian McKenzie. Jenkins, a freshman, rushed for 156 yards and three touchdowns while McKenzie, a junior, had 176 yards and one TD. The Cougars dominated, finishing with 366 yards on the ground.

As a result, BYU won in a runaway. And Lewis was thrilled. "It was something you can't explain," said Lewis. "I finally got to beat them. You make that game so important. You lose one game, and it lasts a year. You go 0–4, and it lasts a lifetime."

In the 1997 NFL Draft, every team passed on Lewis, and he settled on signing an undrafted free agent contract. Though he was disappointed, he was, as usual, upbeat and undaunted. "I've been through this before," said the former walk-on. The eternally optimistic Lewis ended up playing nine seasons in the NFL, becoming a three-time Pro Bowl selection for the Philadelphia Eagles. He caught the game-winning touchdown pass in the 2005 NFC Championship Game but suffered a foot injury on the play that prevented him from playing in Super Bowl XXXIX against the New England Patriots.

Because of his charisma and fluency in Mandarin Chinese, the NFL sent Lewis to Taiwan and throughout Southeast Asia as an ambassador. He gave interviews and helped out with football clinics. In 2003 Lewis was also the Super Bowl color analyst for Chinese radio, with a potential audience of 1.3 billion people.

After his football career ended, Lewis wrote a memoir, *Surround Yourself with Greatness*. He is married to former BYU volleyball star Michele Fellows Lewis. Both Lewises were inducted into the Utah Sports Hall of Fame in 2013. He currently serves as an associate athletic director at BYU.

75 2001: A BYU Space *Odd*-yssey

BYU opened the 2001 season, and ushered in a new era, at home on a sweltering August afternoon against Tulane. In head coach Gary Crowton's debut, the Cougars scored 70 points in a victory over the Green Wave—just months after legendary coach LaVell Edwards retired after 29 years at the helm of the program.

As BYU continued winning that season, it almost seemed as if it would never lose again. On September 8, 2001, the Cougars traveled to Berkeley, California, and thrashed the California Golden Bears 44–16 to improve to 3–0. On the strength of that victory, BYU burst into the national rankings at No. 24. BYU was averaging 55 points a game, and quarterback Brandon Doman and running back Luke Staley were toying with opposing defenses.

While at the time almost everyone figured Crowton would lead the Cougars for nearly three decades, just as LaVell had, it was the man coaching on the opposite sideline who would go on to have a major impact on BYU's future. That would be Tom Holmoe, a former Cougars defensive back whose days as Cal's head coach were numbered. That loss to BYU, ironically, pretty much sealed his fate in Berkeley. By the end of the season, Holmoe's coaching career was done.

Who could have guessed that just three years later, Crowton would be gone and Holmoe would be on the verge of being hired as BYU's athletic director? And who could have guessed that, 10 years later, Holmoe would lead the program into independence?

Then again, it was Crowton who hired Bronco Mendenhall as BYU's defensive coordinator before the 2003 season—and, of course, Mendenhall replaced Crowton as the Cougars' head coach. Holmoe was instrumental in the decision to hire Mendenhall.

Following that September 8 win over Cal, BYU was looking forward to a showdown on September 15 at No. 16 Mississippi State. A victory in Starkville would be huge for the program.

But three days later, on the morning of September 11, everything changed. The Twin Towers fell, and the Pentagon was engulfed in flames. We began to hear stories about true heroes—not ones who score touchdowns—risking their lives to save others, in New York City and Washington, DC, and also aboard a plane that crashed in a remote part of Pennsylvania. Thousands of lives were lost. It was a surreal day, filled with shock and sadness.

Suddenly, sports didn't seem that important. There were reports of the possibility of athletic events being postponed, including the BYU–Mississippi State game. On that day, practice started with the coaches and players on the practice field kneeling in prayer.

After practice, Crowton addressed the situation with reporters. "It's a hard day," he said, his voice cracking with emotion. "You feel fortunate for what you have. The players are aware of what's going on. They fought through it pretty well."

As it turned out, both professional and collegiate games throughout the country were postponed that weekend. BYU moved its game with Mississippi State to December 1, and pushed back its regularly scheduled game at Hawaii from December 1 to December 8.

After the Cal game, the Cougars didn't play again until three weeks later, on September 29, at UNLV. BYU trailed the Rebels by three points with 1:41 remaining when Doman converted a dramatic fourth-and-4 play at the Cougars' own 37-yard line, then capped a 91-yard drive with a 21-yard scramble into the end zone with 1:12 remaining. BYU won 35–31. Judging by the way the Cougars celebrated that night after the game, sports still mattered.

BYU won eight more games—including a close win over New Mexico and its defensive coordinator, Mendenhall—and the Cougars would go on to post a 12–0 mark and break into the top-10 rankings. BYU was hoping for a BCS berth. But in a dramatic 41–38 triumph at Mississippi State—the game originally scheduled for September 15—Staley suffered a broken foot on the game-winning drive. Later that week, BYU was unceremoniously released from BCS consideration. And without Staley, who would go on to win the Doak Walker Award, emblematic of the nation's top running back, the Cougars dropped their final two games—at Hawaii, and to Louisville in the Liberty Bowl. Without Staley, BYU's offense wasn't the same. And a season that started with so much promise shattered.

BYU's 2001 football odyssey opened on a sweltering August afternoon in Provo with the Cougars scoring 10 touchdowns and 70 points against a Conference USA team, Tulane. It ended on a frigid New Year's Eve at the Liberty Bowl, where the once-mighty BYU offense could manage only one touchdown—on a tackle-eligible pass play—and a field goal against the Conference USA champions, Louisville.

The weather conditions in those two games paralleled the stark contrast between the performance of BYU's offense in those contests: scorching hot and icy cold. It turned out to be Crowton's only winning season at BYU. An odd season, indeed.

76 Glen Tuckett

If an athletic program mirrors its athletic director, then BYU reflected Glen Tuckett, who ended his 17-year tenure as the school's athletic director in 1993.

During his years as AD, Tuckett's undying optimism was the guiding force of one of the top athletic programs in the nation.

He spoke of things that seemed improbable, and many times the improbable happened.

During his time as athletic director, BYU produced an improbable NCAA Tournament victory over Notre Dame and a trip to the Elite Eight (1981), an improbable expansion of what was then known as Cougar Stadium to more than 65,000 seats, an improbable national championship in football (1984), and an improbable Heisman Trophy winner (1990).

Tuckett arrived at BYU in 1959 as a baseball coach. "Glen has made enormous contributions not only to BYU and football but to sports in general," said Coach LaVell Edwards. "Not only locally but nationally." Tuckett served on many NCAA committees, most prominently as the College Football Association chairman, which worked out television contracts with ABC and ESPN. He's a member of the Utah Sports Hall of Fame and the BYU Athletic Hall of Fame.

Tuckett is remembered as a visionary man, as well as a hard worker who desired to carry the message of BYU's "bigger picture" to everyone. "I feel that it would be desirable for us to assume a more paramount role with our athletic teams as a missionary tool," Tuckett once said. "Sports participation is a universal language, and I am firmly convinced that a winning athletic program at BYU is one of the great missionary tools available to us. I have facetiously said for years that when we consistently have our football team at 9–2, 10–1, etc., that the missionary tool we will make [will make] the Tabernacle Choir sound like they are singing out of tune."

Tuckett never let anyone forget that BYU is a church school, and he reveled in that fact. "Purely for athletic reasons now: if we wanted to enroll every good Mormon athlete in the world," he once told *Sports Illustrated*, "plus every good, big athlete we convert to our church—just stash them here on our campus, put them on this team or that…think of it. All the king's horses, as they say, couldn't stop BYU."

Tuckett managed to mold a successful program through a positive attitude and patience. He recalled the days when he'd try to schedule football games with prominent schools and they wouldn't return his calls. But that changed. "I said once we get Notre Dame here," he said, "they can bronze me and send me back to Murray [Utah]." In 1993 it happened. Notre Dame played at BYU for the first time.

1977 Silk Bowl

Before the 1977 season opened, BYU made it clear that if it won the conference championship, the school would not play in the Fiesta Bowl, which was scheduled for Christmas Day. Christmas fell on a Sunday that year.

Sure enough, the Cougars won the WAC in 1977, and they snubbed the Fiesta Bowl for religious reasons. (Years later, in 1996, the Fiesta Bowl returned the favor by snubbing the 13–1 Cougars for Bowl Alliance—precursor of the Bowl Championship Series—reasons.)

With the 1977 Fiesta Bowl out of the question, BYU had no bowl to play in. So athletic director Glen Tuckett told the Cougars to "go east, young men." To the Far East, that is, on a goodwill trip that was planned before the season. The team had accepted an invitation from the Japanese government.

BYU played in two games in Japan against Japanese All-Star teams at the end of the 1977 season in the Silk Bowl, which was an exhibition contest only. "It was a great experience for the team, a great trip for the kids," Tuckett remembered. "You don't get to go to Tokyo very often."

During the 10-day excursion to Japan, the coaches and players ate sushi, visited shrines, and easily won their two games. And what was the quality of Japanese football? "They know the game pretty well, but they were just overmatched," Edwards said. "They were competitive...guys. The night before the game I remember thinking, *This would really be big if we lose.*"

The Cougars must have been a big hit in Japan. The following year, BYU defeated UNLV 28–24 in the school's regular-season finale, in Yokohama.

Even after he retired at BYU, Tuckett wasn't done playing a role in Cougars athletics. A couple years after retiring from BYU, Tuckett received a phone call from then–Alabama president Roger Sayers, whom Tuckett had worked with on an NCAA committee. The Crimson Tide football program had just gone on probation for the first time in school history, and Tuscaloosa sat under a cloud of depression. Sayers told Tuckett he was flying out to Salt Lake City to visit with him. But presidents of major universities don't fly thousands of miles out of their way just to eat lunch. Sayers had an offer for Tuckett—to become Bama's interim athletic director. He had a short list, and Tuckett's name was the only one on it. So at age 67, Tuckett took the job during the 1995–96 sports season. Not only did Tuckett assist with the appeal, which resulted in fewer sanctions than were originally handed down by the NCAA, he mended the broken hearts of Tide fans.

Tuckett also accomplished one other important feat while he was in Tuscaloosa. He found Alabama's schedule was filled up for the next 10 years, except for one hole in 1998. Knowing BYU was looking for a nonconference opponent, he spoke to BYU administrators, who jumped at the chance to line up a date with the Crimson Tide. "We needed a home game," Tuckett remembered, "and I signed the contract. I didn't talk to anybody [at Alabama] beforehand about it. As athletic director, I just did it."

Ironically, years earlier, when Tuckett was at BYU, he had inked a home-and-home agreement with Alabama. Under the terms of the contract, the Crimson Tide were scheduled to visit Provo in 1995 and then host BYU in 1996. But when the SEC expanded in 1994 and Alabama needed to make room in its schedule to play one more conference game, BYU allowed Alabama out of its contract. He set up, in 1998, perhaps a once-in-a-lifetime shot for BYU to play Alabama. The Cougars fell to the Crimson Tide 38–31. But for Tuckett it was a win-win situation.

77 Max Hall

Max Hall grew up an Arizona State fan. That made sense, considering his uncle, Danny White, played quarterback for the Sun Devils before going on to star with the Dallas Cowboys.

Following an outstanding prep career in Arizona, Hall signed with the Sun Devils and redshirted before serving a mission and transferring to BYU. Once he arrived in Provo, he was indoctrinated about the quarterback tradition at BYU. "This place is sweet. I've got to go out and perform," Hall said at the time, after spending the 2006 season as a redshirt. "Having guys to learn from like John Beck, and guys to look back at like Steve Young, Jim McMahon, and Robbie Bosco, it's just awesome. It's really a blessing for me to be here."

That was prior to the 2007 season, when he would take over one of the most high-profile roles in college football as a BYU quarterback. Before that, the last time the Cougars had entered a season with a starting quarterback with no Division I experience was 1995, when junior college transfer Steve Sarkisian took the controls. Not only had Hall never taken a Division I snap, he hadn't taken a snap in a game in four years, since he was in high school, after being a missionary for two and redshirting two more.

But Hall was confident. He had reason to be, because he had a bevy of talent and experience around him at running back and wide receiver, as well as on the offensive line. "I've been waiting for this for a long time," Hall said. "I feel so confident because of our team. We have a great team, and I think we're going to win a lot of games."

And that's exactly what Hall did. He became the Cougars' all-time winningest quarterback, leading BYU to 32 victories in three seasons as a starter. He surpassed Ty Detmer, who won 29 games as a starter.

Detmer knows how hard it was to win that many games. "When you're the quarterback, you rely on everybody around you to do their jobs," Detmer said. "It shows the consistency you played with. It shows you're durable. The ultimate goal of the quarterback is to help your team win the game. Max has done that."

Hall warms up for 2008 game action.

Hall beat archrival Utah twice and upset No. 3 Oklahoma in the 2009 season opener in Dallas. He finished second in BYU history in passing yards (11,365), touchdowns (94), completions (903), and total offense (11,569 yards).

He signed as a free agent with the Arizona Cardinals and won his first career start in the NFL. But he suffered injuries as a rookie, and subsequent decisions severely affected his life.

In 2014 Hall's world came crashing down after his arrest for shoplifting and drug possession—he happened to be wearing a BYU T-shirt in the infamous mug shot—in Arizona. That event revealed to the world his addiction to painkillers. "I just wanted to keel over and bury myself and never come out," he said of that dark time. "I got knocked down pretty hard. That was the hardest thing to get up from. I thought about just staying down and not getting back up."

But Hall received help for his addiction and received strong support from the BYU family. He's now coaching at a high school in Arizona. "My No. 1 focus right now, and it has to be every day when I wake up, is to stay sober," Hall said. "In order to do that, there are things that I have to do. I still have bad days. I'm not perfect. I still make mistakes. I'm still working to improve my relationship with my family and all that stuff. That doesn't happen overnight. It starts with hitting my knees. If I can do that and keep myself right and continue to get more sobriety time, I can help a lot of people. It's something that's got to be on my mind every day. I have to wake up every day and make a decision that I'm going to be sober. I've got to call a sponsor. I've got to go to a meeting. I've got to read some material. I've got to talk to someone about it to keep myself in check. Every once in a while I take a drug test just to keep myself in line. Whatever I need to do to focus on it. It's cliché, but it's day-to-day. What matters is that today, I stay sober."

78 The NFL Hall of Fame Sculptor

Former BYU reserve running back Blair Buswell, who had one modest carry in his Cougars career, wasn't destined for greatness on the field. But as the chief sculptor for the Pro Football Hall of Fame, he's created the busts of some of the greatest ever to play the game.

Buswell has sculpted the likenesses of legends such as John Elway, Michael Strahan, Deion Sanders, John Madden, Eric Dickerson, Dan Marino, Bill Walsh, Terry Bradshaw, Ronnie Lott, and Barry Sanders, to name a few.

But one bust he produced had special meaning for him. Back in the 1980s, when Steve Young was trying to establish himself as a great professional quarterback and break out of the enormous shadow cast by his predecessor, Joe Montana, Blair Buswell believed Young would one day be in the Pro Football Hall of Fame. When Buswell told Young that, Young laughed. "He thought it was the funniest thing he had ever heard," Buswell recalled.

Buswell met Young when they were teammates at BYU, and they became good friends. He closely followed Young's career with the San Francisco 49ers. Yet Buswell had more than a passing interest in Young's Hall of Fame candidacy in 2005.

Buswell's prediction—and wish—came true when Young was elected to the Hall of Fame. The enshrinement took place in 2005 in Canton, Ohio, and Young was presented for induction by his father, LeGrand "Grit" Young. Prior to that, Buswell and Young spent considerable time together to make sure the bust had just the right look. Buswell unveiled the final product for Young and his wife, Barb, and the couple's two young sons, inside his Pleasant Grove [Utah] studio weeks before the enshrinement. The Youngs were thrilled with the way it turned out.

For Steve Young, being inducted into the Hall of Fame was a supreme honor. And to have his friend be the artist to depict him made it even more special. "It's because Blair was the one who's done it for so long and Blair was the one who told me 15 years ago, 'I'm going to do yours for the Hall of Fame,'" Young said. "That's kind of a neat little story. We've had fun with it, too."

All those years, Buswell had a feeling he would be sculpting Young's bust for the Hall of Fame. "I just kept telling him if he kept up the way he was playing, we'd spend some time together doing it. It's been something I've been looking forward to for a long time."

Barb Young and others close to the Young family provided their input to the project. "Blair did a good job taking 10 years off of Steve," Barb said with a laugh.

It took Steve Young a while to get used to the idea that he would become a member of the Hall of Fame. "It seems like my tail was on fire, then I retired. I never felt like, 'Oh, this was a Hall of Fame career,'" Young said. "I had it in my mind, and a lot of good things happened, but I think because of San Francisco and Joe Montana and the Super Bowls and the expectations and everything, I don't think I ever stopped long enough to say, 'I'm headed to the Hall of Fame.' For me, when it came around, it was the first time my life was slow enough and my tail wasn't on fire anymore and I could stop and say, 'Hey, this is really cool.'"

Buswell's non-HOF work includes the statue of John Wooden in front of Pauley Pavilion at UCLA, Robert Neyland in front of the Neyland Stadium at Tennessee, and Charlton Heston in the National Cowboy & Western Heritage Museum.

79 Quarterback Pioneers: Virgil Carter and Gary Sheide

As the years pass, they've kind of become the forgotten ones. But they should be remembered. Without Virgil Carter and Gary Sheide, there might have been no Quarterback Factory at BYU. At a place where pioneers are honored and held in high esteem, Carter and Sheide were football pioneers in Provo.

Carter, nicknamed the Blue Darter, is regarded as BYU's first great quarterback. Playing for Coach Tommy Hudspeth, Carter led the Cougars to winning seasons in 1965—including the first of many Western Athletic Conference championships for BYU—and 1966.

As a two-time WAC Player of the Year, Carter set six NCAA records (including most total offense in a game (599 yards)), 19 WAC records, and 24 school records. He led the nation in touchdown passes and total offense in 1966.

A highly intelligent student, Carter was named BYU's Outstanding Senior in the College of Physical and Engineering Science and was a Scholastic All-American for two years. He later played professionally for the Chicago Bears and Cincinnati Bengals.

Sheide, a junior college transfer, came along in 1973 out of Northern California when second-year coach LaVell Edwards was installing an offense focused on throwing the ball. Edwards' experiment with the forward pass involved Sheide as the guinea pig. Or, rather, the triggerman.

Before arriving in Provo, Sheide didn't know anything about BYU, other than it was looking for a quarterback who liked to sling the football early and often. "I knew it was a church school. But I didn't know what church," Sheide said. "I was an off-the-wall guy

Exorcising the Devils

At one time, Arizona State was to the Western Athletic Conference what BYU was to the WAC after the Sun Devils left for the Pac-10. In the late 1960s and 1970s, ASU perennially and routinely wreaked havoc and mayhem in the WAC.

That's why the Cougars' 21–18 victory over the Devils in Provo on November 9, 1974, was so historic. In fact, it may have been the turning point of BYU football. "I'd have to say this is the biggest win I've had at BYU," LaVell Edwards said after the game.

During their 16 years in the WAC, ASU posted a 71–18 record, produced players such as John Jefferson, J. D. Hill, Bob Breunig, Curley Culp, and Mike Haynes. "They ruled the roost for a lot of years," Edwards said.

In his third year at the helm, Edwards and his Cougars hosted the vaunted Sun Devils. The victory led to BYU receiving its first-ever bowl berth—the Fiesta Bowl—at the end of the season.

A 55-yard interception return for a touchdown gave ASU an 18–14 advantage late in the third quarter. That's when quarterback Gary Sheide led a nine-play, 80-yard drive that included a key fourth-down run by Jeff Blanc. Capping the drive was a game-winning nine-yard touchdown pass from Sheide to Tim Mahoney. BYU's defense limited ASU to 76 yards rushing and 108 yards passing.

from California. I don't know, maybe I needed them and maybe they needed me. It could be it was fate."

As a senior in 1974, Sheide helped the Cougars climb out of an 0–3–1 start to win seven games in a row (the longest winning streak in BYU history at that time), including wins over Arizona and Arizona State. BYU earned its first bowl berth.

BYU became a national darling that season. For the first time, a national magazine—*Sports Illustrated*—produced an in-depth article on the Cougars football program, titled "Oh What a BYUtiful Mourning...Given Up for Dead, Brigham Young Is Making a Lively Try for a Title."

The national media compared Sheide to Joe Namath of the New York Jets, partially because he wore the same number, 12,

"The attitude about ASU in the past was, to a certain degree, the way people in the WAC viewed us later," said former BYU assistant coach Dick Felt. "ASU had always been a stumbling block for us. We'd always be down 42–0 at halftime. We looked at ASU as the benchmark at that time. We looked at their program as one to become like in terms of success."

That ASU was the standard upon which to measure other programs in the WAC was never lost on Edwards. "When I became the head coach at Brigham Young, one of the first goals I set for our program was to make us competitive with Arizona State University," Edwards wrote in his 1980 book, *LaVell Edwards: Building a Winning Football Tradition at Brigham Young University*. "Some of my most vivid memories involve standing on the sidelines watching strong Arizona State teams run over Brigham Young teams. I figured if we could become good enough to compete evenly with Arizona State we could play with anybody on our schedule. Almost everything we did for a few years was related to beating Arizona State."

In 1974 Edwards finally achieved the breakthrough win his program needed. Four years later, ASU bolted for the Pac-10 and BYU became the perennial king of the WAC for the next 20 years.

and because he had similar physical characteristics and mannerisms. Sheide became BYU's first Sammy Baugh Trophy winner, awarded to the nation's top passer. Six future Cougars would also win that award.

In the first half of the Fiesta Bowl, Sheide led a couple drives that produced field goals, but he sustained a separated shoulder as the Cougars fell to Oklahoma State 16–6. He was drafted in the third round by the Cincinnati Bengals but was waived due to shoulder problems.

Carter and Sheide proved that with the right kind of quarterback, the potential in the passing game was unlimited at BYU.

80 Married with Children at Bowl Games

BYU bowl trips are unlike those at any other school. Many Cougars players are typically older, having served missions, and dozens of them are married. Some have children. And when the players go to bowl games, they are allowed to bring their wives and children, which can create quite a scene at times.

Rich Rodriguez remembered playing BYU in the 1998 Liberty Bowl when he was Tulane's offensive coordinator. One of his memories involved witnessing the school's entourage. "We had a function at the hotel, and there's all these little kids running around, and I said, 'Man, [the BYU] coaching staff has a lot of kids,'" Rodriguez remembered in 2016. "They said, 'No, those are the players' kids.'"

When the Cougars played in the Fight Hunger Bowl in San Francisco in 2013, linebacker Alani Fua brought his wife, Malaysia, and their two young sons. It meant spending Christmas in a hotel room.

Some families celebrate Christmas, and open presents, before they arrive at the bowl destination. It's too tough to lug gifts in suitcases, after all. "They limit us to just one bag per person," defensive lineman Byron Frisch said before the 1999 Motor City Bowl. He had two children at that time.

Anytime BYU goes to bowl game festivities, it's sure to turn heads. "As the Brigham Young University entourage trooped into the lobby of the Hyatt Regency last week, [BYU] athletic director Rondo Fehlberg looked around and grinned," wrote Whit Canning of the *Fort Worth Star-Telegram* on the 1996 Cougars preparing for the Cotton Bowl. "'That flight we just got off was probably the strangest team charter those [airline] folks ever saw,' he said. The evidence, indeed was around him: football players walking through the lobby carrying babies in their arms, wives pushing strollers up to the registration desk, blue-clad fans looking a bit like Scoutmasters organizing a field trip. It looked more like a mass migration from Middle America than the arrival of a hard-nosed juggernaut with 13 victories. It was in fact a gathering of 'the Saints'—Mormons, followers of The Church of Jesus Christ of Latter-day Saints—a fact that stamps the Cougars as a unique powerhouse in college football. Their victims have enjoyed the distinction of getting their noses bloodied by a team that contains 36 Eagle Scouts and many players who have spent two years in locales around the world on church missions, at their own expense."

Yes, bowl trips at BYU are a family affair.

81 The Block(s)

BYU's Eathyn Manumaleuna started every game at nose tackle as a true freshman in 2007. His final play as a freshman is simply known as the Block. With three seconds remaining in the 2007 Las Vegas Bowl, Manumaleuna blocked UCLA's potential game-winning 28-yard field goal, preserving a dramatic 17–16 Cougars victory. "For a game to end on a play like that, with that kind of surge and that kind of effort, is unbelievable," said quarterback Max Hall.

Manumaleuna got his fingertips on Kai Forbath's field goal attempt, which fell just short of the crossbar as time expired. "It was ugly, but I'll take it," said linebacker Bryan Kehl. "That was close.

Too close for comfort. We needed to make one more play, and our will, our heart, our desire won the game."

What does Manumaleuna remember about that block? "I just remember that with three seconds left, I saw the UCLA sideline going crazy, thinking they were going to win," he said. "They had a pretty good kicker. Honestly, I thought we were going to lose. It was the last play, so I knew we had to give it all we had. I really didn't watch the kicker kick the ball. I didn't see the ball. I just jumped. It was lucky timing, I guess. The kicker kicked the ball pretty low. I barely tipped it. It felt good."

That last play was emblematic of the team philosophy instilled by coach Bronco Mendenhall. "What I saw was an incredible surge. We sent all 11 [players], which is a desperation block," Mendenhall said. "They looked at each other before they went back out, and a couple of them thought they would be the one to get it. I saw enough of the tip to see it start spiraling. But I wasn't sure then if that would be enough. It was close to the crossbar, and I didn't know if it went through or not at that point. It will be a great play to use as an example for our program for a long time, because it was a play of will."

Prior to the snap, Brett Denney was shouting encouragement to Manumaleuna. "He was giving me inspirational advice," Manumaleuna said. "He told me to go all-out. He pumped me up and I was able to get a good push. I don't know how I jumped; I don't have a high [vertical]."

UCLA's reaction was much different, of course. "I feel they got lucky," said Bruins defensive back Chris Horton.

With the victory, BYU extended its winning streak to 10 games and finished its second straight season with an 11–2 record. Not long after that game, Manumaleuna left for an LDS mission to Oklahoma City.

Early the following season, defensive lineman Jan Jorgensen executed another game-winning block in the waning seconds.

Jorgensen managed to knock down a 35-yard extra point attempt by Washington's Ryan Perkins to cap a thrilling 28–27 victory over the Huskies.

The blocked PAT was preceded by a three-yard touchdown run with two seconds remaining in the game by Washington quarterback Jake Locker, who chucked the ball high in the air in celebration after his score and incurred a 15-yard unsportsman-like conduct penalty. On the ensuing PAT, Jorgensen penetrated Washington's line and got his hand on Perkins' potential game-tying PAT kick. "It was a very similar situation [to the UCLA game]," Jorgensen said. "I thought about that right when they scored. I was like, 'We're going to block it. We've been here before. We're going to do it.'"

With that win, the Cougars not only snapped their dubious nine-game nonconference road losing streak, but they also extended their overall winning streak to 12 games.

Manumaleuna returned prior to the 2010 season. He certainly wasn't forgotten during his two-year absence from the program. A local artist, George Durrant, captured Manumaleuna's memorable block in a painting that hangs in BYU's Student Athlete Building.

Manumaleuna was surprised that so many people brought up that play to him during his mission. "Because of where I served, I didn't think anyone would know about it," he said. "There wasn't a day that went by that I didn't think about it at least once."

82 Learn and Sing the Cougars Fight Song

The Cougar Song
Brigham Young University
Clyde D. Sandgren, 1932

Rise all loyal Cougars and hurl your challenge to the foe.
You will fight, day or night, rain or snow.
Loyal, strong, and true
Wear the white and blue.
While we sing, get set to spring.
Come on Cougars it's up to you. Oh!

[Chorus]
Rise and shout, the Cougars are out
along the trail to fame and glory.
Rise and shout, our cheers will ring out
As you unfold your victr'y story.

On you go to vanquish the foe for Alma Mater's sons and daughters.
As we join in song, in praise of you, our faith is strong.
We'll raise our colors high in the blue
And cheer our Cougars of BYU

Every true BYU fan knows the words to BYU athletics' anthem, "The Cougar Song," which is played and sung at sporting events in Provo. It is popularly known as "Rise and Shout."

Fans traditionally remain seated for the first verse, then they "rise and shout" with the chorus. At LaVell Edwards Stadium, the song is played by the band after every Cougars touchdown.

The song was written in 1932 by Clyde D. Sandgren, a 1937 graduate of BYU. While "The Cougar Song" was composed in 1932, it was not copyrighted and presented to BYU until 1947. Sandgren dedicated the song "to all BYU students who so valiantly served their country in World War II." Prior to "The Cougar Song," students and alumni sang "The College Song," written in 1899 by Annie Pike Greenwood. This song is still sung at alumni events.

After graduating from BYU, Sandgren earned a law degree from St. John's University and became a partner in the New York law firm Burroughs and Brown. In 1947 Sandgren returned to Provo to set up his own law practice. Years later, he served as alumni association president and general counsel and vice president of BYU before his death in 1989.

In the 1990s the lyrics of "The Cougar Song" were altered slightly in order to be more politically correct. The line "Loyal, strong, and true" was changed from "Stalwart men and true."

83 A 54-Foot Buzzer-Beater to Win a Championship

Kevin Nixon hadn't shot well during the BYU-UTEP Western Athletic Conference Championship Game in Fort Collins, Colorado, in 1992. But Coach Roger Reid sent him to the floor with 2.4 seconds remaining. The Cougars trailed the Miners 71–70 and needed to go the full length of the court to have a chance to win.

BYU inbounded the ball from underneath its own basket. Nixon received the pass about 15 feet inbounds, dribbled upcourt, and hoisted up a 54-foot prayer that hit nothing but net, leaving

UTEP and its legendary coach, Don Haskins, stunned. That shot gave BYU its first-ever WAC tournament title and another trip to the NCAA Tournament.

Immediately following the game, Nixon said of his shot, "I knew it had a chance to go in. I had an idea it would be near the basket." That shot received an ESPY nomination for Shot of the Year.

"With 2.4 seconds left, anything can happen," Nixon recalled. "And I'm living proof of that. It's a shot that you dream about, getting a chance just to take, let alone making it."

Reid called three timeouts to design a play that might work. The first play he drew up had Nixon inbounding the ball. Instead, Nixon was instructed to let it fly if he got the ball. "I knew I didn't have a lot of time," he recalled. "I figured I had enough time for one or two dribbles. My plan was to get a couple dribbles in and hope and pray for the best."

After his shot went in, Nixon ran around on the court as his teammates chased him and mobbed him. Unfortunately, the Cougars went on to lose to Louisiana State and Shaquille O'Neal in the first round of the NCAA Tournament.

But that wasn't the only game-changing shot of Nixon's career. That famous shot in the WAC tournament overshadows what Nixon accomplished several months later in Hawaii.

In November 1992 the Cougars faced No. 9 Oklahoma in the prestigious Maui Invitational at the Lahaina Civic Center. Nixon snatched a long offensive rebound with about three seconds remaining, and amid a pair of defenders, he coolly knocked down a 14-footer as time expired to propel BYU to a 76–75 upset of the Sooners.

"I bet if you polled BYU fans, they'd say, 'Oh, yeah, I kind of remember that now,'" Nixon said of his shot to beat Oklahoma in Maui. "But the WAC championship and that whole thing kind of overrides everything, and the Maui shot gets lost in the shuffle a little bit."

Kevin Nixon's heroics in Hawaii didn't stop with the Oklahoma game. In the second game of the 1992 Maui Invitational, the Cougars faced All-American and future NBA star Anfernee Hardaway and the Memphis Tigers. Hardaway finished with 37 points, but Nixon struck again. He hit a three-pointer to tie the game at 63 with 1:09 to play in regulation. Then, in overtime, he drained another three with 56 seconds remaining to put the Cougars up 69–67.

Nixon finished with 14 points, and BYU ended up winning 73–67 to earn a spot in the Maui Invitational Championship Game against No. 1–ranked defending national champions Duke, which had Hall of Fame coach Mike Krzyzewski and stars such as Bobby Hurley, Grant Hill, and Cherokee Parks. The Cougars fell 89–66. "Everyone expected us to get beat all the way through," Kevin Nixon recalled. "To upset Oklahoma and Memphis and go to the championship game was a little crazy."

That he played at all in the Maui Invitational was a minor miracle. "Before that tournament, I was having some back problems," he said. "I didn't know how much I was going to be able to play because of my back. The long plane ride to Hawaii didn't help. I wasn't sure how much I was going to play and how well I would play. I ended up having a really good tournament—at least the first two games."

84 Taysom Hill

When Taysom Hill, who signed with Stanford and then-coach Jim Harbaugh out of high school, decided during his mission that he would attend BYU instead, the Cougars already had a top quarterback prospect on their roster—Jake Heaps.

Hill was in the Los Angeles International Airport in December 2011, on his way home from serving a mission in Sydney, Australia, when he learned Heaps was transferring.

Hill, a Pocatello, Idaho, native, chose to attend BYU partly because Harbaugh had left to coach the San Francisco 49ers. Also, Stanford didn't allow incoming freshmen to enroll until June or August. Stanford's coaches wanted Hill to come back five months early from his mission, something Hill didn't want to do. So he explored his options instead.

As it turned out, Hill had one of the most star-crossed careers of any BYU athlete. He won 23 games as a starter; rolled up 9,744 yards of total offense, which ranks No. 4 in school history, one spot ahead of Jim McMahon; passed for 6,929 yards and 43 touchdowns; and rushed for 2,815 yards and 32 touchdowns, making him the most prolific rushing QB at BYU and No. 5 all-time amongst rushers. All told, he accounted for 75 touchdowns.

But part of Hill's legacy will be the question: What could he have accomplished had he stayed healthy? Hill suffered four season-ending injuries and, eerily, three of them came against the Aggies—in 2012 (knee), 2014 (leg), and 2016 (elbow), each in Provo. Hill's 2015 season ended with a Lisfranc injury in the season opener at Nebraska.

In the closing moments of BYU's 6–3 victory over the Aggies in 2012, a communication mishap from the Cougars sideline had

Hill, then a freshman, rushing up the middle instead of taking a knee. USU safety Brian Suite drilled Hill's knees. Hill limped back to the huddle and finished the game. The following day, it was announced that Hill would be sidelined for the final seven games with a knee injury.

Late in the first half of the 2014 game against Utah State, Hill, who was a Heisman Trophy candidate at the time, faked a handoff and scrambled right. Suite rolled up on Hill's leg as he tackled him. Hill limped off the field and left the game with a fractured leg. And his season with over just five games into that season. Oddly, the two tackles by Suite against Hill happened at almost the same spot on the field.

In the 2015 season opener at Nebraska, Hill injured his foot while running for a touchdown in the first half. Hill continued playing into the second half, though he had been diagnosed with a Lisfranc injury.

The following February, Hill announced he would be returning to BYU, though he had options to play elsewhere as a graduate transfer. The NCAA granted Hill a medical redshirt to play one final season at BYU.

Hill was limited during spring drills, and just prior to the spring game, he learned about the unexpected death of his older brother, Dexter. Hill decided to switch his jersey from No. 4 to No. 7 for his final season—to honor his brother.

Many wondered if Hill would change his style of play to avoid injuries in the future. "I just want to win. This is the conversation I've had since my freshman year here, right?" Hill said. "You guys ask, 'What are you doing to stay healthy? Are you going to slide?' My response is, 'I'm going to do what it takes to win a football game.' That's my mentality."

Due to the rash of injuries he suffered, Hill wasn't as fast in 2016 as he had been in 2015 and earlier. But he was still a physical play maker. Hill's final play in a BYU uniform epitomized his approach to the game: Early in the fourth quarter in the Cougars' 28–10 victory over Utah State in the regular-season finale, Hill tried to hurdle an Aggies defender at the end of a 12-yard run. He crashed hard to the turf, with his weight coming down on his left elbow. Two days later, the school announced Hill had suffered a left elbow strain and that his BYU career was over.

Hill, who could do a 430-pound front squat, will be remembered for his ability to stiff-arm would-be tacklers and fight for extra yards on third downs.

One of BYU's greatest quarterbacks, Heisman Trophy winner and offensive coordinator Ty Detmer, called Hill "probably the greatest athlete to play the quarterback position here."

When Coach Bronco Mendenhall left BYU for Virginia at the end of the 2015 season, he gushed about Hill, who he tried to recruit to Charlottesville. "We prefer to have a running threat, if possible. If [he] was a superhero, our quarterback would look like Thor, really," he said. "That kind of guy. So if you're asking 'What do we want?' We want a Thor-terback."

85 Bands of Brothers

The BYU football program has referred to itself as a Band of Brothers—and that works both figuratively and literally. Dozens of sets of brothers have played football at BYU, some at the same time. Once, Coach LaVell Edwards was talking to Joy Bellini, the mother of stars Mark and Matt Bellini. "You've given us Matthew and Mark. Where are Luke and John?" Edwards cracked.

Four Doman brothers (Kevin, Bryce, Cliff, and Brandon) and four Reynolds brothers (Lance Jr., Dallas, Matt, and Houston) have played for BYU. There have other talented brother combinations with the following surnames: Staley (Dustin and Luke), Collie (Zac and Austin), Kehl (Ed and Bryan), Young (Mike, Steve, and Tom), Whittingham (Kyle, Cary, and Fred), Poppinga (Brady and Kelly), Oates (Brad, Bart, and Barry), Denney (Ryan, John, and Brett), Heimuli (Lakei and Hema), Payne (Matt and Mitch), Warner (Fred and Troy), Raass (John and Stan), Kaufusi (Steve and Rich; Bronson and Corbin), Marquardt (Michael and Daniel), and Pochman (Ethan and Owen)—to name just a handful of examples.

In 2006 BYU had seven sets of brothers on its roster at the same time: Rex and Sam Doman, Erik and Ryan Freeman, Braden and Brock Hansen, Hala and Temana Paongo, Manase and Matangi Tonga, John and Andrew Beck, and Jeff and Tom Sorensen.

From 2013 to 2016, identical twin brothers Mitchell and Garrett Juergens played for BYU. Naturally, some would get the twins mixed up. And some just admitted they couldn't tell them apart. One day during fall camp in 2015, offensive coordinator Robert Anae and Mitchell Juergens ran into each other in the Student Athlete Building.

"Are you the healthy one or the hurt one?" Anae asked him.

"The healthy one," Mitchell said.

Weeks later, after BYU knocked off nationally ranked Boise State in a thriller, Garrett Juergens showed up at church Sunday and was enthusiastically greeted by fellow LDS ward members. "Nice catch!" some of them said. Problem is, it was his identical twin brother, Mitchell, who had hauled in Tanner Mangum's 35-yard touchdown pass with 45 seconds remaining to put the Cougars ahead for good 28–24.

"For a second, I want[ed] to play it off just not to make them feel awkward," Garrett said, smiling. "But that could [have gone] on for the whole season. I [had] to correct them. I had to tell them, 'That's my twin brother, not me.'"

At the time, Garrett was injured and couldn't play. "He was playing for me," Garrett said of Mitchell. "When I broke my collarbone, it was harder on him than it was on me. I was controlled and he came into the locker room and started crying. To say we have twin telepathy would be a lie, because I can't feel his pain. But emotionally we feel everything for each other. He knew how bad I wanted a good fall camp. To see me go down, he knew how hard it would be for me. I [knew he was] playing for me a little bit because he [wrote] my number on his arm. [It was] awesome to be out there with him, even though I [couldn't] be out there."

Isn't that what brothers are for?

86 Derwin Gray

As a popular safety at BYU in the early 1990s, Derwin "Dewey" Gray knew how to whip sellout crowds in Provo into a frenzy. "I distinctly remember running out on the field and waving my arms, and 60,000-plus people would go crazy," Gray said. "I remember one game where, at the end, one entire section of the stadium was chanting my name."

That was a validating experience for a non-LDS African American young man from San Antonio, Texas, who was raised without a father and around family members who struggled with substance abuse and found themselves in and out of jail.

On top of that, Gray grew up with a stuttering problem, and he lacked confidence in himself. At that time, his savior was football. "I had seen so much dysfunction and violence that football for me from the age of 14 wasn't a game, it was a job," Gray said. "It was a passport to get me out of where I was. In many ways, I wasn't religious, but football was my God. The religious side didn't matter to me because football at that time gave me everything I needed. It gave me identity."

During his four years in Provo, Gray learned to adapt to a new culture on a predominantly white LDS campus. He enjoyed playing for a legendary coach, LaVell Edwards. In 1990 against New Mexico, Gray recorded three interceptions—tying a school record—including one he returned for a touchdown. He recorded 19 tackles in a game at Penn State in 1991. BYU is also where he met his wife, Vicki, a track athlete who specialized in the javelin.

Ironically, it wasn't until after he left BYU—while playing in the NFL—that he found religion. Since retiring from football after a six-year NFL career, Gray graduated magna cum laude from Southern Evangelical Seminary with a master of divinity degree.

In January 2010 he became the lead pastor of the Transformation Church, with campuses south of Charlotte, North Carolina. The Transformational Church has been recognized by *Outreach* magazine as one of the fastest-growing churches in the United States.

Gray—touted as the Evangelism Linebacker—is an eloquent, charismatic speaker. He has written a handful of books, and he writes a blog titled *Just Marinating*.

The man who used to stammer his way through interviews as a player has delivered speeches in places such as India, Germany, and all over the United States. The man who barely got a high enough score on his ACT to get into college has not only earned a master's degree but is working on a doctorate degree, and received an honorary doctorate degree.

"I view myself as a spiritual football coach," Gray said. "Life is the game, God is the team owner, and I'm a coach. People need to hear and understand the gospel in real terms. Everybody wants to hear your story. Within my story is everybody's story." Gray never imagined 20 years ago that he'd be a church pastor. "I am as surprised as anyone with the unfolding journey that God has me on," he said.

Gray played in the NFL from 1993 to 1998. But what he has accomplished off the field is just as impressive. Gray has had to overcome plenty of obstacles along the way. "The very things

Derwin Gray gets his game face on before his Indianapolis Colts face the Dolphins in 1995.

you think are your disadvantage, God will use in your life to your advantage," he said. "I didn't grow up with a father. It made me long for my Heavenly Father, which now makes me, according to my wife, a great father. I grew up as a compulsive stutterer. Now I get to speak around the world because of the power of God."

Gray appreciates the role BYU played in his life. "It was very good for me to go to BYU because it gave me some social skills that are helping me now," he said. "I respect the LDS culture and the commitment to the cause to which they live by."

Gray, who once could get BYU fans excited about a football game, now stands in front of crowds on a different stage, devoting his life to getting others to come closer to God.

"There are a lot of people who helped me get to where I am. Jesus teaches us that He's going to help you," he said. "That pattern in my life is, I want to wake up every morning and say, 'Whose life can I make better today?' The more I do that, the better my life gets."

87 LaVell's 200ᵗʰ Victory

It seemed only fitting that the game in which LaVell Edwards earned his 200th career victory (something only 13 other men had accomplished at the time in the history of college football—men such as Paul "Bear" Bryant, Amos Alonzo Stagg, Joe Paterno, Bobby Bowden, Bo Schembechler, and Tom Osborne) would be a wild and wacky high-scoring affair against a WAC opponent.

Edwards will always be remembered for his teams' heart-pounding finishes, and BYU's 49–47 triumph over New Mexico on September 24, 1994, was just that. The win didn't come easy.

The outcome remained in doubt until late after the never-say-lose Lobos' constant comeback attempts, and their attempt to keep Edwards stuck on 199 career wins.

In the end, though, LaVell got LaVictory. He was doused with a large jug of liquid, carried around the field on the shoulders of his players, and was even seen giving high-fives to fans. He actually got emotional.

But in the pressroom afterward, he felt more like relaxing than celebrating. His postgame comments were typically droll. It wasn't like he had passed an incredible milestone; it was like he had just come out of surgery after passing a gallstone. "It becomes a nagging problem," he said about all the talk and hype surrounding No. 200. "I'm glad we've gotten it taken care of. It's a feeling of sheer relief."

One of the players he could credit for the win was tight end Chad Lewis, who caught a 21-yard second-quarter touchdown pass from John Walsh, blocked a field goal, and recovered a UNM onside kick with minutes remaining. The only thing he didn't do was hoist Edwards onto his shoulders during the postgame party. "I tried," Lewis explained, "but some of the other guys boxed me out."

Still, the game was far from a one-man show for BYU. Running back Jamal Willis rushed for 204 yards and two touchdowns, including a 39-yard fourth-quarter gallop. Hema Heimuli scored three touchdowns. After his 31-yard TD catch, Heimuli chucked the ball into the crowd and the Cougars were promptly penalized 15 yards for unsportsmanlike conduct. "It's been a lifelong dream of mine," Heimuli said of throwing a ball into the stands. "I knew LaVell was going to yell at me, which he did."

Walsh completed 18 of 24 passes for 228 yards and three touchdowns. "I'm just happy with the way we played as a team," Walsh said. "I wish [the 200th win] would have been last week." Yes, one week earlier, with fanfare surrounding the impending milestone, BYU lost at home to Colorado State, 28–21.

BYU led New Mexico 49–33 before the Lobos scored two quick touchdowns to cut the deficit to 49–47. On UNM's ensuing onside kick, the ball bounced off a BYU player. "It just came squirting out," Lewis said. "I was standing there, and there it was. It bounced right to me. I jumped on it then got up as fast as I could because there were punks all over me trying to get the ball away."

For Lewis, he was willing to do whatever it took to get LaVell Edwards his 200th victory that day. "I'm just so honored to be a part of it," he said. "LaVell's my hero. He was when I was growing up, and he still is. I love LaVell."

88 Shades of Blue and Uniform Changes

Just before the turn of the century, BYU's colors and uniforms underwent a drastic facelift. In August 1999 the school ended months of speculation, announcing it was altering the image of its teams by switching uniform colors from royal blue to navy blue, or what former BYU president Merrill J. Bateman famously termed "the darkest shade of royal blue."

Partnering with Nike, the school also introduced tan as an accent color and unveiled a new family of logos. The football team wore new uniforms with a tan trim, blue helmets, and a white "bib" on the home version.

Leave it to conservative BYU to make a bold fashion statement. It was a controversial move. "I don't know why we changed," BYU offensive coordinator Norm Chow said at the time. "[Utah coach] Ron McBride said they look like LaVell must have taken the team to Red Lobster and forgot to take their bibs off."

The decision to change BYU's sports identity wasn't taken lightly. The entire process took three years to complete but was especially intensified over an 18-month period when BYU retained the services of Sean Michael Edwards Design.

The New York City firm, which also designed new looks for the Denver Broncos and Utah Jazz, among others, came up with logos BYU men's athletic director Val Hale said Cougars fans would appreciate. He explained that a lot of research had gone into the new logo designs. Interviews were conducted with athletic administrators, fans, coaches, athletes, and alumni to determine needs and priorities. Many respondents also felt a departure from bright royal blue was necessary.

Fortunately for BYU, the bib experiment lasted only one year. "It was Nike's suggestion that we try it. They wanted to see if they could differentiate their product from other products, and we were the guinea pigs," President Bateman explained. "In the end, the NCAA made the rule you couldn't use the bib because they thought it was confusing."

One of the reasons for the change was to increase the sales of merchandise. Apparently it worked. Sales of BYU-related items in 2003 were 40 percent higher than they had been in 1998, the last full year that royal blue apparel was sold.

The Cougars' football uniforms stayed relatively the same from 2000 until the end of the 2004 season. But BYU's record from 1999 to 2004 was a mediocre 40–33, which included a 12–2 campaign in Coach Gary Crowton's first season, and three straight losing seasons from 2002 to 2004.

When Bronco Mendenhall was hired at the end of the 2004 season, he wanted BYU to return to its roots by bringing back traditional uniforms and the traditional *Y* logo. "This is the look of the future, and it reflects the past," Mendenhall said before the 2005 campaign. "This isn't about BYU having new uniforms. This is about honoring tradition. This is about respect for and accountability to the coaches and players who have made BYU one of the pillars of college football. They represent a tradition of over 30 years of excellence, both on and off the field."

BYU and Nike approved the change in the spring of 2005, but Nike informed the school there was not enough time for the uniform change prior to the football season. Mendenhall called upon Edwards, who used his considerable clout and spoke with Nike. The next morning, the request was granted and the Cougars returned to their traditional uniforms—though staying with the navy blue color—in the fall of 2005, in time for Mendenhall's debut as head coach.

In 2009 BYU reintroduced royal blue throwback uniforms, and later blackout jerseys debuted in 2012. Both have been used sparingly.

While blue—either navy blue or royal blue—are synonymous with BYU sports, the Cougars also wore orange accents for a couple seasons in the early 1940s.

89 BYU and ESPN

Dating back to the mid-1980s, BYU and ESPN have forged a strong relationship. Both institutions helped each other reach new heights. About the time the fledgling all-sports network debuted in 1979, the Cougars were breaking onto the national scene. When ESPN began broadcasting live regular-season games in 1984, the first one it aired was a game on September 1, 1984, between BYU and Pittsburgh. The Cougars won 20–14 in dramatic fashion, to kick off a season that ended in a national championship. At one time, several of ESPN's highest-rated college football games involved BYU.

BYU's Bowl History

Year	Bowl	Site	Score
1974	Fiesta	Tempe, Arizona	Oklahoma State 16, BYU 6
1976	Tangerine	Orlando	Oklahoma State 49, BYU 21
1978	Holiday	San Diego	Navy 23, BYU 16
1979	Holiday	San Diego	Indiana 38, BYU 37
1980	Holiday	San Diego	BYU 46, SMU 45
1981	Holiday	San Diego	BYU 38, Washington State 36
1982	Holiday	San Diego	Ohio State 47, BYU 17
1983	Holiday	San Diego	BYU 21, Missouri 17
1984	Holiday	San Diego	BYU 24, Michigan 17
1985	Citrus	Orlando	Ohio State 10, BYU 7
1986	Freedom	Anaheim, California	UCLA 31, BYU 10
1987	All-American	Birmingham	Virginia 22, BYU 16
1988	Freedom	Anaheim, California	BYU 20, Colorado 17
1989	Holiday	San Diego	Penn State 50, BYU 39
1990	Holiday	San Diego	Texas A&M 65, BYU 14
1991	Holiday	San Diego	BYU 13, Iowa 13
1992	Aloha	Honolulu	Kansas 23, BYU 20
1993	Holiday	San Diego	Ohio State 28, BYU 21
1994	Copper	Tucson,	BYU 31, Oklahoma 6
1997	Cotton	Dallas	BYU 19, Kansas State 15
1998	Liberty	Memphis	Tulane 41, BYU 27
1999	Motor City	Detroit	Marshall 21, BYU 3
2001	Liberty	Memphis	Louisville 28, BYU 10
2005	Las Vegas	Las Vegas	California 35, BYU 28
2006	Las Vegas	Las Vegas	BYU 38, Oregon 8
2007	Las Vegas	Las Vegas	BYU 17, UCLA 16
2008	Las Vegas	Las Vegas	Arizona 31, BYU 21
2009	Las Vegas	Las Vegas	BYU 44, Oregon State 20
2010	New Mexico	Albuquerque	BYU 52, UTEP 24
2011	Armed Forces	Dallas	BYU 24, Tulsa 21
2012	Poinsettia	San Diego	BYU 23, San Diego State 6
2013	Fight Hunger	San Francisco	Washington 31, BYU 16
2014	Miami Beach	Miami	Memphis 55, BYU 48 (2 OT)
2015	Las Vegas	Las Vegas	Utah 35, BYU 28
2016	Poinsettia	San Diego	BYU 24, Wyoming 21

So it was only natural that when the Cougars decided in 2010 to go independent, they formed a long-term partnership with the Worldwide Leader in Sports.

BYU became the only school to sign an exclusive contract with ESPN. One of the stated reasons for going independent was exposure, which ESPN provides. "This is just a tremendous day for ESPN to be back in business with BYU in a formal basis. It's a tremendous addition to our college football schedule," said Dave Brown, ESPN vice president of programming and acquisitions. "We're anxious to rekindle that partnership and be able to come back to BYU with every game here over the next eight years. That's something we're really looking forward to. We have had a great relationship with BYU over the years, thanks in part to LaVell Edwards, who gave us so many signature games in the past that really put ESPN on the map in terms of being a college football destination network."

Not only does ESPN own exclusive rights to broadcast BYU home games, but it provides BYU with the financial foundation to be an independent. According to estimates, BYU earns between $3.2 million and $6 million per year, between $800,000 and $1.2 million per home game, for football. As part of the contract, the Cougars are guaranteed four home games a year on ESPN channels.

In addition, ESPN is instrumental in helping BYU with scheduling both home and road games, and securing bowl ties. Scheduling is a difficult, painstaking process filled with discussions, negotiations, and contracts. As an independent, BYU must schedule 12 regular-season games every year. For athletic director Tom Holmoe, the scheduling process takes up a significant amount of his time, but the influence of ESPN makes it a little easier. "I work on football scheduling several times each week. Opportunities come along and I have good dialogue with other schools, and on occasion conferences," Holmoe said, adding that he talks extensively with his football coach about scheduling. "We talk through

BYUtv

As an independent football program, BYU is in a unique position, and faces a unique dilemma. Amid the unsettled landscape of college football, featuring conference realignment machinations with schools severing longtime rivalries and league affiliations, the Cougars are considered a Power 5 program in terms of history and accomplishments.

Making independence possible for BYU is an eight-year broadcasting deal with ESPN signed in 2011, as well as its own television network, BYUtv, which boasts state-of-the-art facilities and state-of-the art capabilities. BYUtv is light-years ahead of what any other school in the country currently has in terms of resources. That's a big part of the BYU-ESPN partnership.

BYU's football program is receiving unprecedented exposure in terms of the number of games on national TV. Fans across the country, and around the world, are able to watch the Cougars play on a regular basis thanks to ESPN and BYUtv. BYU has been on the ESPN family of networks numerous times.

For years, as a member of the Mountain West Conference, BYU had many of its games broadcast on channels that many viewers had never heard of, let alone had access to. In 2011 the BYU–Oregon State game showcased the vast capabilities of BYUtv. Because BYU has its own HD broadcast truck, the school was able to work with various entities—the Pac-12, Fox Sports, and Oregon State—to

issues such as home versus away games, travel distance, placement of games, and bye weeks. So much of scheduling is a matter of finding balance. Our contacts at ESPN call regularly about potential schedule opportunities and to discuss possible matchups. This is another example of how the ESPN contract is a win-win situation for BYU."

Former coach Bronco Mendenhall saw firsthand the impact of ESPN on scheduling. "The power of ESPN has absolutely amazed me to this point, of what teams will do to get on ESPN," Mendenhall said. "ESPN is ESPN. People move games to be on ESPN. They'll move from a date to get on ESPN."

produce and televise the contest in Corvallis. That live broadcast, on KBYU, was the highest-rated college football game that weekend in the Salt Lake market.

BYU Broadcasting senior coordinating producer Mikel Minor worked for six years at ESPN producing *SportsCenter* before returning to his alma mater. "People are tired of me saying this, but it's been validated by all of my associates at ESPN who have been coming to Provo and doing the games," Minor said. "They see our HD truck, they see our facilities, and they say nothing else exists like this in the country. It's so unique that a university has this quality of facilities. It's so similar to ESPN. And to have state-of-the-art resources that you have access to, it makes my job so much easier."

On game days, BYU and ESPN pool their resources, sharing cameras and other equipment. ESPN allows BYUtv to produce pregame and postgame shows, even tossing back and forth between the pregame show and the ESPN broadcast. Then BYUtv urges viewers to watch the game on ESPN.

"It's a great setting to do [a college football broadcast]. The atmosphere in and around the stadium is great," said ESPN producer Steve Ackels. "It's a collaborative effort by ESPN and BYUtv to put on the best broadcast that we can. We realize that we're a team. There are cameras and equipment that we can share on site that make the broadcast better."

Among the challenges of independent scheduling is enduring a frontloaded schedule against Power 5 conference opponents. It's difficult to schedule those types of opponents in the month of November, when most teams are hip-deep in conference play. "Obviously schools are in the homestretch of their conference schedule in November, so scheduling games can be a challenge," Holmoe said. "We are working with some conferences to consider occasional exceptions that would benefit both parties. It's one of the realities of being an independent football program. There are certainly pros and cons, but the exposure has been fantastic—even better than I thought it would be."

Football in the 1890s and the Birth of a Rivalry

Officially, BYU started its football program in 1922. But the sport traces its beginnings at BYU to some 30 years earlier. In the 1890s, when the school was known as Brigham Young Academy, it played a variety of sports. Back then, the forward pass was illegal, Provo had a population of 6,000, and the school had an enrollment of just a few hundred students.

The first football game between Brigham Young Academy and Utah occurred in April 1896 in Salt Lake City, with Utah winning 12–4. When the game ended, according to reports, fans from both schools started brawling. According to Brigham Young Academy, the fight that took place was started by locals who provoked and badgered BYA fans who had traveled north to support their team. When they had enough of the verbal abuse, they retaliated. Afterward, according to one writer, "the hoodlums looked like they had been through a sausage mill."

Utah counts the six football games played against BYU in the 1890s as part of the overall series record, while BYU does not recognize those games because they happened when the school was known as BYA.

Even earlier than the first football game, BYA and the University of Utah met to play baseball for the first sporting event between the two institutions in the 1890s. The scoreless game ended with a bench-clearing brawl. That's all it took. That's how the BYU-Utah rivalry began.

When it came to football, BYUA and LDS Church leaders feared the dangerous nature of the sport. Numerous people around the country were killed in those days while playing football, and President Theodore Roosevelt threatened to outlaw the game. So the school dropped football, later bringing it back in 1922. It took BYU 20 years to register its first victory over Utah in football.

91 Edwards' NFL Influence: Mike Holmgren, Andy Reid, and Brian Billick

Not only did LaVell Edwards make a major impact on college football, but his influence also extended into the National Football League. Two of his quarterbacks, Jim McMahon and Steve Young, led their teams to Super Bowl titles, and one of his tight ends, Brian Billick, ended up leading the Baltimore Ravens to a Super Bowl championship as a coach. In fact, one of Edwards' former players has been involved in almost every Super Bowl since the mid-1970s.

One of his quarterbacks coaches was Mike Holmgren, who was on Edwards' staff from 1982 to 1985. Holmgren went from BYU to the San Francisco 49ers, where he served as quarterbacks coach and, later, as offensive coordinator. He coached Steve Young both with the Cougars and the 49ers. He also coached Joe Montana. In 1992 Holmgren became the head coach of the Green Bay Packers, where he played a key role in the development of Brett Favre. Holmgren led the Packers to a victory in Super Bowl XXXI. Later, as the head coach of the Seattle Seahawks, he took the franchise to its first Super Bowl appearance.

Edwards hired Holmgren from San Francisco State after receiving a recommendation from a friend. "He didn't have a lot of college experience," Edwards recalled. "He was with us for four years. He did a great job."

Holmgren once said of his four seasons with Edwards: "Coach Edwards took a real chance in hiring me as a high school coach basically to coach the quarterbacks at BYU. And a lot of my philosophy today is based on the way he treated people, the way he did things. It was an honor to work for him."

One of Holmgren's assistants at Green Bay was former BYU offensive lineman Andy Reid, who would go on to become a successful NFL coach in his own right with the Philadelphia Eagles and Kansas City Chiefs. Reid's teams have always seemed to have roster spots for former BYU players, such as Chad Lewis, Reno Mahe, and Dan Sorensen. "The kids that I've had…I do make a conscious effort of bringing them in because I'm a little partial," Reid told KSL Radio in 2013. "Fifty-one percent of me believes I love BYU, and I have 51 percent of the vote, so that's a good thing. I can bring these guys in and give them an opportunity."

Reid credits Edwards for introducing him to the coaching profession. "Well, he actually asked me if I ever thought about being a coach when I was still playing," Reid said. "At that time I hadn't. He's the one that kind of led me in that direction. I took a look at it. He gave me an opportunity to be a graduate assistant up there after I was done playing. I loved it. So that's the direction I headed."

In 2003 Reid told *Sports Illustrated*'s Peter King that his coaching style was shaped by Edwards. "The Philadelphia Eagles did not collapse after they dropped their first two games this season, and the roots of their resilience reach back 24 years and a couple thousand miles, to the soil of Provo, Utah, where Andy Reid, a Brigham Young tackle, was becoming a man," King wrote. "While protecting quarterback Marc Wilson against Utah in a November 1979 game, Reid got into a scuffle with a Utes cornerback near the BYU sideline. One poke led to another, and Reid, who could be a fiery sort in those days, cursed loudly at his opponent. Before Reid jogged back to the huddle, Cougars coach LaVell Edwards got in his grill.

'He grabbed me, very upset, and he said, 'Don't ever use that kind of language again!' What bothered Edwards was not just the profanity itself but the fact that Reid had lost his poise. You did not lose your cool when you played for LaVell Edwards because to him losing poise meant losing football games. 'If you were a player under LaVell Edwards,' Reid said, 'you had to be calm, levelheaded, and smart. That's what he was.'"

92 Big Signing Day Surprise

Heading into signing day 2015, BYU shocked the college football world by signing a player nobody had heard of, with no highlights, no recruiting service stars, and no playing experience. And who was then serving an LDS mission. What was even more intriguing was that the signee was named Motekiai Langi, and he stood 6'7", weighed 410 pounds, and hailed from Liahona, Tonga.

News of Langi's signing went viral on social media due to his enormous size—and the fact he'd never played football before. "We're going to play him at nose tackle first. We normally require a two-gap player that can be big enough to handle both A gaps," said Coach Bronco Mendenhall. "He might be a three-gap player. Maybe we'll just have him lay sideways off the snap and block the whole thing out. There must be some way he can do something. It will be fun. He's sincere, hardworking, and humble. What an adventure. Why not?"

How Langi got to that point sounds like a Hollywood creation. Mendenhall offered Langi a scholarship just 15 minutes after meeting him a little more than a week earlier in Provo—just days before Langi entered the Missionary Training Center to prepare for an LDS Church mission to Arizona.

It actually started two years before, when Mendenhall sent defensive line coach Steve Kaufusi on a recruiting trip to Tonga,

Samoa, Fiji, and New Zealand. Kaufusi watched Langi play a pickup game of basketball, because they don't play football in Tonga. "Steve thought he was light on his feet and could play football," Mendenhall said.

Mendenhall remembered Kaufusi's evaluation of Langi, but meeting him made quite an impression. "I shook his hand, and his hand went almost up to my elbow," Mendenhall said. "I thought, *How can this guy not be something?*"

At first, Mendenhall had no intention of offering Langi a scholarship but rather was going to invite him to walk on after his mission. But after 15 minutes, Langi was suddenly part of BYU's recruiting class.

"Football is a game and it can be learned. I can't make someone 6'7" and 410 pounds," Mendenhall said. "I think if I'm any kind of coach at all, and our staff is, there's got to be something we can teach that guy to do. The story's out. You can't hide 6'7", 410. Everyone right now is booking flights [to the Pacific Islands], I'm sure. Or they think I'm crazy. One of those two."

Langi is scheduled to return from his mission in 2017. To date, nobody knows how his story will play out. There's only one thing anybody knows for sure about him—he's one big recruit.

93 Brandon Doman

At Skyline High School in Salt Lake City, Doman ran the option to near perfection. Many didn't believe he would fit in at a dropback passing school such as BYU. But when LaVell Edwards was recruiting Doman, he told him he reminded him of another option quarterback, Steve Young. Yeah, *that* Steve Young. "Steve has definitely been my idol," Doman said when he was in high school. "But trying to be like him is a high expectation."

Once Doman signed with BYU in 1995—passing up offers from Nebraska, Michigan, and Notre Dame, among others—observers figured the Cougars would capitalize on Doman's athletic ability and convert him to a wide receiver or defensive back. But Doman was determined to play quarterback. His three older brothers also played for the Cougars, but none played that position.

Before enrolling at BYU, he served a mission to Argentina and then spent a few years languishing on the bench as a backup quarterback. He saw the field a little as a receiver too, in 1999. Frustration set in, and Doman almost transferred to archrival Utah. Ultimately he stayed in Provo. And toward the end of the 2000 campaign, when Doman was a junior, he finally got his shot after quarterbacks Bret Engemann and Charlie Petersen went down with injuries.

Turned out his first start would be in Edwards' final home game, the same day LDS Church president Gordon B. Hinckley announced that Cougar Stadium would be known as LaVell Edwards Stadium. Doman led the Cougars to a 37–13 victory over New Mexico.

The following week at Utah, in Edwards' final game, the Cougars squandered a big lead then found themselves with a fourth-and-13 situation deep in their own territory. Doman completed a pass for a first down, then another. He ended up scoring the game winner to send Edwards out with a career-ending victory.

"Those last two games, for Coach Edwards, were remarkable experiences," Doman said. "I'm just happy I had the chance to be a part of it. I'm honored. I think about all of the great moments in the history of the program. I don't know if it could have gotten any bigger than to play in his final home game when the stadium was named after him and then the last game of the season at Utah.

What an honor to be his quarterback at that time. To finish up that way was a great blessing."

When Doman was a senior, in 2001, Gary Crowton took over the program, and Doman, teaming up with running back Luke Staley, ran roughshod over opponents. The Cougars scored 70 points in Crowton's debut. Not only was Doman able to pick up yardage with his legs, but he also developed into an accurate passer (he finished with a career completion percentage of 62 percent, threw for 4,354 yards and 35 touchdowns, and rushed for 673 yards and 11 touchdowns).

As part of a midseason Heisman Trophy campaign, BYU created a poster of Doman, calling him the Domanator, borrowing from the popular movie *Gladiator* in a pose similar to Russell Crowe's character, Maximus. Instead of a sword in his right hand, Doman held a football. Instead of Rome's Colosseum, Edward Stadium stood in the background.

Doman led BYU to 12 straight victories to open the 2001 season, and he became the first returned missionary quarterback to capture a conference title for the Cougars. Overall, Doman won his first 14 games as BYU's starting quarterback. But when Staley suffered a season-ending ankle injury after BYU's 12th victory, against Mississippi State, the Cougars dropped their final two games.

The following spring, Doman was drafted by the San Francisco 49ers in the fifth round of the NFL Draft. After spending a couple years with the 49ers, he returned to BYU as its quarterbacks coach and was instrumental in the development of John Beck and Max Hall. He was promoted to offensive coordinator in 2011 but was let go at the end of the 2012 season.

94 BYU in the Movies

Hollywood has never made a movie about BYU football, but the Cougars have, in a way, been part of cinematic history. In fact, BYU played an unnamed role in one of the most popular sports movies of all time, *Rudy*, based on the true story of Notre Dame walk-on Rudy Ruettiger. The movie was released in 1993.

Director David Anspaugh decided to film a few key scenes of the movie during the BYU–Notre Dame game on October 24, 1992, in South Bend. It was the first meeting between the Cougars and the Fighting Irish. The film is set in the 1970s, long before the two schools would meet on the football field. BYU's logo, uniforms, and players aren't shown in the film.

On that game day, it was a beautiful fall afternoon in South Bend, as if it were scripted. When Notre Dame scored on a fumble recovery in the end zone in the first quarter, the crowd stood and cheered. That footage serves as the reaction when, at the climax of the movie, Rudy takes the field for the first time as a Notre Dame player against Georgia Tech.

As it turned out, life imitated art that day. Unsung Cougars backup wide receiver Tim Nowatzke, who hailed from Michigan City, Indiana, about a 45-minute drive from Notre Dame's campus, caught a touchdown pass in the third quarter in front of family and friends who attended the game. As filmmakers were depicting Rudy's famous moment, Nowatzke became BYU's version of Rudy that day.

The American Film Institute has rated *Rudy* No. 54 on its list of most inspiring movies of all time, including all genres. BYU is indeed part of that movie, even though the school is never mentioned or shown.

In an interesting development and connection between *Rudy* and BYU, Rudy Ruettiger was baptized as a member of the Church of Jesus Christ of Latter-day Saints in January 2017. His introduction to the church came after attending the BYU–Notre Dame game in 2013. Rudy met some of the Cougars players and started asking questions about the church.

Meanwhile, 7'6" Shawn Bradley, who played basketball for the Cougars for one season before becoming the No. 2 overall pick in the NBA Draft, played a supporting role in the third-highest-grossing sports movie of all time, *Space Jam*, released in 1996, which took in $230 million at the box office. It featured Bradley saying lines such as, "He probably doesn't even have it anymore," referring to Michael Jordan.

USA Today Sports' Brace Hemmelgarn offered this explanation for Bradley being in the film: "Shawn Bradley certainly didn't make it into the original *Space Jam* on talent. He was in it because he was the awkward, tall white guy who was okay laughing at himself."

The highest-grossing sports movie of all-time, *The Blind Side*, stars Sandra Bullock, who won the Academy Award in 2010 for her portrayal of Leigh Anne Tuohy. The movie is an adaptation of the best-selling nonfiction book *The Blind Side*, and while the movie makes no mention of BYU, the book based on the movie does.

The protagonist, Michael Oher, must vastly improve his high school grades in order to qualify to play college sports at Ole Miss. Oher ends up taking BYU independent study online courses called Character Education, described by author Michael Lewis as having "magical properties: a grade took a mere ten days to obtain and could be used to replace a grade from an entire semester on a high school transcript." Lewis called the process "the great Mormon grade-grab."

Years later, BYU instituted a policy that prevented athletes from other schools from taking BYU's university-level independent study courses because of abuses that had taken place. In 2010 the

NCAA disallowed teenagers from using such courses offered by BYU to improve their grades.

And finally, football scenes in the R-rated movie *The Last Boy Scout*, starring Bruce Willis, was filmed during the 1990 Holiday Bowl between BYU and Texas A&M. That BYU is part of this movie is ironic on several levels—many Cougars fans won't watch R-rated movies, and BYU always has dozens of Eagle Scouts on its roster every year. But that actual Holiday Bowl game was as violent as an R-rated movie for BYU. Quarterback Ty Detmer had both his shoulders separated in a 65–14 loss.

95 The BCS Creators

No, BYU was never a BCS buster. But the Cougars' success played a role in helping create the Bowl Championship Series, and the Bowl Alliance before it. When it comes to the upstarts of college football, BYU blazed a trail for other unheralded schools to follow.

In 1984 the upstart Cougars, then of the Western Athletic Conference, won the most controversial, improbable, and disputed national championship in college football history. Back then the bowls had rigid tie-ins to particular conferences, and setting up a No. 1 vs. No. 2 title game was difficult to achieve. Thus the two major polls determined which team finished No. 1. BYU's mythical 1984 crown caused an uproar among the major conferences. That title didn't sit well with the college football establishment. It marks the last time a team from a non–Power 5 conference has won a national title in football.

By being the only undefeated team in the country that season, the Cougars improbably rose to No. 1 in the final national rankings, with a 13–0 record, to claim a much-disputed national championship.

Critics said BYU's schedule wasn't worthy of a title. But there was no way for the Cougars to prove they were the best team. While Oklahoma and Washington met in the Orange Bowl, BYU was relegated to the relatively new Holiday Bowl to face a 6–5 Michigan squad.

BYU's 1984 championship, and college football's co–national champions in 1990 and 1991, prompted the establishment of the Bowl Coalition in 1992. The goal was to set up a championship game between the top two teams and provide favorable bowl matchups for the major conferences.

In 1995 the Bowl Alliance replaced the Bowl Coalition. But in 1996 BYU disrupted the status quo again. The Cougars challenged the Bowl Alliance by posting a 13–1 record and earning a No. 5 ranking in the polls. The Bowl Alliance did not select BYU to play in one of the major bowls. The Fiesta Bowl appeared to be a natural fit, but the Bowl Alliance bypassed the Cougars and instead awarded its two at-large bids to No. 6 Nebraska and No. 7 Penn State. BYU ended up in the Cotton Bowl, and as a result, the Cougars missed out on an $8 million payday.

The WAC threatened a lawsuit, and Senator Bob Bennett (R-Utah) argued during Senate hearings in 1997 that BYU had been robbed and that the Bowl Alliance was at risk of violating antitrust laws because of the monopoly it had on bowl games. Coach LaVell Edwards also testified before Congress about the inherent unfairness of the bowl system and its impact on recruiting. Under pressure from Congress, the Bowl Alliance adjusted its system to allow teams from non–Power 5 conferences to play in one of the major bowls.

In 1998 came the Bowl Championship Series, which was a selection system that set up bowl games between 10 of the top-ranked teams. It also created a scenario in which the top two teams could play in the BCS National Championship Game.

In 2001 BYU once again exposed problems with the system when it posted a 12–0 record, rose into the top 10 in the national rankings, won a conference championship, had the nation's highest-scoring offense, and yet was officially eliminated from BCS consideration—just days before the Cougars were to conclude the regular season at Hawaii.

"It really aggravates me," then–BYU coach Gary Crowton said. "From a motivational and timing standpoint, I think it's really not a very fair way to do it. It's almost like they [the BCS] want to demoralize us to the point where we don't win and then it takes the pressure off them."

By not playing in a BCS bowl, BYU missed out on a payday of as much as $13 million. The Cougars ended up playing in the Liberty Bowl, which pit the MWC champion against the Conference USA champ, which paid out $1.3 million per team.

As it turned out, BYU—playing without star running back Luke Staley and with the disappointment of being spurned by the BCS—lost to Hawaii 72–45. However, the Cougars' predicament became part of the reason for more changes and more accommodations for the so-called nonautomatic qualifying conferences.

Ironically, in 2004 BYU's archrival, Utah, became the first non-BCS team to play in a BCS game. A few other teams did as well—such as TCU, Boise State, Hawaii, UConn, and Central Florida. Eventually, the BCS was dissolved and a four-team college football playoff was created for the 2014 season.

While the Cougars never played in a BCS bowl, they helped change the way national championships are decided.

96 BYU's Influence on the Passing Game

LaVell Edwards had spent his coaching career on the defensive side of the ball. So when he became BYU's head coach in 1972, and tried to figure out how to win, he looked at what offenses gave him trouble as a defensive coordinator. He decided to pass the ball.

In those days, passing was viewed as a gimmick. As Texas coach Darrell Royal said, "Three things can happen when you pass, and two of them are bad." But Edwards knew BYU's recruiting limitations, and that he couldn't attract fast running backs to Provo. So he focused on finding players who could throw the ball and catch it, receivers and tight ends who were disciplined enough to run good routes.

Edwards brought on a pass-happy former Tennessee quarterback, Dewey "the Swamp Rat" Warren, to run the offense. Ironically, the first season produced the nation's top rusher, Pete Van Valkenburg.

But from then on, the Cougars became known for the forward pass. Eventually what emerged was a quick-release attack that rolled up an obscene amount of yards and points. "LaVell Edwards brought the passing game to college football," Gil Brandt, a former director of player personnel of the Dallas Cowboys, once said. "He made it possible for teams with lesser ability like BYU to compete for a championship on all levels."

Over the first 50 years of BYU football, there had been only three seasons when the entire team had caught 100 passes. Jay Miller had 100 all by himself in 1973.

Quarterback Gifford Nielsen, one of Edwards' first great quarterbacks, recalled those early days. "Coach Edwards asked me if I wanted to change the course of college football," he said.

"Everybody at that time was running the veer or running the wishbone, and he wanted to throw. I listened to him, he talked me into it, and it just turned out beautiful."

BYU and Edwards indeed revolutionized football, both for the way offenses were run and the way defenses tried to stop it. "The philosophy on offense was that no matter what they did on defense, they were wrong," Nielsen said. "We got that confidence to have the ability to throw the ball, handle things properly, make good reads, and do so quickly. Then we got to the point where we started to blossom. We got to the point where we had so much confidence we just didn't think we could lose."

Steve Young is one of the greatest quarterbacks to have worn the Y.

Edwards' influence can be seen in many college programs today, with BYU's roots having spread all over the country. Mike Leach didn't play college football when he was a student at BYU in the 1980s, but he hung around football practices, studying the intricacies of the passing game, gleaning insights from assistants Norm Chow and Roger French. When he became a head coach at Texas Tech, Leach unleashed the Air Raid offense. After a successful stint with the Red Raiders, he installed the offense at Washington State. "There are plays that we got from the golden age, back then at BYU, when LaVell Edwards was there," Leach said. "We run it like they did back then, except maybe we've adjusted this route or that route."

Leach has a deep respect for Edwards. "He's easily one of the greatest coaches that ever coached. I think that's indisputable. I know him a little. I'd like to know him a lot better," Leach said. "He's a guy that never overreacted, didn't panic.... He trusted good people to do things. In the end, it was a product, an environment, of trust and focus. It's a foundation that still survives at BYU to an extent. Football-wise, it's very hard to imagine what BYU would be like without LaVell Edwards, and also football in America, what it would be like without LaVell Edwards. I'm not the only person that LaVell Edwards influenced on throwing the football. LaVell has had an impressive legacy."

Edwards' influence affected numerous coaches who either coached with him or played for him, including Kyle Whittingham, Kalani Sitake, Norm Chow, Steve Sarkisian, and Ted Tollner.

West Virginia coach Dana Holgorsen played at Iowa Wesleyan under head coach Hal Mumme and Leach, who was the offensive coordinator. "We still to this day have some stuff in our playbook that goes back to the BYU days," Holgorsen said. "They talked a lot about BYU."

Holgorsen began his coaching career at Valdosta State, where he served under Mumme and Leach. "I was dumb and young and just kind of learning the game of football at that time," Holgorsen recalled. "But a lot of the principles in the passing game were things that all those great quarterbacks were doing back there for BYU, and we took them and stole them and maintain them to this day."

97 Bronco Mendenhall

On a cold, overcast February afternoon in 2005, Bronco Mendenhall sat in his office, optimistically laying out his vision of BYU football to a visitor. Two months earlier, Mendenhall, then 39 years old, had been promoted to head coach of a program that was mired in the throes of three consecutive losing seasons. An ugly off-field incident involving players accused of rape six months earlier had given the program, and the university, a black eye.

Those were dark times for BYU football, and Mendenhall was hired to clean up the mess and bring hope back to Provo. Under arduous circumstances, he wanted to restore glory to a dilapidated program. "I think we're the flag bearer of the institution," he said on that February day, six months before his first game as a head coach against Boston College. "I'm passionate about my faith and I'm passionate about principles of truth and virtue and character. Those things represent BYU and BYU's football program. We're on the front line, representing all of those things. I intend to carry that flag up high, not on the ground. If I do my job right, this place will be one of the most dominant programs in the country, as it once was. I simply go one day at a time, one task at a time, one project at a time, in an attempt to build this program to the greatness that it once knew. I have a very clear idea of what the expectation is. I have a very clear idea of what the demand is and what BYU football is supposed to be. With every ounce of energy that I have and every bit of ability I've been blessed with, I'm driven to return it to that place."

Mendenhall had his detractors at that time, who pointed out that he had never been a head coach before and that he was the second-youngest head coach in FBS football. In his coaching career, he had only been involved in one bowl game.

Eleven years later, when Mendenhall decided to leave BYU for Virginia, he had lifted the program out of ignominious depths. He guided BYU to 11 straight bowl games while never experiencing a losing season.

Two years after being hired, Mendenhall directed the Cougars to an 11–2 record and a Mountain West Conference championship in 2006. He followed that up with another 11–2 season and another league title in 2007. Under Mendenhall, BYU posted five top-25 finishes in the national rankings.

"I remember what it was like when I committed to BYU, and LaVell Edwards, and what I wanted my experience to be like. In those first two seasons I was there, they fell short of that feeling that I wanted," recalled quarterback John Beck. "When Bronco took over, I remember the vision he had for the program. I didn't know what to expect. He didn't know exactly what it was going to look like at the end, but he had an idea of what he wanted to go towards. The first thing was he saw things had been lost. It started with bringing back the old, traditional Y logo. Bronco wanted to make [BYU] a special place. He made [it] what I wanted it to be when I committed there. Something needed to be changed. There were things wrong with the program, but there were so many good players.... Bronco told us, 'If you as a player work hard, are dedicated, and sacrifice and invest your full effort, this is what can happen if you line those pieces up.'"

In later years, as Mendenhall navigated the program through the choppy waters of independence, the Cougars did not reach the

Kai Nacua

During his BYU career, safety Kai Nacua found himself at the right place at the right time. He finished with 14 interceptions, the most at BYU since official defensive statistics were recorded by the NCAA, and tied with Derwin Gray for No. 4 overall at BYU.

It was fitting that his final play as a Cougar resulted in a game-saving interception. BYU was clinging to a 24–21 lead over Wyoming in the Poinsettia Bowl with 1:22 remaining in the game when Nacua picked off Cowboys quarterback Josh Allen deep in Cougars territory to seal the win.

As a junior, his late-game pick-six helped BYU knock off nationally ranked Boise State in Provo. It was one of three interceptions for Nacua in that game.

For all of his ball-hawking plays for the Cougars, some remember him as one of those who threw punches at the end of the 2014 Miami Beach Bowl. BYU fell to Memphis 55–48 in double overtime. A brawl ensued when the game ended, and cameras captured Nacua fighting. During the off-season, he contacted the Memphis coach to apologize, and he was suspended for the 2015 season opener at Nebraska.

As a junior and senior, he was among the nation's leaders in interceptions. And he capped his career with the aforementioned big play at the end of the Poinsettia Bowl.

11-win plateau. But his final season was impressive overall, considering his team was without their starting quarterback, Taysom Hill, and starting running back, Jamaal Williams.

Mendenhall became the second-winningest coach in BYU history, behind LaVell Edwards, posting a 99–43 record. If nothing else, Mendenhall helped rescue the program from the depths of three consecutive losing seasons and pointed it back in the right direction.

"I measure the successes off the field, the anecdotes and stories and images that I've seen over the years with this team," said athletic director Tom Holmoe. "One thing that jumped into my mind was Thursday's Heroes, a program Bronco started. Our team has been able to meet and love some people that need support and are going through challenges. To see our players grasp onto that program and to see their faces, that's part of Bronco's legacy. Years from now, it just gets stronger."

"I feel like I have a unique relationship with Bronco because I got to be his first quarterback and team captain," Beck said. "The program has come so far. He's built a program of wins and bowl games. We worked together when this rebuilding thing was happening. There's more to Bronco than what he did for me as a football player. It's what he did for me as a person."

98 Winning at the Rose Bowl

On an October afternoon at the historic Rose Bowl, BYU beat UCLA in the first meeting between the two programs. Quarterback Steve Young has said the victory over the Bruins was BYU's "coming-out party" on the West Coast, as the Cougars defeated a Pac-10 power that would go on to win the Rose Bowl that season. It certainly earned BYU plenty of respect in that part of the country, if the Cougars hadn't secured it already.

BYU never trailed in the contest, and afterward Coach LaVell Edwards called it "one of the great wins we've ever had." Young wasn't particularly impressive, throwing two touchdowns and three interceptions, but the game helped turn Young into a national star.

After the victory, the Cougars flew back to Provo—all except for Young, who stayed an extra day in SoCal to appear on CNN's *Sports Sunday* program. The win put Young into the Heisman Trophy conversation and the Cougars vaulted to No. 20 in the national polls.

Young ended up second in the Heisman race behind Nebraska running back Mike Rozier, and the Cougars finished the season with an 11–1 record and a No. 7 ranking in the final polls—BYU's highest finish to that point.

At UCLA, BYU seized a 14–0 advantage in the first quarter before the Bruins, led by Steve Bono, struck back in the second quarter. The Cougars led 24–14 at halftime and held on to a 31–21 edge going into the fourth quarter.

BYU scored 6 points in the final period to go up 37–28 before UCLA scored a touchdown with 25 seconds remaining. A subsequent onside kick by the Bruins was recovered by Kurt Gouveia to seal the win.

It stands as the Cougars' only win at the Rose Bowl. BYU has lost four subsequent meetings there against UCLA.

99 The End of the Edwards Era

On the day he announced his impending retirement, on an August morning in 2000 just days before his 29th season at the helm of BYU's program, Coach LaVell Edwards called an impromptu team meeting. "It may or may not be evident to a lot of you, but this is going to be my last year of coaching," Edwards said to a hushed room filled with players and staff members.

"It was a very touching, sentimental meeting," remembered Brandon Doman, who was one of BYU's quarterbacks at the time. "We were stunned and saddened at the same time. It was emotional."

In the afternoon, the school held a news conference, officially launching Edwards' farewell tour. Then–BYU president Merrill J. Bateman called the occasion "an historic day in the history of

Scoring Streak

On a snowy, freezing November day at LaVell Edwards Stadium, an NCAA record came to an inglorious end. Fittingly, in the season finale of a 2003 season plagued by offensive ineptitude, BYU watched its 28-year-old streak of 361 games without being shut out end with a 3–0 blanking to archrival Utah.

"I never thought that would ever happen. I didn't think it would be possible," said senior linebacker Mike Tanner. "I thought there'd be some way we'd get points on the board. We didn't, and that's frustrating. That's kind of the way the year has gone."

Of course, the elements that day in Provo had something to do with the pathetic performances in Utah's 3–0 win. Bitter-cold temperatures and blowing snow made it nearly impossible for anyone to move the ball— including Utes quarterback Alex Smith, who would go on to be the No. 1 overall pick in the 2005 NFL Draft.

BYU's streak of not being shut out began after a 20–0 loss to Arizona State on September 25, 1975. The last time the Cougars failed to score at home was September 26, 1970, a 17–0 loss to UTEP.

"I don't know if I had ever been a part of team or even seen a game three zip as far as I can remember," Tanner said. "It's just really hard when guys lay it on the field. I envisioned a 7–3 victory and it didn't happen. It's sad. You don't want to lose to Utah, especially in your last game. No one could have ever told me that if Utah scored three points, we'd lose."

"That's a tough one to lose because that's a wonderful streak that BYU should be proud of," said BYU coach Gary Crowton. "It will be hard to break. What we want to do is start a new one first game next year."

"It was a phenomenal number of games that they had not been shut out," said Utah coach Urban Meyer. "That tells you what type of football team we're playing against. For many years they've been good on offense, and have struggled a little bit this year. We came out with our A game on defense."

Not only did the Utes snap BYU's NCAA-record streak of 361 consecutive games without being shut out, they also clinched their first outright conference championship since 1957 that day, and handed the Cougars a conclusion to their second consecutive losing season.

BYU started a new no-shutouts streak with the 2004 season, but that came to an end in 2015 when the Cougars were shut out 31–0 by Michigan. And in 2016 the Wolverines broke BYU's NCAA scoring record and finished the season with 366 games without being shut out.

Brigham Young University. This is an historic day in the history of American football."

Tributes began pouring in from all over the country. But Edwards still had one last season to go, and would open the 2000 season against No. 2 defending national champion Florida State.

Edwards had decided his coaching career was over the previous January, weeks after his team lost badly to Marshall in the Motor City Bowl. A news conference to make the announcement was set for a day in February 2000, but Edwards experienced a change of heart and decided to return for one final season. "I knew it was going to be my last. I didn't like the way it ended the year before," recalled Edwards. "We lost our last three games, and we weren't accustomed to that. I decided to go one more time. That's why I announced it at the beginning of the season. I wanted to save the speculation [about the future]. I didn't want to go through all of that."

Edwards had always believed he would finish his last season and then announce his retirement, not the other way around. "Honestly, I had never, ever in my wildest dreams believed I would ever do this," Edwards said during his retirement press conference. "All I wanted to do was to play it out, and when it was time to go, hang it up, take off, and sail into the sunset somewhere."

That season, the Cougars endured a quarterback contro-versy during fall camp. Then Florida State, and Edwards' good friend Coach Bobby Bowden (who retired after the 2009 season), pounded the Cougars 29–3 in the Pigskin Classic in Jacksonville, Florida.

On one play, Seminoles quarterback Chris Weinke rolled out of bounds and inadvertently ran into Edwards' leg. "I took a few stitches on that one," Edwards said. "He was a big guy. Florida State had a very good football team. The fact it was against Bobby, it was a lot of fun."

The Cougars played an arduous schedule, including three trips to the East Coast. At Virginia, BYU rallied from a 21–0 halftime deficit to beat the Cavaliers in overtime. On the other hand, the Cougars were blown out by Mississippi State (44–28), Syracuse (42–14), and Colorado State (45–21).

Enduring plenty of adversity, BYU entered the final two games of the season with a miserable 4–6 record. Nobody associated with the program wanted Edwards to finish his last season with a losing record. Since taking the helm of the program in 1972, Edwards had never experienced a losing season.

Doman, who had languished on the bench as the third-string quarterback most of the season, was named the starter going into the home finale against New Mexico. Before the contest, then–LDS Church president Gordon B. Hinckley addressed the team, urging them to send out their coach in the right way. "This is your last chance to get a victory for LaVell on his home field," President Hinckley said. "Don't muff it."

On the field prior to kickoff, President Hinckley announced that Cougar Stadium would from that point on be known as LaVell Edwards Stadium. Edwards was genuinely surprised by President Hinckley's pregame announcement that the school's board of trustees had decided to change the name of the stadium. "I thought you had to be dead [to have such an honor]," Edwards said. "During that game at Colorado State, maybe they thought I was."

With Doman at the controls, the inspired Cougars drilled the Lobos 37–13 (future BYU coach Bronco Mendenhall was UNM's defensive coordinator at that time). The following week, the Cougars beat Utah 34–27 in Edwards' career finale. Although BYU finished with a mediocre 6–6 record and no bowl game appearance, that game stands as one of Edwards' most cherished memories. "The Utah game, the way we ended it…we've had so many unbelievable endings through the years," Edwards said. "That ranked up there as one of the best. One of the most improbable. It was a good way to end it, really."

100 Grab a Bite in Provo

If you're coming to Provo for a BYU football game, you need a place to eat and relax before kickoff. Okay, so Anthony Bourdain probably won't be bringing his film crew to Utah Valley anytime soon, but there are some very good culinary options in the Provo area.

Bam Bam's BBQ: In the mood for some Texas barbecue in the heart of Utah Valley? This is the place for you. Owner and pit master Cameron Treu has turned Bam Bam's into the official barbeque of BYU athletics.

Located at 1708 State Street in Orem, you can order brisket, pulled pork, sausage links, ribs, turkey, or chopped beef. There are also a variety of sandwich combos: brisket sandwich, pork sandwich, turkey sandwich, chopped beef. Side dishes include baked beans, coleslaw, and potato salad.

We recommend trying the BBQ Swatchos—tortilla chips, nacho cheese, beans, your choice of meat, and sweet BBQ sauce.

Brick Oven: Originally known as Heaps A Pizza, Brick Oven has been a popular college hangout at BYU for decades. It is located at 111 E. 800 North, on the corner of 150 East and 800 North, just off campus.

Brick Oven celebrated its 60th anniversary in 2016. The establishment has been serving students and Utah families since it opened its doors in 1956, when a corner café known as Stadium Lunch was converted into one of the state's first pizza parlors.

Known for its pizza, Brick Oven also offers all-you-can-eat pasta, soup, and salad. You've got to try its signature, homemade Brick Oven Old Fashioned Root Beer, which has been around since 1956. Almost everything on the menu is made from scratch every day.

Legends Grille: Located inside BYU's Student Athlete Academic Center and adjacent to Legacy Hall, Legends Grille offers great food and a great atmosphere. "It's where all of the athletes eat," said Dean Wright, director of BYU's dining services. "It's like going into their own private dining room, which is open to the public." Legends Grille has two levels, and the second level—or both levels—can be reserved for private gatherings.

After taking a tour of all the trophies and memorabilia in Legacy Hall, satisfy your palate with an all-American menu that changes daily, from steak to salmon to prime rib. The walls are adorned with BYU sports photos and memorabilia too. And there's no telling who you might run into.

Legends Grille is open from noon to 2:30 PM and 3:00 PM to 7:00 PM Monday through Friday. It is closed Saturdays and Sundays.

BYU Creamery on Ninth East: The BYU Creamery on Ninth East, called the CONE, is located on 900 East, just south of Heritage Halls. It is the first full-service grocery store on a US college campus, and also features the 9th Street Grill, which offers a variety of hot sandwiches and soups.

But the No. 1 reason most people visit the creamery is, naturally, for its famous ice cream and sundaes. The Creamery features dozens of flavors, including some unique to BYU, such as Rose's Sneakerdoodle, LaVell's Vanilla, Bishop's Bash, Woosh Cecil, and Blue & White. Ice cream can be purchased in quantities of three gallons, half gallons, five quarts, and eight-ounce cups.

Tucanos Brazilian Grill: Not only does Tucanos bring all-you-can-eat skewers of varieties of meats to your table, it also offers delicious salads and fresh fruit. The cheesy potatoes and grilled pineapple are Tucanos favorites.

For years, Tucanos has provided the pregame meals in the press box at LaVell Edwards Stadium. It is considered by many to be the best pregame meal in college football.

Tucanos is located in the Shops At Riverwoods, at 4801 N. University Ave. in Provo.

Burgers Supreme: Many consider Burgers Supreme to have the best hamburgers in Provo. Located at 1796 N. University Parkway in Provo, this establishment offers a wide variety of burgers and sandwiches.

JDawgs: This is a popular haunt for hot dog…um, dawg… connoisseurs, and has become a cult favorite. You can satisfy your craving for a New York–style dawg at two Provo locations—858 N. 700 East in Provo and 287 E. University Parkway in Orem.

JDawgs, started by a BYU student, offers a wide array of condiments (including onions, pickles, banana peppers, jalapenos, and sauerkraut) and its special sauce.

L&L Hawaiian Barbecue: This Polynesian eatery traces its roots to Hawaii and is famous for the plate lunch. Enjoy barbecue chicken and beef, ribs, chicken katsu, shrimp, moco loco and, of course, plenty of rice. Located at 158 W. 1230 North Street in Provo.

Magleby's: Located at 198 S. Main St. in Springville, just a couple miles south of Provo, this is a stylish American eatery with a menu ranging from seafood to a prime rib buffet.

Acknowledgments

It feels like I've been working on this book all of my life. I grew up following BYU as a kid, taping newspaper articles to my bedroom wall and staying up past my bedtime listening to games on the radio, much to my parents' chagrin. I attended BYU as an undergraduate in the early 1990s and I guess I never left. I've spent the past 20 years at the *Deseret News* and the vast majority of stories I've produced have been about BYU sports. Still, anyone who has worked on a project like this knows you can't do it alone. It's a collaborative effort.

For starters, I'd like to thank Triumph Books for entrusting me with this endeavor and ensuring that this book is one that BYU fans will enjoy.

Much of the information contained in this the book has come from covering BYU sports on an almost daily basis since 1993. It also includes material borrowed from articles I've written for the *Deseret News*. I'm grateful to my colleagues and friends at the *Deseret News*, who have taught me a lot about the craft of reporting and the journalism business. Dick Harmon, Brad Rock, Kent Condon, Dirk Facer, Scott Taylor, Brandon Gurney, Tad Walch, Mike Sorensen, and Amy Donaldson, among others, have encouraged me and have been valuable resources during my career.

I also thank BYU's media-relations department, which has been so accommodating to me over the years—setting up interviews, answering questions, granting credentials and parking passes, and tracking down obscure statistics and information. Duff Tittle, Brett Pyne, Kyle Chilton, Ralph Zobell, Norma Collett Bertoch, and Jenny Wheeler have all made my job easier.

My appreciation also goes out to all of the countless coaches, athletes, and administrators I've interviewed over the years. They've been generous with their time, and my favorite part of this job has been getting to know them, learning about their stories, and sharing them.

Finally, I'd like to thank my family for their patience and allowing me to take time away from them to work on this book. My wife, CherRon, and my six sons, Ryan, Brayden, Landon, Austin, Carson, and Janson, inspire me, and I'm grateful for their love and support.

Sources

Newpapers and Magazines
BYU Magazine
Chicago Tribune
Cougar Sports Magazine
Daily Universe (Provo, Utah)
Deseret News (Salt Lake City, Utah)
Detroit Free Press
Fort Worth Star-Telegram
Houston Chronicle
Los Angeles Times
Provo Daily Herald
Salt Lake Tribune
San Diego Union-Tribune
Sport
Sporting News
Sports Illustrated
New York Times
Trueblue Magazine
USA Today

Websites
www.byucougars.com
www.cougarstats.com
www.espn.com
www.heisman.com
www.nfl.com
www.sandiegobowlgames.com
www.si.com

Books

Edwards, LaVell and Lee Benson, *LaVell: Airing It Out.* Salt Lake City, UT: Shadow Mountain Publishing, 1995.

James, Paul, *Cougar Tales.* Salt Lake City, UT: Randall Book Co., 1984.

Harmon, Dick, *Ty Detmer: The Making of a Legend.* Springville, UT: Cedar Fort Publishing, 1992.

Benson, Lee. *And They Came to Pass.* Salt Lake City, UT: Deseret Books, 1988.

Rock, Brad and Lee Warnick. *Greatest Moments in BYU Sports.* West Valley City, UT: Bookcraft, 1984.

Edwards, LaVell and Lee Nelson. *LaVell Edwards: Building a Winning Football Tradition at Brigham Young University.* Springville, UT: Council Press, 1980.

Tittle, Duff. *What It Means to Be a Cougar.* Chicago: Triumph Books, 2011.

Mitchell, Neil. *The Forgotten Years: The Beginnings of Collegiate Football in Utah.* Springville, UT: Cedar Fort, 1992.

Videos

LaVell Edwards: The Spirit of Cougar Football. Provo, UT: KBYU-TV, 2001.

The Greatest Moments in Brigham Young Football History. Philadelphia: Ross Sports Productions, Inc., 1992.

Other Sources

Associated Press

BYU football and basketball media guides